CHINATOWN'S ANGRY ANGEL

Donaldina Mackenzie Cameron, 1869-1968.

CHINATOWN'S ANGRY ANGEL

The Story of Donaldina Cameron

Mildred Crowl Martin

Pacific Books, Publishers
Palo Alto, California

Library of Congress Cataloging in Publication Data

Martin, Mildred Crowl, 1912-
  Chinatown's angry angel.

  Bibliography: p.
  Includes index.
  1. Cameron, Donaldina MacKenzie, 1869-1968.
2. Chinese Presbyterian Girls' Home, San Francisco.
3. Chinese in San Francisco. I. Title.
HQ316.S4M37   362.7'32'0924   [B]   77-2151
ISBN 0-87015-225-4

PACIFIC BOOKS, PUBLISHERS
P.O. Box 558, Palo Alto, California 94302, U.S.A.

Preface

In a time of turmoil when people search for identity, freedom, and social reform it seems appropriate to tell the story of a woman who lived through another tumultuous period. She found for herself and released to others the most coveted satisfactions. Hers is a tale of adventure set against the backgrounds of an unfriendly countryside and the port of San Francisco in the young state of California. She discovered people's behavior was paradoxical. They were bawdy and prudish, compassionate and cruel. Industry moved forward unbridled; cowboys shot up the West and dance hall girls entertained them; the Barbary Coast shanghaied and murdered and lusted; tent evangelists traveled through the small towns of America preaching hellfire and brimstone; and missionaries went half-way round the world to save the souls of the heathen.

In San Francisco's Chinatown the unsophisticated young Donaldina Cameron challenged the savage practice of "yellow slavery," the buying and selling of young Oriental girls. The business was carried out by a small group of lawless Chinese abetted by corrupt white collaborators. The backbone of the Chinese population, like that of the white, formed traditional families and ran legitimate businesses. Their children became honest workers and skilled professionals. They supported Miss Cameron in her lifelong effort to befriend their abused sisters, and, in time, they helped her extend her crusade across America and into the Orient.

The resource materials about this period and all the memories of people who knew Miss Cameron cannot be included in a single book. I am grateful particularly to *Chinatown Quest,* by Carol Green Wilson (Stanford University Press, Palo Alto, California, 1931 and 1950, reprinted in paperback in 1974), an earlier biography of Miss Cameron, to which I make a number of references. *Ventures in Mission* by Lorna Logan (1975) recounts the Mission's heritage, a continuance of social service through Donaldina Cameron House, in the heart of San Francisco Chinatown.

Here Miss Cameron's life is presented from other views, as rescuer of slaves and mother of girls she took to herself as daughters, and as a remarkable woman who speaks to the human condition in any era. Like her British contemporary, Josephine Butler, who championed abused women and girls in London, she was endowed with "an awful abundance of compassion" which made her fierce.

To writer-members of the Occidental Board who took meticulous minutes, composed articles for mission magazines, and kept personal journals, I am in debt for priceless historical materials. For twenty-five of the forty years Miss Cameron carried on her work, she wrote passionate annual reports. But only for a portion of one year did she keep a personal diary. A colleague, Miss Ethel Higgins, spoke of her epic work and of her personal reserve. Donaldina Cameron's story is, she says, ". . . a tale of life and of high adventure, but of one Hope. The . . . years have passed over her but lightly, as years do with those who have 'the Gift,' but through her life have come and gone hundreds of other lives, and to them all she has seemed an angel of deliverance. Further than this we dare not speak, for Miss Donaldina Cameron is . . . Scotch, and to quote one of the interpreters of the Scotch to the rest of the world—'We have a feeling that if we pass too often this way we will come to a door marked Strictly Private, and with fresh paint. So we withdraw.' "

But, from a brief personal friendship with Miss Cameron, from delightful conversations with her niece and nephews, her colleagues and friends, along with gleanings from written records, emerges a beautiful, bold, gentlewoman in action.

As for the conversations quoted in the text, I have recorded verbatim those repeated by Miss Cameron, her relatives and friends. Other quotations come directly from her reports, her diary, notes for speeches, and her writings. A few fictionalized scenes were confirmed as characteristic by those who knew her best.

Donaldina Cameron revealed her own well-spring and her expectation in an early report:

> . . . We do not always walk crowned with laurel . . . "Tis not enough to help the feeble brother rise; but to comfort him after." This we find the greatest responsibility of our Mission work. . . . With simple faithfulness, therefore, let us go forward looking to God for our pattern, then weave it into human life; thus will the world become better.

Acknowledgments

I first called on Miss Donaldina Cameron to secure material for a newspaper sketch. She allowed me to tape our interviews, and later invited me to visit with her and her protégé and companion, Miss Tien Fuh Wu. I owe much to the memories of those times with her, the impact of her paradoxical gentleness and strength, and her delightful recitals of the events of her early life and her long career.

But the story of Donaldina Cameron would never have been written without Miss Dorothy James Roberts, well-known historical novelist, under whom I was privileged to study. She and members of her seminar, Evelyn Berger Brown, Anne Holmes, and Elizabeth Perry, gave invaluable criticism.

I received early encouragement from Scribblers, a group of writer friends, especially Louise Boggess, Necy Hales, Dee Henri, Alice Kennedy, Helen Pryor, Dorothy Shaftner, Dori White, and Louise Zobel.

Mrs. Ernestine Putman and Arthur Flegel kindly read and assessed the manuscript for its historic value.

Members of Miss Cameron's families and her colleagues provided vital information. Miss Caroline Bailey, Miss Cameron's niece, contributed days of her time. She furnished old letters and pictures and recalled details and incidents not otherwise available. Allan Cameron, Miss Cameron's nephew, also recounted family history, as did his brother, Kenneth Cameron. Miss Lorna Logan, Miss Cameron's successor, was an indefatigable source of memories and documentation; Miss Mae Wong and the late Miss

Tien Fuh Wu, two foster daughters close to Lo Mo from childhood, shared many recollections; the Rev. Dr. F. S. Dick Wichman, who introduced me to Miss Cameron, gave me the incen-
tive to undertake the book and every cooperation in obtaining
materials.

I am indebted also to others involved in Donaldina Cameron
House and its historic work: Mrs. Lisette Bates, nurse at Tooker
Home, at "920," and Ming Quong; Miss Hung Mui Chew,
teacher at Ming Quong Homes, and a foster daughter; the Rev.
Dr. Harry Chuck, a pastor of the Chinese Presbyterian Church,
a staff member of Cameron House, and a community leader;
Hilary Crawford, attorney for the Home; Milton Hall, M.D.,
physician to "920"; Mrs. Helen Kee, a foster daughter; Mrs. Wok
Jun Lee Linn, a teacher at Ming Quong Homes; Helen B. Pryor,
M.D., physician to Mei Lun Yuen, Baby Cottage in San Fran-
cisco; Miss Lucille Reber, teacher in Ming Quong Home at Los
Gatos; and Mrs. Helen Wu, nurse in Mei Lun Yuen. Retired
members of the Chinatown Police Squad presented the lawmen's
viewpoint: Captain Peter Conroy, George McArdle, John P.
O'Connor, and Henry Martin Schutzer.

Devoted friends told of their acquaintance with Miss Cameron: Miss Virginia Borland, daughter of one of the Home's
attorneys; Sister Mary Clement Manion, Inspector Manion's
daughter; Mrs. John Durham, niece by marriage of missionary
Lucy Durham; Chester Marquis, associate of Nathaniel Tooker;
Mrs. Esther Shepherd, widow of Dr. Charles Shepherd; Mrs. Jean
Miller, a young friend during Miss Cameron's retirement.

Historian Ching Wah Lee offered facts and lore about Chinatown.

Several librarians, with knowledge, resourcefulness, and cour-
tesy, located obscure and significant data: Mrs. Louise Beck of
the San Francisco Theological Seminary Library at San Anselmo,
California; Mrs. Gladys Hansen of the San Francisco Public
Library, San Francisco, California; Mrs. Eleanor Walker, of the
Palo Alto City Library, Palo Alto, California; Mrs. Catherine
Wynne and Ms. Elena Fiant of the San Mateo County library
branch at Woodside, California; Ms. Beth McNabb of Bay Area

Reference Center, and Ms. Joy Berry of the California Historical Society, San Francisco.

Always, Seldon Martin, my husband, has given steady and affectionate support, and our daughter, Carolyn, has afforded me insight into Lo Mo's feelings as a mother of winsome daughters.

To all these, and to others who for various reasons do not wish to be mentioned, I offer my deepest thanks for their generous contributions to this story.

Contents

List of Illustrations

CHINATOWN'S ANGRY ANGEL

CHAPTER ONE

Prologue
1895-1976

As the young Rev. Dr. Harry Chuck strides down San Francisco's Sacramento Street hill, early sunlight thrusts hot fingers between buildings, burning off a veil of fog. Harry's black eyes glance up at the building he calls home, a square brick fortress with a hundred-year history. The words, OCCIDENTAL BOARD PRESBY-TERIAN MISSION HOUSE, top the entry porch; a sign on a pillar reads DONALDINA CAMERON HOUSE, and on the heavy door are bold numerals "920." Jail-like iron grilles cover basement windows, and tell-tale scars along the first story show where others have been removed.

Harry turns onto crowded Grant Avenue, Chinatown's romantic thoroughfare, speaking to a dozen people in every block. He does not look about him at the street stalls displaying Chinese cabbage and melons and sugared ginger, or into shops where satin mandarin gowns hang, porcelains fill the shelves, and teakwood furniture gleams. Neither does he listen to the babel of Chinese and English and the clamor of traffic in the narrow street.

He has seen the pagoda roofs, the red and gold signs, and the swinging lanterns a thousand times, and they, like the mingled smells of fish and baking sweets and incense, go unnoticed.

Tall and slight of build, Harry slips easily through the crowds, turns into a doorway between shops and takes the stairs two at a time. At the top he waits for his eyes to adjust to the dimness. His rap on a door at the end of the hall is drowned by children's voices and a baby's cry. He tries again. The door cracks open.

"Who is it?" a man's voice asks in Chinese.

"A friend, from Cameron House."

"Come in. Come in." A thin man smiles welcome.

He speaks rapidly to four little girls. Two hop off the only chairs in the room and climb obediently onto a bed. The others, eyes sparkling with curiosity, follow. A woman at her sewing machine watches, silent.

The man motions Harry to one chair and takes the other.

"Mr. Lee said you would come," he begins in Cantonese.

"Yes," replies Harry, in that tongue, "I've been looking for your son. Mr. Lee showed me his passport picture. He is a handsome boy."

"Not so handsome in his ways." The father stares at the floor. "But I can offer little to encourage him."

"He is only twelve."

"He is becoming a man."

"How long has he been running with the gang?"

"Two months."

Harry nods. "He did not take part in robbing the apartment last night. He stood across the street. So far he has no police record. Will he let us help him?"

"What can anyone do?"

"At Cameron House we have a program that most boys his age like. Will he come tonight if I send a friend to get him?"

The matter was arranged. Harry invited the entire family, recent immigrants from Hong Kong, to visit Cameron House, where, he explained, all might find something geared to their needs: "the Best Day of the Week" and other activities for children, English classes and interest groups for adults, and social services and some psychiatric counseling.

The Rev. Dr. Chuck, like his colleagues, who share living and working quarters in Cameron House, is in the business of helping all kinds of people in trouble to get out of trouble. And in Chinatown, where some 32,000 people live in about seventeen square blocks and two hundred immigrants pour in every month, trouble elbows alongside.

Dr. Chuck is among the foremost young Chinese leaders in San Francisco. He is a third-generation Chinese-American, with a heritage in Cameron House reaching back to the turn of the century, when his grandmother and grandfather were married there. He is active in one of the oldest, largest, most turbulent Chinese settlements in the world outside the Orient. With his colleagues in Cameron House he counsels individuals needing help, and families in trouble, such as the immigrant family worrying about a delinquent son. This family, living in one room and supported only by the mother's earnings as a seamstress, is among those who concern the Chinatown Coalition for Better Housing, which Harry heads. He works through agencies, and negotiates with employers for good jobs. Many Chinese, bewildered by crowding, inadequate English, and fear, are chained to jobs that pay no more than fifty cents an hour for twelve-hour days and seven-day weeks.

1974 marked the one hundredth anniversary of the founding of a mission inherited by Cameron House and currently directed by F. S. Dick Wichman, D.D. The last forty of the one hundred years have been invested in community planning and action, youth work, and individual casework. The first sixty years, beginning in 1874, took another tack, but the goal was the same: an intimate caring for, and saving of, persons caught in tragic circumstances. Those persons were immigrants too, slave girls, bought for a pittance in China, brought to woman-starved Chinese men in America, and sold for fat profits as wives, concubines, prostitutes, and household slaves. When a group of Christian women decided to combat the slave trade, they found they had to cross swords not only with wily and obdurate Chinese traffickers, but also with some members of their own race, who spat upon them in the street as they attempted to rent shelter for the first thirteen slaves they induced to run away from cruel masters.

Opposition simply stiffened their resolution. By the 1890's Miss Margaret Culbertson, superintendent of the Home, had developed rescue techniques. The Presbyterian denomination had taken the crusade under its wing and had built a large home at 920 Sacramento Street, where fugitives could be trained and protected.

In 1895 a young assistant, Donaldina Mackenzie Cameron, came to help. After Miss Culbertson died in 1897, Miss Cameron stepped into her place. The crusade accelerated as she hurtled through the cribs and dens of Chinatown, snatching girls from their owners. Eventually she moved across the United States and traveled to China on her quest to slay the monster slave trade.

The "highbinder" tongs retaliated. They planted dynamite on her doorstep. She disregarded them. A Chinese newspaper announced that she had killed her lover and had come to Chinatown to do penance. She threatened to sue, and the story was retracted. The tongs waged a forty-year war of wits and violence with this woman, who was willing to grapple with any danger, horror, or intrigue they could devise.

Called "a woman of rare charm and courage" by a eulogizing press, Miss Cameron once replied, ". . . I do not deserve it. I think real courage means doing difficult things where one has a sense of danger or fear. Very truly, I did not have to combat that feeling. Perhaps my Highland Scotch background has had something to do with it, but I never anticipated danger when I went accompanied or unaccompanied on some of the raids in which I participated in Chinatown."

Whatever her own disclaimers of courage or applause, Donaldina Cameron became renowned as the most loved and the most hated woman in Chinatown, called by her enemies "Fahn Quai," the white devil, and by her girls "Lo Mo," the mother.

Paradoxically, though she readily led the way for police who wielded axe and sledgehammer to crash through a door, or disguised herself as a bent old woman carrying a black umbrella, or climbed through a skylight to reach a girl, slender, well-groomed Miss Cameron remained a gentlewoman, soft-voiced, hospitable, faithful to her "proper" upbringing.

As fortune-seeking pioneers, her large and warm-hearted Christian family had passed along to her, its youngest child, plenty of the Scot's doughty readiness for adventure. She acknowledged an ancestry of sheep-stealing crossed with parson's blood, a blend that equipped her to respond with passion and canniness to any experience that came her way.

"My Creator blessed me," she often said. "I enjoy people." And people enjoyed her. She attracted a succession of suitors, loved several, and lost her heart completely to one.

Over a period of nearly forty years Donaldina Cameron was credited with saving more than 3,000 girls. For many of them she was appointed legal guardian and mothered them in old "920." She counted the salvation and the nurture of her family her greatest achievement and her delight.

"Many of us owe our lives to Lo Mo," says Mae Wong, a daughter. "She gave so much love. Her influence will never end!"

Lo Mo loved every living thing—flower, bird, beast, or human. No baby smiled unnoticed; no cry for help went without her response. Often she sat all night beside a feverish daughter, or distracted a child who had to take castor oil with the story of Billie, the Tailor. Or, if a girl's safety were in jeopardy, she shared her jail cell to protect her.

Miss Cameron's niece, Caroline Bailey, recalled her aunt's humor. Though often she was burdened by life-and-death decisions, in the run of a day "Aunt Dolly always saw the funny side of whatever happened." Her colleagues tell how Lo Mo joined in "downright silly" pranks. But she held the reins of her household and her mission in a firm hand, always the uncontested sovereign of her domain.

At the end of her ninety-eight years, in January of 1968, the California legislature passed Assemblywoman March Fong's resolution paying Miss Cameron this affectionate tribute:

HOUSE RESOLUTION NO. 62

Relating to the memorializing of Donaldina Cameron

Whereas, The Members of the Assembly have been saddened to learn of the recent death of Donaldina Cameron, who for over forty years worked and helped the Chinese; and

Whereas, As a young girl of twenty-five years, Miss Cameron began her social work activities at the Mission House operated by the Presbyterian Church in San Francisco; and

Whereas, Refuge and shelter was provided for girls, who were imported and sold in this country against their will, by her determined fight against the "slave masters" in the notorious tong days; and

Whereas, Her active and persistent intercession with regard to the immigration problems of the Chinese resulted in many persons being able to call this country their "home"; and

Whereas, Because of her concern with the plight of children, Miss Cameron was instrumental in the establishment of the Ming Quong Home for girls and the Chung Mei Home for boys, and it was not a rare occasion that found Donaldina Cameron caring for these sick and homeless children in her own rooms; and

Whereas, As a token of appreciation for her many years of service, the house in San Francisco which carries on activities for young people was named Donaldina Cameron House; and

Whereas, Because she was able to give of herself to all, even "the least of His brethren," and to touch the hearts of so many in the Chinese community, Miss Cameron was lovingly called "Lo Mo" which means "Mother"; now, therefore, be it

Resolved by the Assembly of the State of California, That the Members express their heartfelt sorrow at the passing of this distinguished Californian, who will be remembered for the love and kindness she showed to her fellow human beings, and for the integral part which she played in the history of San Francisco and the Chinese community; and be it further

Resolved, That the Chief Clerk of the Assembly transmit a suitably prepared copy of this resolution to the Donaldina Cameron House, San Francisco, California.

Miss Cameron's spiritual heirs carry her crusade into the social convulsion and gang violence of modern Chinatown. The features of trouble are not the same, but the troubles are comparable to what she faced eighty years ago.

"What Chinatown needs right now is another Donaldina Cameron," says Dick Wichman, director of the house that bears her name, a house still known as a place where hope is born.

CHAPTER TWO

The Shaping

1869-1895

It was natural, perhaps inevitable, that, as Assemblywoman Fong wrote, Donaldina Mackenzie Cameron, called "Lo Mo," the Mother, was "able to touch the hearts of so many in the Chinese community . . . remembered for the love and kindness she showed to her fellow human beings . . . ," and that the underworld snarled at her as "Fahn Quai," the white devil. Little Dolly Cameron was a twig bent to love people unstintingly and to fight what hurt them.

On July 26, 1869 she was born to Allan and Isabella Mackenzie Cameron, pioneers on a lonely New Zealand sheep ranch on the Molyneux River, later the Clutha. Her name was written in the family Bible after those of five sisters and one brother: Annie, Helen, Catharine, Jessie, Isabella, and Allan. Perhaps, being the youngest, she had more love as well as demands to conform to family standards than did her brother and sisters. The Camerons were all much of a piece, tough, intelligent, fun-loving, staunchly Christian.

Donaldina absorbed tales of family history, and regaled her friends with them later. On both sides her parents were well connected.

. . . They were people who gave Scotland its sterling reputation. My mother went to finishing school. She was very beautiful and she knew how to walk. Once on a city street she asked her companion, "What are all those men turning around to look at?" "At you, my dear!"

Donaldina liked to tell about her forebears, who had raised

sheep in the rugged Highlands of Scotland, where they also fought off political subjection, educated themselves, and entertained friends and travelers. Though the austerity of their lives seemed hard, it bred charm. In early childhood she learned to take disappointment by repeating words of the hymn, "Count your blessings; name them one by one." And when a girl finished counting what she did have, how could she cry over what she did not have?

Hard times and the colonizing fever of the 1860's attracted Donaldina's father to New Zealand. He visited the country, found a position as manager of a large sheep station, and sent for his family. The grandparents, particularly Mamma's father, Donald Mackenzie, felt so bereft by the impending departure of their daughter and grandchildren that the youngest granddaughter, Isabella, was allowed to remain with them. The other children sailed with their mother on the rugged six months voyage.

The New Zealand venture was prospering, when her father heard that in California a sheepman could redouble his fortune, not from the gold that had attracted hordes of adventurers, but from the green-gold of the state's lush pastures. When Donaldina was two years old, Papa Cameron went ahead to explore, and found the new land good. He leased acreage in the San Joaquin, California's Great Central Valley, ordered a flock of New Zealand's long-wool-bearing sheep he hoped to breed with a tough American strain, and wrote his family to follow him.

Whether Donaldina remembered arriving in the port San Francisco one stormy morning, or whether the stories came from others, she looked back on events of that day and the next as prophetic of her later adventures.

The steamer felt her way toward port under clouds shrouding the fingers of land that shaped San Francisco Bay. On deck Donaldina clapped her hands as she heard the calls of the seamen, who had become her friends. Excitement and cold pinched her cheeks red, and her hazel eyes sparkled under the curls that escaped her cap. She cocked an ear to the throaty boom of foghorns and the keening of gulls. A fellow passenger picked her up. He was William Greer Harrison, later founder of the Olympic Club and of San Francisco's first orphanage. With him and her family, Dolly watched dark clouds roil like an angry dragon through the Golden Gate.

Beyond a forest of masts, they glimpsed the Embarcadero. Above the water's edge rose a tumble of hills, from which jutted old shanties and new mansions. When the ship berthed, the Cameron flock bounded across the gang-plank onto a land that remembered the brawling gold rush and its turbulent aftermath. From a carriage they caught sight of the Barbary Coast, about which they had heard rumors of wickedness. They looked up Market Street to such shops and business buildings as the older ones had not seen since they left Britain.

They knew little of the revolution precipitated by forty-niner's gold: wealth, energy, industry, and a burst of settlers at the end of the Civil War. But they discovered that San Francisco, once a primitive trading village, had become the most exciting port in the New World. At that hub, men such as the Big Four, Leland Stanford, Charles Crocker, C. P. Huntington, and Mark Hopkins, translated the gold into progress, power, glamor. But they also exploited the immigrant Chinese. This was the San Francisco Donaldina later called "my good grey city."

The family stayed one night in a hotel overlooking the Chinese quarter. Next morning the children peered down on the rainy street at strange-appearing men going to work in a cigar factory. Hunched under black umbrellas, as though in a funeral procession, they padded by, wearing native slippers and dark pajama-like costumes, their long pigtails swinging. Dolly pressed her face against the window long after her brother and sisters had tired, a first hint of her fascination with The City's people of the golden skin and almond eyes.

Papa took his family to the ranch near Berenda and Merced in the San Joaquin Valley, one hundred and fifty miles southeast of San Francisco. Donaldina remembered the ranch house as gaunt and foreboding, a wooden box built for shelter, not for beauty. Shaded by a cottonwood tree, she often sat on a bench by the back door, swinging her feet and looking over miles of undulating grasslands interrupted by a single oak and rimmed by the granite heights of the Sierra Nevada.

Though the Camerons were hospitable to travelers, the wilderness home and her family composed Donaldina's world. She, like her sister, Helen, inherited her mother's grace and dramatic gift, and learned to read aloud from Dickens, Thackeray, and Scott. She listened, enchanted, to Catharine's telling of Scottish legends, and Jessie's recitations, sometimes the whole of "Locksley Hall."

Brother Allan was more playmate than teacher, though he, too, was a student, and dreamed of seeing the world. Papa and Mamma kept current newspapers and books, so that conversation was learned, lively, and contemporary. The family practice of memorizing poetry and scripture influenced Donaldina's expression, both written and spoken, harking back to cadences of the King James Bible, particularly to the Psalms. Her Scottish burr and the style of the classics lent her remarks a hint of mysterious authority.

Her sister, Annie, fifteen years her senior, painted and sewed, but her chief enthusiasms were cooking and party-giving. She taught Donaldina baking and planning for each family birthday, holiday, or guest's visit. No one could forget the roast lamb and lemon meringue pie that came out of the big black range or the decorated cakes and buttery shortbread.

Now and then adventure penetrated the Camerons' isolation. Dolly remembered one summer afternoon when, for relief from the heat, the five sisters wrapped themselves in wet sheets and perched like birds on the corral fence. They saw a cloud of dust approaching. As it boiled along the road toward the ranch, they scuttled to the house. A group of horsemen pulled rein, and Papa went out to meet them. The leader demanded whiskey, which Papa quickly supplied. The men were Tiburcio Vasquez, the notorious valley bandit, and his henchmen. As the band thundered away, Papa gave thanks that the desperadoes had let him off so lightly.

During the winter, when the older children rode to the country school, Donaldina made pets her playmates: a hen she named "Eagie" for the golden eagles she saw flying overhead; a little dog, "Gyptan," given her by an Egyptian sheepherder; numbers of cats; and often an orphaned lamb. She tried to make friends with curious antelope, which approached the corral, by holding out handfuls of grass, but they bounded away like rocking horses. Occasionally she visited with Jim, the sheepherder's cook, her first Chinese friend.

Dolly vividly remembered a soft spring morning when she and Mamma walked the pasture, picking baby blue eyes, and Mamma smiling as she wove flowers into a wreath for Dolly's hat. The family had taken a picnic to the meadow splashed with color and filled with perfume of wild flowers.

Papa lay back on the fragrant meadow and sang the twenty-third Psalm and Old Hundredth. The family listened, wrapt. Only Papa could sing. Mamma and all the children were tone deaf, like the Mackenzies. Dolly, so happy she felt a little sad, sat waist deep in grasses, and looked off to the marbled blues of the Sierras, their peaks crowned with snow. It was easy to believe what her parents told her — God is love and this is His world.

That faith helped her, as a little girl of five, to forgive the valley the tragedy it brought. The hardships of pioneer life, the merciless heat in summer and dank cold of winter, were too much for Mamma. In the spring of 1874 she died. Annie and Helen, then twenty and eighteen, stepped in to mother the younger children and keep the household going.

But the valley had not finished its onslaught. Two dry years shriveled the pastures and starved most of the sheep on the range, except seed stock. When the rains came, they deluged the land. At seven, Dolly was old enough to understand what was happening. On a black night when the storm struck at the farmhouse with angry fists, she heard Papa go to the sheep house to check his flock. He did not return until morning to tell his family what happened.

He had found the folds empty. He rode out in search of his sheep. At dawn on the bank of a swollen stream he found them in the hands of rustlers. The thieves knew he had identified them. As he watched, they destroyed the evidence against themselves by cutting the throats of the animals and throwing them into the raging waters.

He rode the range for hours looking for strays. From the night's exposure he caught pneumonia. He needed months to recover and suffered from severe asthma thereafter.

The Camerons' pioneering days were over. Papa sold his few remaining sheep for fifty cents a head and moved his family to the Willows, a suburb of San Jose, fifty miles south of San Francisco. He worked for other ranchers to support his family. The younger sisters attended Castleman school for girls, and Al went to public school. The San Jose years proved quiet ones, though gregarious Dolly made many friends. With more places to go, she enjoyed dressing up, and sat patiently while her long hair was plaited into two heavy braids that curled at the ends. She was proud of her "best" dress, a white ruffled muslin with a wide sash of Cameron tartan taffeta. Photographs taken in these years seldom reflected her vivacity. She appeared "forebearing," for she hated to pose. Some pictures reveal the over-bright eyes of fever from recurring sinus infections, though otherwise she was healthy.

When she was ready for high school, the family moved to Oakland, where she happily entered into school and church affairs. She made two lifelong friendships with neighbors, Eleanor Olney and Evelyn Browne. The girls giggled at the same jokes and created their own good times.

The Oakland years passed swiftly. When Donaldina was fifteen, the family made another move, a final one for Papa, to the San Gabriel Valley of southern California. Lucky Baldwin, the Horatio Alger of California industry, an entrepreneur in hotels, theatres, racing, ranching, and finance, hired Allan Cameron to manage La Puente, the sheep center of his famous Santa Anita Ranch. In the south, Donaldina again plunged into school and made new friends. She hiked the hills and fields with boys and girls, boated on a pond on the ranch, and rode the spirited horses Lucky retired from the race track. The warm, dry climate cleared her sinus affliction.

After graduating from high school, Donaldina began a teacher-training course at normal school. But before the first year was over, her father's death brought her home. Although the college education she longed for was ended, she quickly put her life back together. She had always taken for granted that she would marry some day; and in the spring of 1888 she decided she had found the right man, George Sargent, a good friend of her brother. A letter written a few weeks before her nineteenth birthday, to her sister, Jessie, teaching in Hawaii, discloses her happy plans.

Puente, June 15th '88

My darling sister:

I know you must be awfully much hurt with me for not writing before but we all seem to have been in a sort of rush for the last long while . . . Jacko darling, how shall I begin to tell you what joy it gave me that you were so cordial about George's and my engagement. You would be glad if you only knew how *very* happy your dear letter made me. I would have written myself and told you, but George loves so to handle his pen and seemed eager to write so I let him. I am awfully glad that you feel warmly to him Jacko for I would hate to marry anyone that some of my family didn't like.

We were delighted with Charlie's Photo. I think he is really very nice looking he looks so awfully kind and "very much man" as old Castillo would say. Oh Jessie how I long to see you both, what fun it will be—my sister Mrs. Bailey. I'm certain I can't keep a conscious look out of my face when I speak of you. Just think if George should happen to have enough money by the time we're married to take a trip to the Islands, but I fear such joy is not in store for me as I may be thankful if we have enough money to keep us comfortable. I'm to have a little chinaman Jessie, imagine, if you can, my entertaining you and Charlie when you come up!! . . .

You will have gathered before now that I'm at home again. It is so unfortunate, I had only been in the office a week when it changed management and the new manager sent away all the new copiests (heard there were ten) myself among the number, they were very nice to me and said that I had done so very well but there was absolutely no work to do as real estate had gone down so terrible. However, having been there will assist me in getting another place and Ano and I are going to town to do what we can towards getting one. I'm so eager for a place, as I think it's a shame to live on poor Al, and I want to begin before very long to lay up for my trousseau. I don't think it likely that we'll be married for nearly two years for I don't propose to live on love, and as both George and myself have good appetites I fear we couldn't even if we wanted to. He's surveying over at the Old Mission just now and gets sixty five $ a month but he doesn't want to have surveying for his business so he probably won't stay there long. Al and he want to get a ranch somewhere in Southern

Donaldina, about 10, wearing a sash of Mackenzie tartan, 1879.

Donaldina, about 19, when George Sargent courted her, 1888.

Donaldina's brother Al, left, and her fiance, George Sargent, about 1888.

Cal. and have cattle and sheep. I wish awfully they could for I know
it would pay very well indeed and stock ranches are so genteel. How
I envy you living on a fine plantation, but Oh my dearest Jessie the
more you have and the happier you are the more sincere joy it will
give me and I hope you will always be happy as it is possible for anyone to be. I feel sure that it won't be Charlie's fault, from all we've
heard of him, if you aren't. . . .

Jessie it was so very, very good of you to have sent the crochet, it's
so very pretty and is to be carefully laid away with a little turkish
toweling "imported" (!) wash rag that Nursy gave me (also a nest
egg) when she was here. Shearing will begin next week. I dread it so
much as Helena and Nursy are away. . . .

This letter is awfully uninteresting and very "Georgie" I fear but
I know you won't mind. Please give Charlie my love and tell him that
since I've seen his Photo I long more than ever to see him. Don't think
for a moment that we get tired of hearing about him. Ano will write
a note on the subject of your clothes.

With dearest love

DODO

P.S. I wrote to my mother-in-law elect last night or rather Ano[1] and
I composed a letter together, don't you envy us? She wrote me such
a sweet ladylike one.

At nineteen Donaldina appeared much in love with George.
He was said to be bright, ardent, and witty. But the pair did not
marry. Whatever the reasons—and no one seems to know them—
Donaldina took a typical Cameron attitude: "Some things we do
not talk about, and it is better that way."

Her social life continued lively, and she welcomed visits from
her long-time Oakland friends, Evelyn Browne and her mother.
A woman of drive and initiative, Mrs. Browne was president of
the Occidental Board of Foreign Missions. She fascinated Donaldina with stories of her work in San Francisco's Chinatown.
After she had succeeded in getting the Y.W.C.A. started, she had
concentrated her efforts on saving Chinese girls who were sold
as merchandise on the slave block. She told thrilling tales of a
Miss Culbertson's rescuing slave girls and bringing them to live
in a mission home.

---

[1] Family pet names: Ano for Annie, Jackie or Jocko for Jessie, Nursy for
Catharine, Helena for Helen, Dodo for Donaldina.

Donaldina found it incredible that children and young girls could be so brutally treated. She turned the conversation again and again to the plight of the Chinese girls in San Francisco.

"Dolly, would you be willing to help in the Home?" Mrs. Browne asked.

"But I'm not educated for it," Donaldina replied in surprise.

"You can teach the girls to sew. And perhaps you can assist Miss Culbertson. Her health is delicate. You are needed, Dolly. Will you come for just one year?"

To be needed in a vital work! And Mrs. Browne had faith in her. Her only possible answer was "Yes."

CHAPTER THREE

Children of Darkness
1895-1896

When the train stopped in San Francisco one April morning in 1895 an excited Donaldina stepped off. She had wakened early, put on a full skirt and frilly blouse and the chinchilla-collared short jacket that Helen told her set off her rosy coloring. She pressed her flower-and ribbon-trimmed hat firmly behind her burnished pompadour with its white streak, tossed a large veil over her head, secured it at the throat, and drew on white gloves.

Fog billowed in from the Bay and sifted down the street. In the station she was surprised to catch friendly smiles from formal San Franciscans. Like her mother's many years ago, her blithe carriage made heads turn. Voices shrilled for hacks, horses' hooves clip-clopped on cobblestones, buggies creaked to curbs and wheeled away, and a streetcar clattered to a stop.

She remembered Annie's caution, "Take a hack this first time, Dolly. It's a big city! And a dangerous place, that Chinatown!"

Donaldina signaled a cab and sprang up the steps before the driver could hand her in. She remembered shivery warnings about Chinatown from her schoolmates in the Oakland days: Stay away! A yellow hand will reach out and grab you. Or, a trap door will open and swallow you up. Surely nothing could be that ominous now. The city looked benevolent and fascinating to a country girl on her way to her first job. As it disclosed itself, she fell in love with it: in the warehouse district huge draught horses and their brawny drivers; men in overalls, carrying strikers' placards and marching in a circle; and downtown, twelve-story buildings, some plain as tailored suits, but the Baldwin and

Grand Hotels as fussy as dowagers. She enjoyed the decorum with which both men and women dressed, wearing hats and gloves; cane-carrying men flashy in spats and jewels. At the end of Market Street, on the Bay's edge, she saw the Ferry Building pointed upward like a tapered finger. The hack jogged onto Grant Avenue, lined with elite shops. Crossing Bush, the street name changed to Dupont. Donaldina was in the Orient.

The first block looked Japanese. The next became China. Pagodas, their peaked roofs banded in flame and black lacquers, etched the sky. Balconies jutted from upper stories; signs in red and gold Chinese characters hung beside shops filled with strange wares. She sniffed at a curious blend of smells on the damp air; fragrance of baking sweets, and bitter scents she could not identify.

The hack lurched off Dupont Street, up a steep hill, and stopped.

"920 Sacramento Street," the driver announced, opening the hack door. "When you learn to speak Chinese you'll call it 'Tong Yun Guy,' " he said. "That means 'China Street.' "

"How lovely." Donaldina paid him. "Thank you for a delightful ride."

He tipped his cap. "Have a care around these parts, Ma'am."

Donaldina stood before her new home, a sturdy bastion of red brick with a domed top. But why the grilles over windows? Were the girls prisoners? Or was danger outside? Her old friends, Evelyn Browne and Eleanor Olney, who were part-time volunteers at the Mission, would tell her.

She climbed the stairs and lifted the knocker. A young Chinese woman opened the door a crack.

"Who?" she asked.

Donaldina gave her name.

The woman scrutinized her, drew back, motioned her to enter, and quickly locked and bolted the door. At the same moment a Chinese girl who had been squatting on the landing rose. The doorkeeper took a step forward and the girl fled. Puzzled by the odd scene, Donaldina did not notice that Eleanor Olney had arrived from the hall until she heard her name called.

The two girls hugged each other and fell into excited conversation. "Come on," Eleanor said and led the way to Donaldina's room. It was furnished with an iron bed, straight chair, and a small table. Like everything else, it was in order, and so clean, so clean. Eleanor closed the door.

"This Home is not like the ranch, Dolly. Everyone is not happy. That was a new girl and she was trying to run away. She's afraid of us. The girls have had terrible experiences. Their owners tell them that we're devils at the Mission."

"Poor dears!"

"Yes. It takes time and a world of patience to win their trust. Some have never known decent treatment!"

She opened a door to a closet smelling of fresh pine. "You know this building is only a little over a year old. Hang up your coat. I'll show you around. Miss Culbertson is attending a meeting."

Eleanor led her through the girls' rooms, hallways, a meeting room, and dining rooms—all Spartan. In contrast, the Chinese Room under the dome was sumptuous with teak, rich rugs, and works of art, gifts of the Chinese Legation and merchants. Mrs. Vice-Consul Owyang-King selected the furnishings, Eleanor explained. She tucked her arm through Donaldina's.

"The little girls are in school, but the older ones are working in the laundry, kitchen, or at their sewing."

Downstairs Donaldina heard the clink of pans and murmur of voices. When she and Eleanor appeared in the kitchen, talk stopped. A girl with a round timid face ducked out of the room like a startled rabbit. One of two girls who were washing dishes gave them a defiant glance. Her partner bent over her work, sulky. Donaldina wanted to go to them, to put her arms around them and wipe away the fear and anger.

A girl stowing utensils in a low cupboard straightened and smiled. "Miss Olney!"

"This is Ah Ying, who has lived here all her life," Eleanor said. "It's her turn to help in the Chinese kitchen." She patted Donaldina's arm. "Miss Cameron is our new assistant, Ah Ying. She loves music. She will enjoy hearing you play the piano."

"Thank you," Ah Ying's eyes shone like onyx. "We are glad

Donaldina Cameron, at 25, when she came to teach in the Presbyterian Mission Home for Chinese Girls in 1895.

you come to us." She introduced the others, who went on with their work in silence.

As soon as they were alone, Donaldina cried, "Oh Eleanor, Ah Ying is lovely. But those others! They look so—so half alive, so unloved!"

"They are. It helps when you get to doing something for them." She opened the gold watch she wore pinned to her shirt-waist. "It's awful to leave you now, but I have to meet my class— see you at lunch."

Donaldina went to unpack, her thoughts sober. Later a young woman came to her room. "Welcome," she said. "I'm Anna, Miss Culbertson's niece. I go to art school and help Aunt Margaret. It's nice to have you here." She held out a bouquet of white roses.

"Thank you. What a lovely thing to do!"

"Do you know you have interesting eyes?" Anna asked. "Like Scotch tweed, green and brown with flecks of gold."

Donaldina laughed. "My accent gives me away. But I don't mind if my appearance proves my heritage, too."

Late that afternoon Margaret Culbertson summoned Donaldina to her office. She was a woman of middle age, thin, weary, her shoulders drooping. She said, "I wish we could visit, but you have come at a time when we are under particular stress. I feel I must apprise you of the risks you will take if you cast your lot with us."

"Risks?"

Miss Culbertson drew a sheet of paper from a folder. She had the air of a woman too tired to explain, and said with an effort, "This is a translation of a letter I had after a recent rescue."

"Your religion is vain," Donaldina read. "It costs too much money. By what authority do you rescue girls? If there is any more of this work there will be a contest and blood may flow. Then we will see who is the strongest. We send you this warning. To all Christian teachers."

Margaret Culbertson replaced the letter. "Today sticks of dynamite were found on our front porch, and in the grating of windows. The police tell us there was enough to blow up a city block." She gave Donaldina a searching look. Would she like to reconsider her decision to help at "920"?

No. Indeed, Donaldina saw added reason to stay. But she wanted to know more, much more about the girls.

Miss Culbertson's thin lips parted in relief. "Let's go to dinner, and afterward we'll begin to answer your questions."

But the superintendent did not finish the meal. The doorkeeper slipped a folded note into her hand. She flattened it on the table and read, "Come get . . ." and an address.

"I know that abominable place," she said. "A girl in trouble. I must go. Excuse me."

Rising, she spoke to the girl waiting table, "Tell Ah Cheng to get a wrap and meet me at the door—at once!"

Donaldina finished her dinner without appetite. She wished she had been asked to help. To watch that frail woman go alone was hard. In the entry she awaited the rescuers. Within half an hour Miss Culbertson and Ah Cheng returned, supporting an emaciated girl who wore a blue satin dress, elaborately embroidered, and clutched a large bundle. She looked at Donaldina with terror.

Miss Culbertson spoke, her voice gentle, "Take her to the kitchen, Ah Cheng. You and Ah Ying persuade her to eat."

Slowly, her hands shaking, Miss Culbertson took off her coat. "Come into my office. I'll send for some hot chocolate and we'll talk while I unwind."

Donaldina hesitated, her glance following the two girls.

Miss Culbertson's brown eyes softened. "Girls who speak her own tongue can help most right now. We'll be here when she needs us."

Donaldina followed, her mind bursting with questions. The note—and now this: A girl swaddled in silk, yet a slave. She had much to ask Margaret Culbertson.

In her office Miss Culbertson said, "This has been a harsh introduction for you."

"What kind of slave was the girl you rescued tonight?"

"A prostitute."

Donaldina's lips parted, but she could not repeat the word. She had never heard it spoken aloud. Nice people didn't. Yet Miss Culbertson—

"Why?" she asked.

"You were not told about our work?"

"Oh yes. I have heard of rescued slaves. But I didn't know 'slaves' meant—I thought the Home cared for orphaned and unprotected girls."

"And so it does! I'd better begin from the beginning. Come see." She raised a green window blind and pointed.

"Up there on Nob Hill stand the mansions of millionaires. And," she pointed down narrow Sacramento Street, with its flickering gas lights, its barracks-like buildings, and beyond, the spire of St. Mary's Church, "in Chinatown are the men who helped them get their wealth. You might say men from both those quarters caused slavery.

"In 1849 Chinese men, like those from other nations, rushed to California to get wealth from 'the gold mountains' and carry it home to China. Few got rich. Prejudice grew against Chinese. White Americans believed their ways the 'right' ones. Chinese, who wore pajama-like sahms, spoke in sing-song, braided long queues, cooked strange-smelling foods and practiced heathen religions were peculiar. Peculiarity was despised. Chinese were forced out of gold fields, their claims jumped, their gold stolen. Some were murdered."

A knock on the door interrupted. Ah Ying, the bright-faced girl Donaldina had met in the kitchen, brought a pitcher of chocolate.

"That smells good," Donaldina said.

As they drank, Miss Culbertson resumed. The Chinese who survived the first persecution had no money to return home. They took the least desirable jobs, building railroads and working the gold fields for white men. More Chinese were imported from their impoverished villages in China to do menial work. Coolies[1] were packed in holds of ships as cargo. Employers paid $100 or more for a man's passage, and indentured him to work out his debt. But in the depression of 1876 American labor wanted even the lowly jobs of Orientals, and the Chinese were rejected again.

"How unfair!" Donaldina said.

[1] Coolie translates "Ku-li," meaning "bitter strength" or "bitter labor."

"Yes, unfair," Miss Culbertson agreed, but absently as though the word had lost its meaning.

In 1882 Congress passed the first of three Exclusion Acts, which forbade most Orientals from entering the United States, excepting certain classes of merchants, officials, and teachers and their families; and wives and children of American-born Chinese. But families of Chinese men outside those categories could not immigrate. Nor could single men send for Chinese wives. The situation encouraged the selling of legitimate entry papers to impostors.

Donaldina said, "They must have been very lonely."

"Yes. There were about 2,000 men for every woman. Intolerable. Chinese tongs (some say they were originally protective societies) had organized in the gold fields, and began bringing in women, calling them 'daughters of joy.'"

"How did they manage that?"

"It was not too difficult. Agents went to China, got possession of young boat girls, or bought girls from poor parents on the mainland. Other families were told their daughters would marry rich husbands, or get an education." Miss Culbertson turned in her chair, as if to get away from dreadful facts. "Smuggling became big business. Teen-age girls were sold in America as wives or concubines. Many were forced into prostitution. Little girls served as household slaves, called 'Mooie Jais,' until mature enough for other purposes." The superintendent paused. "These are the children and young women we rescue and shelter. This is the yellow slave trade we fight."

Donaldina laced her fingers around her cup. "How do I begin to help?"

Margaret Culbertson smiled. "You are helping. Draw up your chair. Here are records of the girls. Some are pupils you will meet tomorrow." She opened a thick ledger, titled, "Register of Inmates of Chinese Women's Home." "This is Chun Loie's story."

Donaldina read the director's precise handwriting:

Mar. 25/92. Chun Loie

I received word in the afternoon that a little girl about 9 yrs. old at the N. W. Cor. of Clay & Dupont Sts. was being badly beaten. I got the police went to the house and brot her to the home—She was in pitiable condition, two cuts from a hatchet were vizable on her head—her mouth, face and hands badly swollen from punishment she had received from her cruel mistress.

Mar. 28. Rec'd. Letters of guardianship for Chun Loie—had the woman arrested for cruelty to children.

Mar. 31st. Went to Police court with Chun Loie. Judge Jouchinson fined her wicked mistress twenty five dollars.

"In three years," Miss Culbertson said, "she has become a cooperative, teachable child."

Donaldina read on through accounts of abused children brought by sympathetic neighbors, and of older girls from brothels. She looked at tragedy and misery she had not known could exist. Such was the story of Sing Ho:

Aug. 15/92. With the assistance of two police officers and Ah Cheng we went to Bartlett Alley and rescued the girl of above name. She is very small of stature—looks like a midget—has an old and peculiar face—give her age as 22 years. Sing Ho says her mother died in San Francisco and her father returned to China—that her parents owed money and that she entered upon a life of sin to pay their indebtedness.

Sing Ho was a victim of the opium habit and after spending a night in the Home decided to return to the brothel—she could neither eat nor sleep.

Further entries told of other girls who spurned rescue. Some tried to run away from the Home.

"Why?" Donaldina asked.

"These are the children of darkness," Miss Culbertson sighed. "Some slaves refused help because owners threatened them with punishment or death. Such threats were not idle. Girls trying to escape died mysteriously or were hideously tortured. Others who asked sanctuary changed their minds when they discovered the Home's requirements. A courtesan accustomed to luxury rebelled when told she must dress in cotton and eat our simple fare; she refused to study or take her turn with chores."

Donaldina asked, "Do you think all this effort is really worth-while?"

"I do think so. Given time and love, many girls outgrow their stunted beginnings. And a number of orphaned children and girls from good homes live here so they can get an education."

Several of the responsive ones, Donaldina discovered, were in her class. Isabel, carried into the home as a sickly baby, had grown into a happy first-grader. Qui N'gun, an eight-year-old mooie jai, who had run away from a cruel mistress three years earlier, developed into a bright, interesting girl of eleven. And Yoke Ying, at thirteen, "a quite good looking and pleasant slave girl," who had made her own escape, fit in happily.

Next day Donaldina was a guest in the schoolroom. Desks in graduated sizes marched in rows facing the teacher's desk, be-hind which Miss Culbertson stood, awaiting her pupils. Dressed in cottons styled in the Chinese manner, they filed in. Donaldina tried to identify some of them. Could that sweet-faced child in the first row be Isabel? Or Qui N'gun, the middle-sized girl who sat straight and curious? Was Yoke Ying among the older pupils who fixed alert and suspicious eyes on the new teacher? All the children seemed solemn and tense.

Miss Culbertson introduced Donaldina, and then let the silence lengthen until everyone was aware that she meant to speak of something serious. She had just learned, she said, that from a gift box of apples, a rare treat intended for all the people in the Home, several fruits were missing. Who stole them? The room echoed with silence. Miss Culbertson turned severe.

"Who took the apples?" she asked a second time and a third, her voice rising. Donaldina flinched. The children must find their director forbidding.

A sigh broke the stillness. A small girl with rosy cheeks and skin like pale gold silk slowly stood up. Tears rolled down her face.

"Tien!" exclaimed Miss Culbertson, incredulous.

"I did it." Tien quaked from pigtails to feet. She brushed at tears and Donaldina noticed a scar on her jaw and others on her arm. Miss Culbertson's eyes fixed on the frightened child.

"How could you, Tien? You must be punished!"

Donaldina thought, "She is so little! She must have been born honest to face up like that." Tien confessed that older girls had put her up to pilfering, promising to share the blame if she were caught. But they did not. Donaldina's sense of justice flared. How could those miserable older girls let that little thing catch it alone? After class Donaldina asked to see Tien's ledger record.

Jan. 17/94. Tai Choie alias Teen Fook[2] was rescued by Miss Houseworth, Miss Florence Worley and some police officers from her inhuman mistress who lived on Jackson St. near Stockton St. The child had been very cruelly treated—her flesh pinched and twisted till her face was scarred. Another method of torture was to dip lighted candlewicking in oil and burn her arms with it. Teen Fook is a pretty child of about ten years old, rosy cheeked and fair complexion.

Donaldina learned about the small culprit's early life. Tien remembered her home in old China, and how, when she was five years old, her father ordered her mother to ready the child for travel. A buyer would pay enough for her to settle his gambling debts. The mother's wailing did not deter him. Tien tottered off with him on tiny bound feet. She remembered the dealer in Canton, a woman who unbound her anguished feet and soaked them in water. Her motive was not to relieve the pain but to make the child serviceable. Tien was destined for the yellow slave market in the United States.

She recalled the long voyage, her re-sale and bondage as a mooie jai "in one of the worst dives in Chinatown." With her owner's baby strapped to her back, Tien did the family washing and cleaning. When she was slow or inept, her "inhuman mistress" punished her with pinches and burns.

Deeply moved, Donaldina set herself to win high-spirited, imaginative, and intelligent Tien. She could be a power for good. Recognizing her promise, Miss Culbertson had interested a missionary-minded businessman in her. Horace Coleman of Norristown, Pennsylvania paid her expenses in the Home and planned to give her further education. When he visited "920"

---

[2] Another spelling for Tien Fuh Wu. The Cantonese Fuk and Northern Fuh and Fu are written with the same Chinese characters. Wu is Ng (surname) in Cantonese.

A "mooie jai" like Tien Wu, in Chinatown, about 1900. (Photo
courtesy California Historical Society)

he showed her much affection, and Tien, in turn, hero-wor-
shipped him. When put upon by others, she threatened, "You
just wait 'til my American Papa gets here. He will give it to you!"

From the first Tien had been a leader. Having few toys in the
Home, she substituted a broken table for a ship to set sail to
China. She made up games, and conducted a Buddhist funeral
for a dead bird. But she was continually in mischief, punished
for it, and therefore at odds with authority. She expected no
favors from the new teacher.

In sewing class Tien fended off Donaldina, averting her eyes
and pretending she could not match a simple seam. She mistook
Donaldina's smile of friendliness for amusement, jerked away
from her affectionate touch, and labeled Miss Cameron an
intruder.

Patience, sympathy, time, Donaldina thought. Surely this fascinating girl would soften.

Though she loved teaching, Donaldina chafed to take part in
rescues. Her first chance came one windy April night. After dusk
the doorkeeper handed Miss Culbertson a card with an address
on Bartlett Alley.

"A young man told me to give it to you. He said, 'Please to
hurry.' "

Miss Culbertson sent for Donaldina. "Do you want to help
with a rescue? This is a vile alley." She indicated the card.

"Of course I want to help."

"Ah Cheng will come to interpret."

The three women dashed down the hill to Stockton Street,
where they found two policemen armed with sledge hammer
and axe. The five white people hurried along the crowded sidewalk. Men of the night in plum-colored silk stepped aside. A
child in a skull cap, with devil chasers jingling about his neck,
darted out of the way. Donaldina noticed crates of vegetables
and bins of dried meats from street stalls locked behind gratings
for the night. Foul odors rose from the gutters; the sweetish reek
of opium seeped around doors.

In dim Bartlett Alley they found the den, its entrance barricaded, windows barred. A knock was not answered. Poundings
brought only echoes. An officer blew his whistle, and three more

Police of the Chinatown Squad aided Margaret Culbertson. They are shown here with their break-in tools, hatchets, sledge hammers, crow bars, and wedges. Standing, left to right, Jesse B. Cook, John T. Green, George Riordan, James Farrell, George W. Wittman. Seated, T. P. Andrews.

police came on the run. Two pried off metal grating from a low window, broke out glass, and led the women inside, while the other men stood on guard outside.

They entered a room lit by a single candle, bare save for a chair, a table, and a bunk set into one wall. A girl, eyes glazed with misery and fear, crouched in a corner. Miss Culbertson rushed to her and helped her to her feet.

"Mission Home," she said. "You come?"

"I come! I come!" The girl gestured to a small wooden box and chattered in Chinese.

Ah Cheng translated. "She says all she owns is in her trunk. She must take it with her."

One officer lifted the box. The other tried the door and found it locked. He crashed his hammer against the lock and kicked open the door into a hall. A Chinese ran toward them shouting, "Stop! Stop! You break my house!"

"Open the street door," the officer commanded.

The glare of the Chinese man swept over the six figures, stopped on the girl, and bored into her face. She cringed against Miss Culbertson. "You!" he screamed. "May all your ancestors curse you, and turn you into a turtle!" He went on abusing her in Chinese. Terrified, the girl whimpered and hid her face.

"Open the street door or I'll bust it!" the officer said.

Still cursing, the Chinese slid back the bolt and put a key into the lock.

The girl sobbed, hysterical. They led her outside, where five policemen surrounded them and helped them pass among crowds from Chinese theatres and people out for late snacks. Some stared, others muttered in Chinese, but none tried to stop them.

Donaldina's thoughts were grim. Her work had truly begun.

CHAPTER FOUR

Fahn Quai

1895-1900

Donaldina looked with new sympathy on her girls, aware of the depravity from which they came. Often she assisted with rescues, and sometimes directed raids, to relieve the Superintendent. In a few months Margaret Culbertson's declining health forced her to take time off, and Donaldina, with some support from Anna, Miss Culbertson's niece, began to manage "920."

She developed closer ties with the Home's sponsors, the Presbyterian Woman's Occidental Board of Foreign Missions. She learned that San Francisco Bay area church women had started crusading against yellow slavery in 1873, the same year Andrew Hallidie's first cable car clanged up and down the Clay Street hill, a block from Sacramento Street.

A number of the founders remained active in 1895, among them Mrs. P. D. Browne, Donaldina's friend, who was president; Mrs. E. V. Robbins, who had braved angry street crowds and been spit upon when she tried to rent quarters for the first girls in 1874; Mrs. Sara B. Cooper, and Mrs. Phoebe Apperson Hearst of the newspaper family.

Under scrutiny at her first Board meeting, Donaldina made a favorable and "modish" impression, wearing a voluminous black voile skirt over a rustly taffeta petticoat, and a purple shirtwaist with leg-of-mutton sleeves. "And they were mutton, not lamb," a lady commented, "the kind that had to be folded in pleats to go under a coat."

The ladies were assured of the new assistant's warmth when a little girl who had recited scripture ran from the platform and climbed into Donaldina's lap. When they visited the children, they noticed they smiled more often than before and sang at play, reflections of Miss Cameron's buoyancy, they told one another.

Donaldina also mentioned changes: "Some of the newly rescued girls come in as forlorn, dejected looking creatures, either too frightened, or else too sullen even to smile. But how truly wonderful it is to see how rapidly they respond to kind words and gentle treatment. I wonder whether we half realize the golden opportunities given us to work for Him who gave His life for us."

Donaldina demonstrated aptness for rescue work and administration, abilities of critical importance in an aide, for Miss Culbertson would never be robust.

When Margaret Culbertson returned from her leave, she appeared stronger. But, as Donaldina's year drew near an end, the Board asked her to remain. The work would be blessed. Her salary of $25 a month, out of which she paid her board, posed no inducement, but it was all the ladies could manage. The decision must rest upon Miss Cameron's dedication and upon her "call to serve."

Donaldina weighed the proposal. Was this the way she wanted to spend her youth? Chinatown was an unlikely place to meet marriageable men. Yet Margaret Culbertson relied on her. If she left, who would assist with rescues? Who would tend the children's measles and whooping cough, the older girls' syphilitic sores and la grippe? Or deal with the ill-tempered young women who would try the patience of a saint?

In the midst of her soul-searching, Charles Bailey, sister Jessie's husband, appeared, expecting to take her home to La Puente. She was torn between homesickness for all the dear faces and country hills and loyalty to her new Chinese family.

"Give me overnight to decide," she said to Charles.

By morning she knew what she wanted to do. She would stay, but first she would take a holiday. In high spirits she went shopping for presents to take home and a few necessities for herself.

Refreshed by two stimulating weeks with family and friends in the quiet San Gabriel Valley, Donaldina returned with new zest. Whenever possible she relieved Miss Culbertson, though the director would not spare herself and refused a sabbatical until almost a year later. She had delayed too long. A few days after she left the Home, her life flickered out.

Looking into the trusting faces of her pupils, Donaldina felt as if the world of "920" had slipped from orbit and fallen onto her shoulders. She declined the superintendency, begging inexperience. She needed more than a scant two years' training, even under "that wonderful woman," Margaret Culbertson. The Board selected a mature person, Mrs. Mary H. Field, as superintendent. Until the children learned to trust Mrs. Field, they looked to Donaldina, calling her "Mama." Appeals for rescue continued, and Donaldina answered. She seemed in demand day and night.

By September of 1897 the strains of Miss Culbertson's illness and death and her new responsibilities overwhelmed Donaldina. Deeply depressed, she suffered what Mrs. Field called a "serious breakdown." She worked her way back to health by putting one foot after another each day, fulfilling her duties.

Writing of that difficult time, she said,

> . . . the beginning of the year was fraught with misgivings, as we took up for the first time this line of the work which had been carried on . . . by our devoted missionary Miss Culbertson. But that the rescue of heathen womanhood is not entrusted to any one individual has been shown by the numbers who still come or send word to us seeking the help and protection of the Home.
> . . . Among those was little Dong Ho, who after long months of abuse at the hands of a cruel and exacting mistress, made her escape one Sabbath morning . . . the poor, homeless little waif found herself received with much the same enthusiasm and joy with which the prodigal son was welcomed at his father's home. Dong Ho's only anxiety seemed to be in regard to the small bundle which she brought, containing all her worldly possessions—a few small, soiled garments, a broken comb, and two little wooden chopsticks. These were her treasures, and she clung to them, fearing that we might take them from her.

And of a Sacramento rescue Donaldina made a rare confession of her own fear, "Terror lent wings to our feet."

The "turtle men" (slave-owners) of the tongs welcomed the

change of staff at "920," hoping to rout Mrs. Field and Donaldina. An owner sent a message purporting to be from a girl wanting rescue. When Donaldina rushed into the apartment, she found, dangling from the ceiling, an effigy of herself, with a dagger in the heart. Discounting threats, she insisted that people who intend violence act. They do not give warning.

Chinatown came to take for granted the flying figures of a slender white woman and her tiny Chinese interpreter. Offenders quailed before her expression, implacable as granite.

Sergeant Jesse B. Cook of the Chinatown police squad and most of his men cooperated, aiding Donaldina to find an address, ordering her admittance, breaking in doors or windows when necessary, and protecting her party.

Yet frequently Donaldina did not find the girls she sought. She discovered that the Mission was ringed by enemies as well as friends. A few police officers accepted bribes to betray her. Slave-owners set watchmen and informers throughout Chinatown and, when warned of impending raids, whisked their slaves into secret rooms, over roof-tops, or into cellars and underground tunnels. Donaldina followed, sometimes catching up, often not. But she was learning to search and to gauge the cunning of her adversaries.

If the Mission got possession of a slave, tongs helped her owner try to recover her through legal and pseudo-legal means. They paid unscrupulous white lawyers for writs of habeas corpus and warrants falsely accusing a girl of theft; they devised fictitious search warrants. If an owner succeeded in gaining custody of his slave, he prevented her from appearing in court on her trial date.

If Donaldina had not been appointed a girl's guardian before her owner appeared at the Home with police escort and genuine search papers, he was courteously admitted. But rarely did he find his quarry. She would be hidden between folding doors in the dining room or behind rice bags in the pantry; or if she were brave enough, in the dark basement or the bowels of the sub-basement. Few girls or their owners dared face the evil spirits they believed might lurk in those black holes.

Understanding judges decided the destiny of many rescued

Chinese girls, placing some in Chinese families, deporting others, releasing wives to Chinese husbands, or appointing guardians, often in the Mission Home, where Donaldina adopted them as wards. With her attorney, Henry E. Monroe, who succeeded Abe Ruef,[1] she appeared routinely in juvenile court, and with the girls involved in criminal charges, in any court where their cases were tried.

In the spring of 1900 a landmark contest between Donaldina and the tongs employed every evasion, trick, and legal recourse that either side could muster. It was headlined by the newspapers of San Francisco, Palo Alto, and Stanford University; detailed by Carol Green Wilson in *Chinatown Quest;* and told in several versions of "920" 's records.

On the evening of March 23, Donaldina went with a young man to rescue a slave girl, Kum Qui, on Baker Alley. She plucked her from a nest of tong men, and rushed her to the Home through a heckling crowd. A week later, her owner and a constable from San Jose, a town fifty miles south of San Francisco, served a warrant charging the girl with grand larceny. They insisted on taking her to San Jose. Impulsively, Donaldina went along.

The party did not reach San Jose, but met a judge midway in Palo Alto, site of Stanford University. Donaldina asked for immediate trial, but the judge refused and jailed Kum Qui. Donaldina shared her cell. Before dawn three men broke in, overpowered Donaldina and ran out with Kum Qui. Donaldina followed the captors and her ward to a waiting buggy, and jumped in with them, but was pushed out onto the dusty road. She raced back through dark Palo Alto streets in search of help.

Meanwhile Kum Qui's abductors had located a Palo Alto justice of the peace who agreed to hold impromptu court. He heard the larceny charge, found the girl guilty, and levied a fine of $5, which her abductors paid. Having gained legal possession of her, the three men whisked her to San Francisco, where they had arranged her marriage.

A ceremony completed, the party hurried to the depot. There

[1] Attorney who had given his services to Miss Culbertson, but later shifted his loyalties and exploited the Chinese.

Miss Cameron, who had been tipped off by a friend, and a police escort stopped them. Kum Qui's husband was placed under arrest, and he, she, and her kidnappers were ordered on trial in Mayfield, a small community near Stanford. Word of the affair had spread. Outraged, Stanford students marched on the jail where Donaldina and the girl had been held, yelling, "Bring your own rope. Tear the place down." Prominent Palo Alto citizens and Stanford professors called a community meeting.

Donaldina appeared and calmly told her story, concluding with the plea, "In the name of the law and public decency I protest against these proceedings and the treatment of a defenseless woman. I make the statement by way of appeal to the Public of Palo Alto."

A *San Francisco Chronicle* reporter wrote:

> Seldom anywhere has a great audience made so wonderful a demonstration of enthusiasm as when Miss Cameron came forward in response to the introduction and told her simple, straightforward story of the experience she had had in attempting to protect her ward. . . . Although low, Miss Cameron's voice was heard in all portions of the room.
>
> The speaker proved by her beauty and modest manner that she was a refined and cultured woman, and it seemed amazing how men could subject such a woman to such vile indignities as she related as having been perpetrated at Palo Alto. . . .
>
> We admire the fearless, heroic, and womanly action of Miss Cameron in her efforts to prevent the abduction of her ward, which was accomplished under the guise of the law.

Through her Chinese friends Donaldina discovered that two years earlier Kum Qui, one of a group of seventy "Oriental Maidens" portraying the Chinese way of life at the Omaha Exposition, had been admitted to the United States by a special Act of Congress, which required them to return to China within six months after the exposition's close. Instead, most were spirited into San Francisco. With this knowledge Donaldina secured the cooperation of Colonel Jackson, Immigration Commissioner of San Francisco. He appointed Dr. John Endicott Gardner, government interpreter, to represent him in the Mayfield trial.

During the questioning Dr. Gardner asked Kum Qui if she

had a registration card. The girl replied, "No." He placed her under arrest. The San Jose constable, still conniving, requested that she be removed from the courtroom. Shortly afterward, he slipped out and drove off with the girl. Hearing a commotion, Dr. Gardner investigated. He and another man leaped into a buggy and followed the kidnapper, overtaking him on a blind road. The runaways were placed under arrest.

Customs officials took possession of Kum Qui, and a federal court appointed Donaldina the girl's legal guardian. When Donaldina reported to her Occidental Board, she expressed gratitude for the sympathy of the people of Palo Alto. Her Chinese daughters in the Home sent this message to the Stanford students who had been good to Miss Cameron, "In all thy ways acknowledge Him and He shall direct thy paths."

On April 27, a front-page article in the *Palo Alto Times* proclaimed that the San Jose grand jury had indicted the justice of the peace and deputy constable and two Chinese. The long investigation of detectives from San Jose and San Francisco was praised. An editorial exulted that convictions "proved people are anxious to have guilty parties brought to light and punished," which would "put a stop to such dastardly proceedings."

Kum Qui was not the only girl from the Omaha Exposition to leave her mark in Chinatown. Police rounded up more than thirty young women, many of whom the court assigned to "920" until their trials. Most, as reported by the missionary magazine, "The Occident," ". . . submitted to the inevitable without much protest. . . . Some of them have occasionally come into the school room or to morning and evening prayers; but most of them spend their time in playing dominoes, dressing their hair, planning their meals and enjoying them, or lying on their beds in utter idleness."

Others of the girls, in Donaldina's words,

. . . distinguished themselves by loud weeping or volleys of Chinese imprecations. . . . When these half frenzied creatures found themselves prisoners they shrieked and beat themselves with their hands; they spat upon the furniture and clean floors . . . the scene was one of horror and yet of pathos. [She continues in the Ledger,] . . . It was nearly four months before the last of these girls taken on

September 27 left the Home. Not one when made free could be persuaded to remain. The government paid their board at the rate of
40 cts. a day per individual.

When the last of the Home's noisy guests departed, Donaldina
wondered what effect publicity about them would have on the
work. She wanted the awful existence of Chinese slavery known.
But she protested attaching a bad name to all Chinese, for she
had found most of her Chinese neighbors to be fine people who
cared for their families and lived respectably.

A newsboy, Frenchie, whose father ran a French restaurant on
California Avenue, brought her inklings of neighborhood gos-
sip. After the exposition affair he had looked up at her, admir-
ingly, declaring, "Boy, you're a regular Carry Nation."

He seemed to know, too, of white slaves she had rescued from
"boarding houses" at the edge of the Chinese quarter, where
both white and "Chinee girls" served. He heard how the managers raged at Miss Cameron, "that interfering S.O.B.!"

But certain madams who claimed "legitimate businesses" with
all-white girl entertainers, silkily informed on their Chinese
competitors. They were outraged when Donaldina occasionally
rescued one of their white slaves.

Frenchie sometimes happened to see "that Scotch woman with
the thick brogue and the rusty hair" dash out on raids. And
when she came back, leading her girls, or an arm about one, not
hurrying, "plain as hell, with more gall than a burglar," he
spread the word, and hoped Miss Cameron might ring him up
to bring her a newspaper. She always smiled and talked a minute
or made a joke and sometimes gave him ten or fifteen cents for
a five-cent paper. She was nice.

The furious tongs felt otherwise: A White Devil, "Fahn
Quai," ruled the Mission!

Donaldina summed up the state of affairs differently:

While the world today is convulsed with war our Home too has
not been exempt from its share of exciting events . . . as some poor
slave girl or abused child made her hasty and terrified flight . . . from
her angry pursuers. Our warfare against the wickedness and cruelty
of these heathen people is sometimes a discouraging conflict, yet as

we look back over the past year we are thankful to see that much good has been done, and many victories gained. . . .

How grateful she was for the young lives entrusted to her who could and did respond. Her daughters gave Donaldina a new name.

CHAPTER FIVE

Lo Mo

1900-1903

Like any mother, Donaldina was proud of her children. Whenever a church or club asked her to speak, she took some of them along. How illuminating for people who knew Chinese only as laundrymen and cooks—or highbinders—to see her daughters in pink sahms, hear them recite scripture, and "sing like little birds."

When the chorus had no accompaniment, Ah Lon (or Lonnie) started the singing. Once she leaned against Lo Mo, tucked a braid in her pocket, and solemnly asked,

"Mama, what would the Mission do without me?"

"I don't know what the Mission would do," Donaldina replied, smothering a laugh, "but I know *I* couldn't do without you."

The performers, who traveled by street car, cable car, or ferry boat, attracted attention. One day on the ferry to Oakland a troupe of eight, ranging from five to twelve years of age, chattered and asked questions.

"It's my turn to sit next to Mama."

"Mama, how long 'til we get there?"

A group of tourists looked curiously from the Chinese children to their white "mama." A woman approached Donaldina.

"Pardon me, Madam. But are these little girls really yours?"

Donaldina smiled. "Indeed they are."

"All of them?"

"Yes."

"You seem so young," the stranger faltered, and returned to her seat.

Later Donaldina told the story with relish, adding, "I hope my Creator will forgive me. But I told the legal truth, you know. Can't you imagine the head shaking that went on when those easterners took home their tale about cosmopolitan San Francisco?"

The girls decided to give their white Mama a Chinese name, making her more their own, and quieting public curiosity. Having grown up among people with little education, they chose the colloquial "Lo Mo," which is freely translated "old mama" instead of "Mo Chun," the more dignified word for "Mother." By the time the commonness was understood, Donaldina's title "Lo Mo" had been adopted with love and pride throughout Chinatown.

In 1900 Mrs. Field resigned, and the Board persuaded Donaldina to become superintendent. Because, for years, she had been the most conspicuous representative of the Mission in Chinatown, the community scarcely noticed a change. Inside "920" Lo Mo continued to mother her children. She turned over daily routine to a new housekeeper, Frances P. Thompson, tall and prim in appearance, but a kind woman who won the girls' trust. Donaldina praised Miss Thompson to her board, as a very efficient matron who taught the girls to be neat, clean and capable housekeepers, which, she felt was as important "and calls for just as much care and patient teaching as do the more intellectual lines of instruction."

Miss Thompson whirled through a program that would have buried a lesser woman. In her report she described a routine of housework that kept "all on the alert, with constant interruptions from callers. . . . Our young cooks soon learn to handle 24 lbs. of rice daily without spoiling, as well as various quantities of meat, fish, and vegetables. . . ."[1] She marveled that a child of 14 was able to take charge of her own bed and room, make her

---

[1] Food prices were on the rise. In her journal, Mrs. E. V. Robbins notes that it cost 5c a day to feed a girl in 1878. By 1902 Board members paid 10c for lunch served them in the Home on meeting days.

clothes, bathe methodically, and attend school. Four girls between 11 and 14 added waiting table for the teachers and cleaning the dining room to their personal responsibilities.

Further, said Miss Thompson,

. . . We have many visitors from the far east who occupy a great
amount of our time. Some days we have entertained as many as one
hundred, during the week of Chinese New Year; and average from
twenty to thirty a day for months at a time, during the period tourists visit our coast.

Our girls cheerfully entertain all who come and request them to
sing, play or recite, at any time of day or night. We often call them
up after having retired.

The Home gained enough notice to become part of every
Chinatown tour, in the year 1900 hosting more than a thousand
visitors from the United States, Canada, and Europe.

Miss Thompson told of a visit from President Theodore
Roosevelt in 1901:

The family had retired, when at half an hour past midnight a
messenger hurriedly announced that the distinguished party was near
at hand.

The gas was turned on, the sleepy household aroused, and all was
in readiness by the time our guests were in the house. Even the babies
were brought down to sing their little songs and hymns, and give
verses of cheer and counsel from the Book of books.

The appreciation showered upon the wee trio quite repaid any
effort that was made to entertain. They were pronounced the most
charming little people they [the presidential party] had ever met.

Everyone in the Home was expected to do all she could for
herself and for others. Each older daughter was put in charge of
one or more younger children, a necessity because of the few paid
employees. And Donaldina believed her daughters would value
the experience when they had children of their own.

The girls also learned sewing and handwork skills to their
immediate and future benefit, according to Miss Thompson:
". . . Darning and soleing many dozen of stockings has kept the
fingers busy [in sewing class]. Pieced and tacked three quilts.
Many dozen of buttons have been sewed on garments brought

in from outside, which contributed a few cents to the girls pleasure. . . ."

In a year pupils made eight hundred buttonhole strips, at five cents per dozen. An older girl sewed for a factory, in ten months' time earning enough for fare to China. The sewing class turned out ten dozen sahms for stores, and made all the bed linens and comforters for the home. The girls, Miss Thompson said, "accomplished a good deal in the way of mending and making new garments. *One* suit consists of four garments. With thirty-five girls in the Home, we are required to make one hundred and forty garments every four or five months, as with constant washing and steady wear they are soon to be replaced. . . . We are a busy people, and withal happy in the work. . . ."

To that Donaldina might have added, "but all work and no play could make Jill a dull girl." Recalling her childhood joy on the San Joaquin meadows, she planned outings for the little girls. In Golden Gate Park they first saw a green and flowering world. They ran on cool grass instead of the concrete of their play yard, fed ducks on the pond, and watched the wonderful new Dutch windmill turn in the breeze. Lo Mo bought them peanuts, telling them to eat all they wanted, but to put the shells back in the bag so they would not litter the beautiful park.

Autumn brought golden days that burned off summer fogs and lured the family to the beach. Lo Mo removed her high-buttoned shoes and long black stockings, tucked her skirts into a fisherman's wrap above the knee, and waded in the surf with the children. Afterward she let them bury her feet, then wriggled them until the sand fell away. When her toes appeared, the girls screamed with glee.

Though "920" was not intended for young children, Donaldina could not bear to turn away infants, nor those born to girls who were pregnant when rescued. Going from one part of the house to another, she often paused to cuddle "my babies," to pat a head, kiss a cheek, or dance a toddler on her knee.

In a family of fifty young rivals, Lo Mo knew the importance of giving time apart to individuals. On busy days she took a child with her on errands. A ride on a street car or a cable car, which five-year-old Tien Wu had called "that little house that goes up the hill by itself," could be delicious adventure. Out of those intimate times a child learned, "I am special to Lo Mo." Mrs. Kelley, secretary of the Board, observed, "The spirit of the family was never sweeter and more Christian-like in its tone. . . ." Little children mentioned in Donaldina's report reflect that climate.

Little Yute Ho Ji . . . made her debut into public life a few weeks ago when she appeared before the Grand Jury of this city to bear witness to the fact that even tiny children are brought into this country as slaves. She made such an impression upon that august body that several members soon visited the Mission to see for themselves what was being done in the way of rescue work.
   . . . May is three years old now, and somewhat precocious for her years. Not long ago some older children took candy to church to beguile the long hours of Chinese service which they do not understand; they were corrected for this small offense and May heard their reproof. Later she said to Chin Mooie, who takes care of her, "When I get to be a big girl, I won't eat things in church, if I do people will say I don't have good teaching at the Mission Home."

The family also faced sorrow among its youngest:

A death which touched us exceedingly was that of . . . (Mrs. Ng Sing's) dear little daughter "Margaret," born two days before Miss Culbertson left the Home and named by her—her last name-sake. She was a beautiful and wonderfully winning child who drew to herself hosts of friends. None who were present will forget the beautiful funeral of this Christian Chinese child—the small, snow-white casket covered with exquisite flowers—her own picture laid at the end, and a lovely engraving of the Madonna and child, which she loved, placed at the head by her father—the sweet singing by the children from the Home who had been her little friends who were present.

Many Chinese were impressed by the Christian ceremony, with its fearless and hopeful attitudes toward death. Some remembered that in China their dead babies had been thrown over the city walls where dogs could be heard growling and fighting over the bodies.

Lo Mo believed that her daughters learned much about life and death from their Bible study—a half hour morning and evening and thirty minutes during the school day. And they practiced kindness outside their home circle. Known as a "public-spirited woman," Donaldina kept up with world affairs. The Spanish-American War and the Boxer Rebellion in China dismayed her and she encouraged her daughters to contribute through the Red Cross. Kum Ying, secretary of the Junior Red Cross Society, told of its first meeting.

The girls of the Presbyterian Mission have organized a Red Cross Society. . . . We are going to change our officers every six months. And we try to help the soldiers all we can by sewing for them. And we always remember them in our prayers, because we think that they are right and we know that God will help the right. We are very glad that the American soldiers are not fighting for land or money, but to make men free.

Secretary Kum Ying

Suey Leen, the eleven-year-old orphaned daughter of a fine family, had come to the Home a year earlier, knowing no English, but sent this letter to a soldier.

Dear Soldiers:

I write These letters for you. I am very Sorry you go to war. I hope God help you. I live These Country. I Give These text for you: "Be thou faithful unto death and I will give thee a crown of life." I was born in These Country. I am native daughter. God bless you, goodbye.

Suey Leen
[Called the "Sweet Singer" of the Mission]

Donaldina felt particular sympathy for girls whose ragged backgrounds limited their happiness. She tried to offset early handicaps. "Because of my childhood family I have a great deal of love," she said, "and I can pour it out."

She poured out love to Tien Wu, who continued resistant, wringing her patience dry. One chill morning Tien got into trouble through a friend's mistake. The girl, who rose at six o'clock to prepare breakfast, persuaded Tien to help, lest evil spirits bother her when she was alone in the dark.

Before daylight the two girls went downstairs to the Chinese kitchen, lit the kitchen lamps and stoked the cookstove. They chattered, their voices shrill. Tien began chopping meat and vegetables.

Suddenly her companion shrieked, "Devils! Devils! They come for us." She pointed to a window where two white-clad figures pounded. She fled, screaming.

Tien recognized Miss Cameron and a guest. As she went to let them in from the fire escape, she noticed the time, two hours earlier than rising time.

On hearing the chopping noise, Donaldina had feared that slave owners were trying to break in. In her relief at finding no danger she berated Tien. What was she doing here in the middle of the night? All that racket! Had she no consideration for others? She was to go to her room at once!

Tien flipped her long queues over her shoulder, "You don't need to tell me what to do!" she retorted, "I was here long before you came!"

She banged out, her rebellion mounting. In her room she rushed to open the window, took off all her upper clothing and sat down, allowing the fog to billow over her. She sucked in deep breaths of wet air. The hubbub wakened her roommate.

Tien cried, "You go next door if you get cold. I show that Miss Cameron. She gave it to me for nothing. I catch pneumonia and die. Then I come back in a spirit and taunt her!"

Next day Tien complained, "I didn't even catch cold, but some day I pay her back."

Soon she experienced another kind of confrontation with Lo Mo. For several years Tien had adored an older girl, Yuen Qui, who was a translator and an able helper on raids. Donaldina loved her sweet disposition and congenial company.

Yuen Qui caught tuberculosis and was bedridden for weeks. Tien, disconsolate, hovered near her friend. One morning as Tien stood at her bedside, the girl's face changed. Frightened, Tien called Donaldina, who recognized that Yuen Qui was dead. Donaldina threw herself on the bed beside her, sobbing. Tien perceived the real Lo Mo, a mother deeply mourning her beloved daughter. Impulsively she went to Donaldina.

"Don't cry, Lo Mo. I help you."

Tien kept her word. From that day she seemed to understand Lo Mo's feelings, some of which Donaldina expressed in a report to her Board:

There are lights and shades in all lives, and we have had our share of both in our life here; but the darkest shadow in many years was that which fell over our Home . . . when dear Yuen Qui, the lovely, wise and capable young interpreter of our Mission began to fail in health—suddenly and relentlessly did this shadow deepen and darken until it became to us the darkness of death. . . . The loss of Yuen Qui in our work is irreparable. We feel that no other will ever be quite what she was, and what shall we say of the deep personal loss to us, of one whose every thought and act seemed to be for our help and comfort? Her life among us was a blessing to all and her memory will be a constant benediction. Her sun went down while it was yet day, it went not down behind a cloud, but melted into the pure light of heaven.

Tien tried to take Yuen Qui's place. Not that she could keep out of mischief. But her recognition of Donaldina's love for the dead girl, and for herself, poured self-esteem into her life. She asked to help as interpreter on raids. Accepted, she developed into a quick and shrewd assistant.

Like most of the girls, Tien delighted in the Home's frequent weddings, "some brilliant occasions, some very quiet ones." Chinese men still outnumbered women in America, and girls prepared to be happy wives and mothers were much sought. Donaldina became an Oriental matchmaker for her daughters. She selected young men of high caliber; they must be Christian and show themselves able to support a family financially.

Mrs. Field had once said, ". . . If we were to speak of an Anglo-Saxon institution we might say lightly there had been several serious cases of heart trouble but as the Mongolian does not allow that useful muscle a place in his matrimonial arrangements we will say simply that we have had . . . weddings."

Donaldina could not agree. Suitability did not always assure compatibility. She required a courtship period which gave the partners time to become friends. Often genuine romance flowered. If love failed to unfold, she did not encourage them to marry.

The photograph that Tien Wu, about 16, sent to "my American Papa," 1900.

Yuen Qui, who died in 1900, interpreter and friend to Lo Mo, and adored by Tien.

The wedding of one former mooie jai was an occasion to re-member. The girl had run away from a cruel mistress five years earlier and "proved to be a bright refined child." She accepted Christianity, learned American cooking, for several years or-dered for the girls' table from the Chinese butcher and vegetable man, and served as doorkeeper.

When she wanted to marry, Lo Mo chose ". . . a splendid Christian man who has a large beautiful store . . ." in southern California. The pair fell deeply in love, and, because the bride-groom paid all wedding bills, this well-to-do merchant expected a lavish affair.

On the wedding day everyone tumbled out of bed before dawn. Donaldina and several older daughters boarded street cars to go to the wholesale flower market at Fifth and Harrison Streets. They carried home armloads of white blooms—roses, dahlias, and chrysanthemums, and then departed in the opposite direction for Golden Gate Park. Lo Mo's friend, the crusty Scot, John McLaren, the park's creator and superintendent, gave standing orders to his gardeners to prune greens for Miss Cameron.

Back at "920" Miss Thompson reported that the big cake was cooling and the Chinese sweets ready. With branches and vines the decorators made a green bower of the bare meeting room, enlarged in 1900 and called "The Chapel." They twined posts and stair railing and covered a trellis and arch on stage. Younger children helped tuck in white blossoms, while Donaldina ar-ranged an enormous bouquet for the wok in the entry and a bowl of roses on the dining table.

The fragrance of flowers and baking spread through the Home. Toward evening Donaldina retreated to her room to rest and to change into her silk dress. She thought how fortunate it was that the bride had been rescued before she was sold into prostitution. But for others who had come out of the most de-basing slavery their new faith had worked miracles. Chinese girls traditionally wore red for weddings, but the Home's brides dressed in white, symbolic of purity. And rightly so.

Even girls who had been forced into prostitution experienced a cleansing of spirit at "920," and in their white wedding gowns glowed with happiness just as the bride did that night. Lo Mo lingered over a memory of the bright, earnest face of a rescued slave of whom she said, "The past, with all its sin and contamination, seemed to have fallen from her like a mantle. No one would ever imagine her history."

That evening nearly a hundred guests gathered. Chinese were enchanted by ceremony and prized invitations to weddings in the Home. Because the girls had no fathers, it was Lo Mo who rounded the newel post with the bride on her arm when the Lohengrin wedding march began.

After the ceremony, the guests enjoyed a Chinese-American reception. Lo Mo had ordered a carriage for the bride and groom, and provided rice to be thrown. Like any mother of the bride, she shed tears as her daughter was driven away, as did the excited girls.

Inevitably, to a beautiful woman who gave so much of her sympathies to other couples, romance came again to Donaldina.

CHAPTER SIX

Another Direction

1900-1904

Between 1900 and 1904, the year Donaldina became thirty-five, she was, perhaps, involved in more dark and bright encounters than at any other time in her career. She met the deepest love of her life, mothered several hundred girls, and fought crucial battles against the highbinder tongs.

Donaldina's romance began during a weekend with sister Jessie, her husband, Charlie Bailey, and little daughter, Caroline, in the small town of Alhambra, near Pasadena, in southern California.

Early Sunday morning she slipped outdoors. Her eyes traced the jagged spine of the Sierra Madres, dark against the pale sky. Light stabbed between the peaks, and as the sun rose, its glow suffused the valley and drowsing town.

A thrilling promise for the day. She loved family visits, and doted on her only niece, Caroline, with her bright mind, beautiful curls, and beguiling Cameron charm.

Caroline was up early, too, eager to put on the new white organdy dress "Aunt Dowey" had made her. The family walked to church. Charlie tipped his derby hat, his steel-blue eyes twinkling, and took Jessie on his arm. Caroline caught her aunt's hand, and the four started down the street bordered by young camphor trees. Donaldina stopped to admire the home of Gail Borden, dairy magnate, and his beautiful flowers and grounds, watered by a new kind of underground sprinkling system.

Inside the square church Caroline leaned happily against

Donaldina and smoothed her full skirt. Birdsong and the hum of bees came through the open window, and she looked about to see what the ladies wore. She later told her aunt the exact number of buttons up the long row on her neighbor's high-necked blouse and the designs of all the elegant yoked dresses.

Services in this little church stimulated Donaldina. The young bachelor minister, the Rev. Ben Bazata, a good friend with whom she rode horseback and had long talks, "preached the gospel" in a solid way that satisfied his older parishioners. She described Ben as "homely and attractive, with a glorious baritone voice" and a zestful charm that attracted young people. His widowed mother and two younger sisters kept open house in the parsonage. Matchmaking minds in the congregation hoped in vain to pair Ben and Dolly.

On this particular Sunday Ben's younger brother, Charles, a student at Occidental College in Los Angeles, was visiting, and the Bazatas, Baileys, and Donaldina had dinner together. Charles, a big blond football player, never ran out of what the girls called "silly crazy things to say."

Witty herself, and free for a few hours from "920" 's demands, Dolly enjoyed the party. She and Charles fell in love almost at once. The Scottish Camerons and Bohemian Bazatas came out of the same mold—alike in family solidarity, cordiality, pleasure in the out-of-doors, and dedication to their faith. Charles, Ben and his sisters, Anna and Aloisia (who adopted the American name, Jennie) sang at home for fun, and as a quartet for public programs.

With the Bazatas, Dolly felt young and happy. She and Jennie became close friends, and went into "gales of giggles" at slight provocation. When time allowed, the young crowd rode burros up Mount Wilson, camping at overnight stations.

As their romance flourished, Donaldina and Charles found five hundred miles between them a hardship. But both were as committed to their work as to each other. Charles had little time and less money to meet her in San Francisco, though Donaldina once wrote, "Charles took lunch with me today." She was reticent, but her family knew from the glow about her that this dream of her own was a precious thing. They marveled that she met horror and evil each day without turning sour. She kept her conviction that "people are wonderful and dear."

Whether Donaldina influenced Charles's choice of a profession, no one knows. But midway in their courtship he decided to enter the ministry and to train at Princeton, New Jersey's Presbyterian seminary. He covered the sorrow at parting with a show of nonsense. As Caroline watched, he picked up an old silk hat of her father's and setting it on his head at an angle, strutted around the room roaring funny songs.

But both Donaldina and Charles felt apprehensive about being separated by a continent for several years. In May of 1903 Donaldina wished she could share the inspiration of General Assembly with him. That body, the highest judicatory of the Presbyterian denomination, held its annual meeting in Los Angeles. The Rev. Dr. Henry Van Dyke, a Princeton professor and author of *The Other Wise Man,* which had deeply moved her, was moderator, and gave the keynote address on "Religion in Relation to Human Rights," in Immanuel Presbyterian Church.

Donaldina found Dr. Van Dyke charming, distinguished, and elegant in his swallow-tail coat. His message, urging simplicity, appealed to her as right for the times, "The word of living men— that is what we need." How fortunate that Charles was training under professors like that!

At the General Assembly Donaldina's little singers were beautifully received, called "a flower garden of Oriental children." She introduced her work to many fine people, among them the Tookers: Nathaniel, a missionary-minded man of affluence, and his daughters, Mary and Gertrude. His son was a medical missionary to China.

Charles and Donaldina did not meet again until August of 1904, on her furlough. She had served the Home for nine years, four of them as director. Strain had brought her to the brink of collapse. Her understanding Board and her friends gathered a fund and gave her a sabbatical year abroad. She planned to meet Isabella, the sister in Scotland, whom she had never seen, and to visit China. Before she sailed, she and Charles would share a wonderful week in New York, where she could stay with friends.

Friends also arranged for a free pass from San Francisco to New York, with a stop-over in Minneapolis, where a married daughter needed her counsel. Though her funds were meager, she could not resist buying parting gifts for some of the youngest children, who were not easily consoled when they learned she was to leave them for a whole year. Wilmina Wheeler would act as superintendent in her absence. By the time Lo Mo had made her preparations and said tearful goodbyes to her children, she was almost too tired to travel.

She visited Jessie and her family in Sacramento before starting across the country, and in a big high-ceilinged hotel with long windows and flowered rugs, Donaldina enjoyed several days of refreshment.

In August heat across western deserts and midland prairies, cooped in a Pullman car's green plush seats by day and curtained berth by night, she sweltered. Windows could not be opened lest cinders and smoke blow in. Minneapolis was a welcome oasis, and the visit with her daughter satisfying. Afterward, Miss Emma Page, another friend to Chinese, insisted that Donaldina spend a week in her lodge on Lake Minnetonka. There she relaxed on walks among the "temples of trees," swam and boated on the lake, and rested beneath pines sighing in the wind. She was ready to meet Charles.

Mrs. Lyman Kelley, an Occidental Board member, had arranged for a shipper in New York to help Donaldina, and he booked her on a freighter that carried live beef from Philadelphia to Liverpool and accommodated a few passengers.

Sailing time was disappointingly near. It allowed her and Charles only one day together in Philadelphia instead of the week they had planned. The lovers' brief time was full of emotions pent up during their long separation. They had so many decisions to crowd into a few hours that the light-hearted happiness of earlier times was impossible to revive. Since they last met each had taken on sobering responsibilities. Donaldina's sisters were growing older, and would need family support. Helen was nursing patients recommended by her family doctor. Kathie's love for children had drawn her into orphanage work, and Annie, always the center of the family, raised chickens and made soap to sell. But the years were encroaching upon them. Someone should stand by. Brother Al had married and his hands were full with his own growing family. Only Dolly was free.

Charles had to support a widowed mother; he had no money of his own and could look forward to years as an underpaid young clergyman. Both Donaldina and Charles felt strong religious "callings" to their separate careers. How, and when, dared they marry?

During their precious day together they reviewed every aspect of their dilemma, believing they could surely find a way to meet their obligations and join their lives. At dusk, when they went to the pier where Donaldina's steamer, the "Merion," was preparing to sail, they had found no solutions.

For hours they paced the wooden planks, scarcely hearing the river port sounds. Gulls keened, tugboats hooted, and departing vessels sounded their gutteral warnings. Voices, the clip-clop of horses' hoofs, and the rattle of wagons surged around them unnoticed. Gradually the day sounds faded. In the damp air night breezes whispered a thin melody through ships' smokestacks and cranes. Occasionally a creaking buggy paused to discharge passengers, who stared curiously at the handsome young couple striding the docks, arm in arm. Donaldina looked more frail than ever before, and less rosy. Charles had matured into a rugged handsomeness. Intent, looking into each other's eyes from time to time, they walked away from the shadowed wharves, then back toward the freighter. Near midnight they stopped at the foot of the gangplank.

What they said or did belongs to the secret memories a Cameron did not talk about. But later Donaldina let it be known to her intimates that she and Charles had concluded they could never blend into a shared life what God required of each of them. Their hard decision then became an easy one. The will of God was indisputable. And, somehow, it must be for the best.

*   *   *   *   *

That first night of her voyage, as the steamer slid down the river toward the sea, Donaldina forced her thoughts away from Charles and their fateful decision. She must consider her blessings. In thirty-five years had she not lived more fully than some women do in a lifetime? The Lord must have further plans for her if He asked her not to marry Charles.

The pain of that obedience was a fresh wound. She would start healing by responding to whatever came her way. Like Moses she seemed to have been asked, "What is that in thine hand?" The answer: the work at "920." She looked back over her past five years. Life and death and happiness had been at stake every hour. She remembered reading, "God has a thought for every life he sends into this world." Sometimes she wondered what his thought was for the poor Chinese slave girls He brought to her very doors. They should be given from the fullness of lives such as hers and thus be led up to Him.

As she once wrote, whatever God's thought was, her duty seemed plain, her privilege and opportunity great. She would say, "Yet will I rejoice." And begin rejoicing over a dear child like Ah Ching, who was a member of the quartet. Her voice and those of Ah Tye, Lonnie, and Margaret blended with a sweetness that often brought tears.

On a rainy day during an epidemic of bubonic plague in San Francisco in 1900, nine-year-old Ah Ching had slipped through quarantine lines to "920," outside the plague area, looking for help for her dying sister. So frantic was her plea that Donaldina, dressed as an old Chinese woman and sheltered by a black umbrella, went with her into the forbidden zone: through a friend's shop, upstairs to a skylight, and across several roofs, and down another stairway to the apartment Ah Ching called home.

She and her sister, orphans, had been cared for by a Chinese family who did not call a doctor though the girl was dying. They believed her body was possessed by evil spirits, and had put her outside the door on three hard wooden chairs. Donaldina called a physician who diagnosed not the plague, but a ruptured appendix. He allowed both the sister and Ah Ching to be moved to "920." The sick child lived only three hours.

Her sister, amazed by the kindness shown to a dying person, wanted to remain with Lo Mo. After a hard struggle Donaldina persuaded Ah Ching's friends to surrender her, and was appointed the child's guardian.

Often, Donaldina noted, ignorance took pathetic tolls. One of the girls in the Home had been so terrified of inoculation against the plague that she had jumped out of a second-story window and broken her ankle. Allowed to get up after ten weeks in bed, she fell and broke the ankle again, which took another six weeks to heal.

Donaldina admired a young girl, Bow Yoke, who had been put through many stormy court appearances and had shown unusual courage. She was saved by Donaldina's counsel, Henry Monroe, "our splendid, faithful lawyer, whose assistance and advice so courteously and freely given for the past eight years has made it possible for us to win many cases which seemed almost hopeless."

After some time in the Home, Bow Yoke went to China, where she became a native helper in the mission cause. At least once a year she sent Mr. Monroe a gift or a letter and to Donaldina she wrote,

Dear Miss, I am still staying with Mrs. Clark on Manno, at work, look after the children, have twelve dollars every month is so, and before I was find my mother, sister and brother they are very glad, then I will speak with them where the place I live, then she cry and very sorry for sinful. I will thank you very much and kind to me, will always be remember you forever. I hope you will keep in good health and strong, perhaps after I will go back to San Francisco, again can you help for me?

Sincerely yours,

Bow Yoke

Lo Mo had cherished a letter from Moon Ho, a girl rescued from Isleton and sent to the Victoria Home in Hong Kong. Translated, her letter read:

My Much Loved Mother: It is now some months since I left you, but even when I sleep I do not forget you. I do not know whether you are now well and happy, but here in school I am both well and happy, so I beg of you not to be anxious about me, because I am so far away from you it is very hard to write to you. It is also difficult to remember. Now I am writing these few words to wish you peace. Now I write this letter hoping that you will answer it and tell me of your welfare, then I shall be glad. I pray God always to give you peace. I am in the second class at school. I hope you will always pray for me and ask God to make me wise, to understand his word. I also pray that God will make your scholars obedient, this will make me glad. I should like them all to write to me, then I shall know better how to write to you. Now I wish all of you peace, for this is what my heart desires for you.

Moon Ho

Donaldina thought with gratitude of an aide, Frank Kane, of the Pacific Society, who, when others had hesitated, helped rescue Chyo, a young Japanese, now at San Rafael working in a lovely home, happy, independent, and well cared for. What a contrast to the forlorn little painted creature with a tinsel crown on her small drooping head who had been brought to Donaldina at midnight two years earlier.

Donaldina rhapsodized in her report:

Well might these rescued and transformed lives be compared to the beautiful story of Michael Angelo's statue of David. Carved with exquisite grace and perfection of form this wonderful work of art has stood for centuries admired by thousands of pilgrims from all over the world who visit Florence every year. But the very thrilling thing in the story of this noble statue is that it was the stone's second chance. A sculptor began work on a splendid piece of marble, but lacking skill he only hacked and marred the beautiful block of stone, and at last cast it aside as quite worthless. It lay thus abandoned for years. At last Angelo saw it and at once perceived its possibilities. Under his skillful hand the rude block of stone was transformed into the fair and marvelous beauty which appears in the statue of David.

Thus it is with many a human soul whom the world has cast aside as lost. The Great Master Sculptor can take and mould from it a character of beauty fit for His kingdom above.

But what of girls who never got a second chance? Donaldina could not bear to think of slaves who dragged through lifelong captivity. Some, like Suey Lon, were sold and resold over fifteen years. Planning to put Suey Lon on the market again, her owner disguised her in American clothes and hid her for months in a dank barn near the Delta town of Isleton. A kind-hearted constable found her, emaciated and aged-looking, though not thirty years old. No longer a profitable slave, she would have been left to die of starvation had not Donaldina been summoned.

Fifteen years' survival was rare. The average prostitute plied her trade for only five or six years; most of them were dead of disease by twenty. A few courtesans, pampered with much that was "dear to the hearts of Chinese girls—fine clothes, jewelry, feasting and no hard work," lived longer, if they were not overtaken by venereal disease. Ninety percent of all prostitutes were thought to have contracted one or more forms. Fearless of infection, Donaldina nursed her afflicted daughters, washing and dressing their sores herself.

She had tried to convey to her Board and to others a picture of conditions created by the slave trade. She knew she could not bluntly tell decent people, people who thought it cruel to rap a child across the knuckles, all she saw of cold-blooded depravity. So she spoke in polite terms of "slavery," "a life of shame," "house of ill fame," the "blackness of iniquity."

The places she saw in her mind's eye were parlor houses and cribs. Parlor houses, most of them on main streets, such as Dupont, or in dark byways of Ross Alley and Waverly Place, were furnished sumptuously in teakwood, embroidered silk cushions, hangings, and soft couches. Girls wore rich clothes, made up their faces with rice powder and rouge, perfumed the palms of their hands, and piled shining black coils of hair atop their heads. They were trained in seductive "arts." Some teetered about on "yellow lilies," bound feet four inches long that would fit into teacups. The girls walked with a sinuous swaying that pleased their customers.

Men slavers usually managed parlor houses along with gambling or opium dens, but occasionally courtesans who had bought their own freedom set up elite establishments. Their "entertainment" commanded a fee as high as a dollar. White men or middle-class Chinese patronized most of the parlor houses, for wealthy Chinese could own several wives or slave girls. The Home rarely made rescues from places like these.

Often Donaldina and her team raided cribs, which served males of any nationality or age. In some dives men paid twenty-five to fifty cents, and boys a special rate of fifteen cents. Such brothels lined dingy, fifteen-foot-wide alleys, and proliferated along Jackson and Washington Streets. A crib resembled a barn stall, some twelve by fifteen feet, often divided by curtains into two rooms. Two to six girls staffed a crib. They wore uniforms of the trade—blue or black silk blouses trimmed with embroidered green-blue banding.

In *Barbary Coast,* Herbert Asbury described a scene typical of those which sickened Donaldina:

. . . The only entrance to the crib was a narrow door, in which was set a small barred window. Occupants of the den took turns standing behind the bars and striving to attract the attention of passing men. When an interested male stopped before the crib, the harlot displayed the upper part of her body and cajoled him with seductive cries and motions.

"China girl nice! You come inside, please?"

She invariably added to the invitation this extraordinary information, seldom, if ever, correct:

"Your father, he just go out!" (some of the Chinese considered it an honor to possess a woman whom their fathers had also possessed.)

More loudly, the girls cried their wares:

"Two bittee lookee, flo bittee feelee, six bittee doee!"

When a consignment of girls arrived from China, slavers put them on the block in a secret place, where enemies like Donaldina would be unlikely to find them. The girls were stripped, inspected, and examined like cattle. When sold, each passed her purchase price (usually in gold coins) through her own hands to the seller and signed a contract. Some spelled out elaborate terms. A cryptic agreement read:

For the consideration of [whatever sum had been agreed upon], paid into my hands this day, I, [name of girl], promise to prostitute my body for the term of ———— years. If, in that time, I am sick one day, two weeks shall be added to my time; and if more than one, my term of prostitution shall continue an additional month. But if I run away, or escape from the custody of my keeper, then I am to be held as a slave for life.

(Signed) ————————————————

Cribs and dens in a San Francisco Chinatown alley. (Photo courtesy Caxton Printers, Ltd.)

A Chinatown slave girl, caged and compelled to cry her wares.
(Photo courtesy Caxton Printers, Ltd.)

A bill of sale for a nine-year-old girl was printed in the *San Francisco Call,* one of the papers Donaldina read:

BILL OF SALE

Loo Wong to Loo Chee

April 16—Rice, six mats, at $............................ $ 12
April 18—Shrimps, 50 lbs., at 10c........................ 5
April 20—Girl 250
April 21—Salt fish, 60 lbs., at 10c...................... 6
                                                         _____
                                                         $273

Received payment

Loo CHEE

At about the time Donaldina began her work, two slave dealers were said to have kept a hundred girls under the age of fourteen penned in the rear of a building; and a woman stocked half a hundred for ready supply to individuals or to brothels.

Mortality rates of their stock were high. In the early years a worn-out or diseased slave was stored, alone, in a "hospital," a bare room with scant food and water, until her demise. In the 1900's sick girls were encouraged to escape to one of the missions in Chinatown.

Small humanity, Donaldina thought, ironically. Confronted with the meager progress her Board had achieved in thirty years, and she in nine, she wondered how the monstrous traffic could be dealt its death blow. Perhaps, as she sought salvation for slave girls, she felt like Moses, who complained, "Thou layest the burden of all this people upon me . . . it is too heavy for me."

In her deep discouragement the words she had written to her Board two years earlier came back to her:

. . . It took only four years to set the negroes free throughout the whole of the South; for twenty-five years a few women have been wrestling with the Chinese slavery problem and it seems no nearer a solution now, than it did more than a quarter of a century ago when the rescue work was first organized. True, much *has* been done toward *lessening* the evil, but it does still exist in all its hideousness. To free the *negro* the entire forces of a great people united, and no sacrifice either personal or political was considered too great toward that end.

Could not the Christian people of our State, with the same conse-
crated effort and firmness of purpose, lift the stigma of slavery from
the Chinese community and give to the Oriental women and girls in
our midst, the privileges which we so richly enjoy.

She recalled the struggles for freedom: Forlorn little Mae Tao,
after the merest farce of a hearing, had been dragged away by
her uncle, while her shrieks of distress drew crowds from all
directions. The judge was appealed to but he wavered on trifling
technicalities of the law. And the child still existed in heathen
slavery on free soil while a Christian Home stood open to receive her.

"Is this justice?" Donaldina fumed.

And what of Yuen Ho's young husband, shot by a highbinder
after he helped her escape? Sure that he was dying, he had sent
for Lo Mo and cried, "Oh, don't let them spoil my wife." He
survived, but for months could not work. To support them his
wife sewed early and late. The couple's strength was inspiring.

Attorney Monroe had pursued one involved case through
forty-seven hearings. He was able to win freedom for a young
woman, but could not recover the baby taken from her earlier,
and she finally returned to China alone.

Infuriated by thwarted justice, Donaldina occasionally got into
hot water. When she disregarded an order to release a girl, she
was cited for contempt of court, and went through several stormy
hearings before her case was dismissed. Her audacity in dodging
a court order once caused her arrest. In tears she appealed to her
attorneys, who posted bail to save her from jail.

In one of her darkest hours she had written:

The Chinese themselves will never abolish the hateful practice of
buying and selling their women like so much merchandise, it is born
in their blood, bred in their bone and sanctioned by the government
of their native land. Enactment by law does not reach this evil as it is
impossible to get any Chinese evidence into court on account of the
danger of life and property involved by incurring the enmity of the
powerful and revengeful Highbinder Tongs.

Donaldina had tried to explain away her seizure and holding
of minors.

. . . it was necessary . . . in a way to break the *letter* though not the *spirit* of the law when we rescued a Chinese child for there was no written law to uphold us in entering a house and carrying off a child— then, too, before it was possible to carry out guardianship proceedings, the ever available writ of habeas corpus would in many cases deliver the child back into the custody of the Chinese until the matter could be settled in the Superior Court—in such cases we seldom or ever won our case.

To end the predicament Attorney Monroe proposed an amendment to state law which would empower a judge to assign temporary guardianship of a child until a hearing. The state legislature passed a bill to that effect, but the governor vetoed it as unnecessary. The bill was presented and passed a second time by the legislature. Donaldina and her friends pressed for action. In her words,

A member of the Board knew the State Controller, whose duty it is to personally bring many bills and documents to the Governor for his signature. The good offices of this friend were besought; he agreed to lay the matter before Mr. Pardee [governor] personally. Many letters, telegrams and telephone messages passed back and forth between the Mission Home and the capital of the State, for we all felt that much was at stake. Our friend appeared before the Governor with our bill and prepared to use all his influence to get it signed, but he was too late. Governor Pardee had already signed the bill and it had become a State law! So that is how we can go boldly into any house where we believe a slave child is and take her away.

The enemy's armor had been pierced. Donaldina praised her Board and all her legal friends, including Mr. Pence of Salinas, Mr. Belcher of Marysville, and Mr. Drew, of Fresno, "But the largest debt of gratitude and greatest tribute of praise is for our own Mr. Monroe, who has done *so much* for us this year as in the twelve years past, during all of which time he has attended to the legal work of the Home." The girls called him "Our Abraham Lincoln."

In another report she wrote:

We must pass now . . . to the no less important . . . stories of the young Japanese women who have been helped and protected during the year, fourteen in number. . . . The three under our care at present are, Yorki, Roe and Asa, all bright, interesting girls, helpful and willing about the house work and their studies. Asa . . . only fifteen . . . was brought to San Francisco by an agent of the notorious ring of Japanese men, who make a business of importing these young girls. Mr. North who represents the United States Government in . . . immigration, has done much to suppress this traffic and kindly cooperates with the Mission. . . . We feel that this branch of the work . . . is of growing importance and calls for special prayer and effort.

Donaldina quoted a "pretty poetical letter from the father of Asa . . .":

Dear Superintendent: The springtime has come and how are you? We feel exceedingly grateful to you, dear madam, that you have kept my daughter safe and happy under your wings as a loving mother hen protects her young from all danger. Having not the opportunity to see you I am obliged to write a few lines to express our sincere thanks to you for what you have done for my own daughter. Very sincerely yours, Isuki Yamasaki.

She added, "In closing this imperfect record of the events of the year I must add a few words in tribute to the faithful, loving service rendered by the dear Christian girls in the Home—they who *live* the religion of Jesus Christ in their daily lives as well as professing it. . . . Truly 'the beauty of the Lord' rests upon the lives of many of the converted . . . girls. . . ."

Fifteen hundred girls, it was estimated, had been delivered from slavery during the Board's thirty years' war. Donaldina challenged the ladies further:

So in truth the responsibility of uprooting this great evil and relieving the wretched condition of the oppressed class, the Chinese [and Japanese] slave girls, rests with you. . . . Was not the commission given to us as well as to the prophet long ago? Have not we been sent to bind up the broken-hearted, to proclaim liberty to the captives and the opening of the prison to them that are bound?

Yes, her direction was clear.

CHAPTER SEVEN

Respite and Retreats
1904-1906

Though Donaldina's attention had been wooed away from "920" for four weeks, she slept lightly, listening for a child's cry or the shrill of a telephone. In quiet hours her mind turned to Charles: "I must tell him . . ." or "We must plan . . . ," and then grief: they would share no future.

Early the first morning at sea she had walked the freighter's deck alone, forcing her thoughts toward the future. She welcomed the ten-day Atlantic crossing as a time to gather her powers. Two fellow passengers provided pleasant distraction: Lucy Minegorod,[1] a vacationing social worker, and Mike Ferguson, an elderly gentleman, who took a young woman on each arm and walked them miles around the decks.

Donaldina was not a good sailor. But calm September seas and the heavy ship were kind. She waked mornings to see sunshine streaming through the porthole, to hear the rumble of water, and the faint lowing of cattle in the hold.

Often she and Lucy climbed into the peak of the bow, sheltered from the breeze and salt spray. Rocked by the "lift and scend" of the steamer, they talked for hours and took long naps. By voyage end Donaldina was more rested than she had been for years.

She watched shadows on the horizon approach until Ireland and then England grew real. In Liverpool a "very British" family friend and his young son, in school uniform, waited on

---

[1] Later Superintendent, Department of Nurses, U.S. Public Health Service. She and Donaldina corresponded for years.

the windy wharf. They helped her make a train north to Inverness in Scotland. From there, Aunt Catharine, her mother's sister, took her home to the Highlands. In the village of Beauly, she was Dolly again, a daughter of the Camerons and the Mackenzies, walking the soil of the country that claimed her lifelong citizenship.

Beauly, in a latitude parallel to that of Labrador, was "frightfully cold," but fireplaces warmed every room of Aunt Cath's stone house, Glen Oran. The two women shared what they called "a mutual love feast," a visit after years of letter writing and news carried by family travelers. The family had described her aunt as homely. Donaldina thought she resembled Queen Elizabeth I. A conscientious Victorian, she read the Bible to her two maids and added gleanings from the *Inverness Courier,* "world news that was fit for the others to hear." Dolly met other relatives about whom she had heard all her life.

Donaldina was surprised by a visit from Dr. Abram Halsey, a secretary of her Presbyterian Board of Foreign Missions, and his wife, who were touring Europe. With pride she introduced her relatives.

Isabella, Donaldina's sister who had remained in Scotland when the rest of her family emigrated to New Zealand more than forty years earlier, came to Aunt Cath's from Huntley, Aberdeenshire. It was an emotional meeting. The sisters "got on famously."

Bee, Isabella's pet name, took Dolly to the home of "Nurse, a wonderful permanent member of the family" and heart of her older sisters' and brothers' lives in Scotland. Their departure so distressed Nurse that she became ill. To see Donaldina now and hear from all her charges, grown to maturity, came as a benediction. She sent messages to each, and from a display on her dresser chose a cherished plate for Jessie, whom she remembered as the baby of the family.

As Bee and Dolly tramped the glens and moors, purple with heather, Dolly found it easy to hear the chants of druid priests sighing on the wind. In villages established for more than 1400 years, kirks reminded her of forebears who had helped to wear the hollows on steps and floors.

Bee, having lived always with tradition, was amused by Dolly's ecstasies. But she indulged her, driving her along the Royal Mile from Edinburgh Castle to St. Giles, the Presbyterian Cathedral, and on to the Palace of Holyrood. When they met a parade of kilted bagpipers, Dolly joined the children, running after them to the skirl of the pipes.

The old aunts told Dolly of her Grandpapa, with a household of girls, one of them Donaldina's mother, and party clothes to pay for. On one occasion when a bill arrived from the cobbler, he exclaimed! "I'm ruined! And all from patent pumps."

The Scotland visit ended in the home of Aunt Annie, "a spinster with a great sense of humor, who lived in an adorable little stone house" at Nairn. Aunt Annie reminded her of heirlooms she had seen at home, marble-sized stones called millprieves, that an ancestor had found in a nearby peat bed. Thought to have been used by druid worshippers in the first century B.C., they were carved with snake-like symbols and said to be unlucky omens.

Friends and relatives took their American guest on long walks and to play occasional games of tennis or croquet. But eating became an occupation. Tea was served in bed, followed soon by a hearty breakfast. About one o'clock came a formal lunch, in the afternoon tea and refreshments and a full dinner at seven or eight at night. Donaldina ate and ate until she was considered "nice and plump."

While staying with Aunt Annie she met Great Aunt Jess Mackenzie, the grande dame of the family, who expressed surprise to find her niece from the western wilderness able to speak the king's English. As a girl Aunt Jess had been a beauty, but gave up marriage in order to keep the family home open. Her brother, Sir William Mackenzie of the British East India Company, sent his children from India, asking her to enroll them in school. Aunt Jess retained both charm and spirit, and rallied her social circle for Dolly's pleasure.

Early in December Donaldina said her farewells to Scotland, expecting to be entertained in London through the holidays by a cousin, Ewen Mackenzie. But he was ill and she spent a sad time in unaccustomed solitude, until other cousins rescued her. With them she attended a fashionable wedding at the Trocadero, where she wore her party clothes, a gay, wide-brimmed hat, a long dress of white nun's veiling cut in slim, contoured lines, and a silk pongee coat. She had a wonderful time.

Through Aunt Jess's nephew, like his father, Sir William Mackenzie, a part owner of the British East India Company, Donaldina was booked for the Orient on the steamship "Mombasa" under command of Captain Stephenson. A lifelong friend of the family, a career officer in the Royal Naval Reserve who had been a personal friend of the late Queen Victoria, Stephenson was eager to introduce Donaldina to eastern ports.

The "Mombasa" left England the first week of January 1905. Several missionaries and a lively group of young people returning home to India from school organized a masquerade dance to celebrate the new year, a mixer such as Donaldina had not enjoyed since girlhood. A gentleman gave her a tiger's claw, souvenir of a hunt in Indian jungles.

The Atlantic warmed along Spain's coast. Beyond Gibraltar lay the Mediterranean, the Romans' Middle of the Earth. Donaldina would have liked to follow Paul's journeys and set foot in the Holy Land, but her only view of Bible scenes came early one cloudy dawn along the Gulf of Suez.

As the sun rose, clouds began to roll back, like the Biblical parting of the Red Sea's waters. A mountain believed to be Mount Sinai was revealed, bathed in red and gold, a jagged pyramid in the desert wilderness. Donaldina imagined the awe of the children of Israel before its grandeur.

The "Mombasa" anchored several times in the Near East, and Captain Stephenson took Donaldina ashore in his private gig, introducing her to Chinese officials and merchants. She discussed the slave trade, explaining how dealers in China and America sometimes routed their victims to eastern ports. She offered co-operation to block the world-wide traffic, and hoped action would follow the courtesy shown her.

In Calcutta Donaldina's cousin, Patrick Cameron, manager of the Hong Kong and Shanghai Bank, and his wife, Gertrude, entertained her in their lavish marble home, and showed her the city's camel cavalry, the Black Hole of Calcutta, and street bazaars.

Another cousin, David Cameron, a bachelor who had visited La Puente, arrived by elephant from his tea plantation in Darjeeling ready to accompany her to Agra and the Taj Mahal. But Patrick, who had a social position to protect, forbade the unconventionality of a woman's traveling alone with a man, be he cousin or no. David returned alone and Dolly saw the glories of the Taj Mahal, that most beautiful tomb in the world, through Gertrude's stereopticon.

In Rangoon she joined children sliding down a hillside on banana leaves, and delightedly watched playful monkeys in the trees. More of the globe-trotting Cameron and Mackenzie cousins, as well as Chinese friends, appeared in each Oriental city: Singapore, Hong Kong, Canton, and Shanghai.

In the terraced city of Hong Kong she was greeted by the secretary to a former Chinese consul general in San Francisco whose wife the Home had befriended. A boy Lo Mo had known in the Occidental School near the Home took her to call on his mother, a traditional lady who entertained her with the exquisite formality of tea pouring, as her son interpreted their conversation.

On the soil of mainland China Donaldina experienced excitement as great as that of reaching Scotland. She wished she could explore the more than three and three-quarter millions of square miles of Chung Hwa Min Kuo, translated, "Central Flowery People's Nation," but knew that it would be impossible to do it in three months' time. She did visit friends in Kwantung (Canton) province, from which most of her girls came.

Donaldina was introduced to Canton by Evelyn Burlingame, former teacher of Chinese in San Francisco, and her housemate, Dr. Mary Niles of Canton Christian Hospital, co-founder with Lucy Durham of work for blind Chinese. Miss Durham, a Wellesley graduate in art, had furnished money to open and maintain the station until the Presbyterians took it over. Her hostesses guided Donaldina through their mission compound and along the twisting, narrow streets crowded with sedan chairs carried by coolies, and with pigtailed Chinese merchants hawking their wares. She visited Evelyn's school in the nearby city of Sz Pai Low, where she scarcely recognized a beautiful bride as the girl she had rescued and sent to China three years earlier.

Miss Durham made arrangements for a trip up the Pearl River (also called the Si, or West, River) on a family houseboat stocked with chickens, a dog, and pig. Scrupulous cleanliness made the elbow-to-elbow living acceptable. Donaldina saw rural China: hills and flooded rice fields, villages with thatched-roofed houses of peasant farmers, boatmen poling their craft upstream.

She met two California Chinese. Sing, a former servant of southern California friends, the Unruhs, beseeched her to take his twelve-year-old son back to San Francisco and educate him. With sorrow she explained that her Mission sheltered only girls and that none housed boys. She did not say that prejudice against Orientals prevented public schools from admitting Chinese boys. She determined to change that miserable situation.

A rescued daughter, N'gun Ho, waited for Lo Mo, who had described her as "the Madonna" because of the beautiful serenity in her face after her conversion. In China, as a nineteen-year-old bride, she dutifully subjected herself to her mother-in-law. Her letters had revealed how her husband's family and the villagers ridiculed and rejected her because she practiced Christianity. At last she won her mother-in-law and became a "Bible Woman" to her people.

Time allowed one more important stop, Shanghai. Donaldina had hoped to see a cousin, Sir Ewen Cameron, who had visited her family during her girlhood, brought gifts, and told fascinating stories about the Orient. But he was in England. As president of the Hong Kong and Shanghai Bank, Ewen had arranged the largest loan his bank had ever made to a foreign state. In recognition of this service the imperial Chinese government had given him the official title of mandarin, the first bestowal of that rank on a non-Chinese, and he had been knighted by the king of England. Donaldina was shown through his imposing bank and the trade center for all central China.

She found Shanghai a picturesque port "up from the sea" on

the Yangtze river: street peddlers, skinny water carriers balancing buckets that weighed nearly as much as they, on a pole across their shoulders; women patiently preparing food and cooking it outdoors over charcoal stoves; bookkeepers with abacus and brush.

She marveled at the curve and grace of Chinese architecture, exquisite silks and ivory, artists she saw painting and carving. Vestiges of China's 4000-year-long history appeared everywhere—proof of human grandeur and human mortality. Yet one thing seemed missing. Individuals lacked value. Oh! that these wonderful people could embrace her Saviour, who cared for each soul! Yes, the missionary goal was right—if China could be saved, the world would follow.

In Christian churches she found records of sorrow, tributes to martyrs killed in the Boxer Rebellion. When would her world learn the message of the Prince of Peace? And the children! How many she had seen, the latest in the Mission school of Amy Law, who had received numbers of daughters from "920."

Again in Shanghai, Donaldina talked about the slave traffic. Because Chinese custom and law still permitted the sale of girls and women, she knew she could not cut off the raw material of slavery at the roots. But she could appeal to upright Chinese officials to cooperate with American laws. She made graphic the hideous fates of Chinese females imported illegally into America. She could not estimate her effectiveness, but she knew she had established valuable connections with staff members of Christian schools, churches, and homes. They agreed to advise one another of girls traveling the Pacific.

The "China Mail," on which Donaldina sailed from Shanghai, touched port in Japan and Hawaii, and in July steamed through the Golden Gate. Rosy and happy, she felt more excitement about this harbor and her family than about any port or people in the world.

Her sisters and niece and some of "920" 's daughters waited on the dock, and back at "920" her children rushed to greet her. As she was distributing gifts, answering questions, and exclaiming, "How you have grown!" the telephone rang.

"It's for you, Lo Mo. Someone in a hurry."
Donaldina was home.

*   *   *   *   *

In July of 1905 Donaldina picked up her work again. During her absence, Wilmina Wheeler and Frances Thompson had kept peace in the Home, and held the enemy at bay. Miss Wheeler wrote that the public believed, "the back of Chinese slavery is broken, but if so the life of the tyrant has not departed . . . little did I realize that my work would of necessity be one largely of defense."

Donaldina had scarcely disappeared from sight when the first tong man invited a girl to dinner. On her behalf Miss Thompson declined. Not discouraged, owners sent other invitations, delivered by women "friends," by suitors, by slaves imploring their former friends to visit them. A young merchant asked to marry an attractive girl, Kum Ying. To prove his good standing he paraded friends, an American lawyer and a justice of the peace. Displaying a marriage license and a permit, purportedly from the United States marshal, he demanded to see Kum Ying. Suspicious, Miss Wheeler phoned the marshal. The papers proved fraudulent. The party withdrew, hissing its wrath.

Many persons faked relationships to Lo Mo's wards. An abandoned baby, found by Miss Culbertson years earlier, and now of marriageable age, suddenly acquired devoted foster parents. The impostors planned to sell or marry her off and pocket a fee.

A bold turtle man asked to see his former slave. When pressed to know his errand with the girl, he said, "O, I just want to see her face once more." Actually he hoped to make arrangements for her marriage to a dissolute gambler and had offered his services for a consideration.

Miss Wheeler received a note, supposedly from two little girls, who claimed their parents planned to sell them. They threatened to "make ourselves dead." When rescuers responded, the children were surprised and one so terrified that she leaped through a second-story window, imitating a method of suicide common among Chinese women. The letter had been forged by an enemy of their father, who hoped to embarrass him.

Nevertheless, Miss Wheeler had rescued nine Chinese girls and eight Japanese during the year; she had welcomed thirty more, many of whom stayed briefly until they could return home, marry, find work, or go on to school. But brothels flourished openly, and girls continued to be smuggled into the country, which told Donaldina that good influences in Chinatown were not holding their own. The highbinder tongs had escalated their power again.

The original tongs (a Chinese word meaning associations) were respectable organizations. But later ones had harassed The City for more than fifty years. In 1851 a group of Cantonese from districts, or counties, of Kwantung province, China, formed the first of many traditional Kong Chow (Canton) Associations. Later representatives of each association organized the Chung Wah Wui Kwoon, "Meeting Hall of the Chinese People," also called the Chinese Six Companies, or the Chinese Benevolent Association.

Soon individuals from small family clans or associations who felt unjustly treated by Chinese leadership as well as by white Americans began to form tongs, which some say were at first fraternal societies. They turned renegade, abandoned the tradition of arbitrating differences, settled their grievances by violence, and staked out territories where they controlled gambling, prostitution, and narcotics.

Two years later two fighting or "highbinder" tongs, the Kwong Duck and Hip Yee Tong, began to oppress law-abiding Chinese in San Francisco. The term "hatchet men" was applied to their hired assassins because they used cleavers for weapons.

By the end of the century, because Chinese could not appear in an American court, the Six Companies acted as a quasi government for Chinese in California. The association gained almost unlimited power to speak and act, to arbitrate disputes at every level, to initiate measures for overall welfare, and to try to keep order. The Association attempted to discipline the fighting tongs, who then numbered about fifty, but with little success.

Presidents of district associations (most of them scholars imported from China for that purpose) governed the Six Companies. By an unwritten law no tong men could rise to the presidency of an association or to the Six Companies' Board of Presidents. But between 1880 and 1905 that rule was broken; hence the tongs gained power and protection to pursue their debaucheries.

Donaldina lacked the power to depose the tongs. Their new strength brought her fight against slavery to a stand-off. Yet the Mission, known to every Chinese colony, attracted runaway girls and troubled people from long distances. Donaldina devoted much time to mediating what she gently termed "domestic infelicity," common in plural marriages and with chattel mates.

She wrote, "A life of slavery from infancy had fostered much of evil and little of good" in unfortunate Chow Kum, a purchased wife of a Seattle storekeeper, who ran away with her small daughter to "920." A rebel, the young woman was unwilling to bend to the Home's discipline and left it. Several times she returned, but again departed, though not without involving an astonishing number of people. Her father arrived from China, and her husband from Washington. Lo Mo received and held counsel with them, with friends of the husband, friends of the wife, community workers, and a detective, whose help she enlisted.

Eventually Chow Kum and her husband were reconciled and moved to Oakland, but not long thereafter mother and child disappeared again. Hoping to recover the little girl, Lo Mo broadcast tracers for her. Months later she got word that Chow Kum was working in a Philadelphia restaurant and sending her daughter to a mission school. Trusting another mission to tend the seeds she had sowed in the thin soil of her runaway's heart, Lo Mo surrendered further responsibility.

She "had to lend a helping hand . . . to . . . a Chinese woman whose mind became deranged owing to the presence in her home of a second wife purchased by her husband while [she] the first wife (a small-footed woman) was still in China."

She and her girl of four and boy two years old, came to the Mission, where

Kindness and peace had a soothing effect at first, but later brooding over her sorrows and worries, and possessed by a fierce jealousy, fits of despair seemed to possess her. The climax came one day when she tried to jump from a window with the little girl in her arms. After that she had to be taken away from the Home.

The boy was placed with a kindly woman and Lo Mo set legal wheels in motion to make the girl, Ah Yoke, bright and a good singer, a ward of the Home so that she might "escape the sad fate of unloved Chinese girls. . . ." She won a hotly contested case.

These times of exasperation, tedium and disappointment in people beyond help were cut short.

The annual board meeting, planned for April 18, 1906, was not held. In her 1905-6 and 1906-7 combined reports Donaldina wrote:

The year [1905] ended with an unusually joyous Christmas and holiday time—the last to be celebrated in that home. The new year of nineteen hundred and six, which was to bring so many unexpected events and strange experiences, began with a change in our housekeeping department by the resignation of Miss Frances Thompson, who had faithfully and efficiently filled the position for six years. . . . Miss Minnie Ferree came to fill the matron's position left vacant by Miss Thompson. She remained with us for sixteen months, a period which included many strange experiences and hardships not counted upon . . . but which, to her credit . . . Miss Ferree met with cheerfulness and fortitude, bravely doing her part during the very trying days which overtook us. . . .

[in 1906] The Home had its usual spring renovating. From attic to lowest basement Miss Ferree and the girls worked, sweeping, scrubbing, polishing; until floors, woodwork and windows shone. The days passed quickly, happily calmly . . . up to the evening of April seventeenth when final touches were given, curtains hung and a beautiful fish net (the gift of a rescued Chinese girl) draped in the chapel room. All was ready for the events of the coming day. The last good nights were said and the family sank into quiet rest.

No premonition had crossed the mind of any one in that busy hopeful household that we were preparing our dear old home for its burial, as it were. The children's songs echoed through the halls and chapel on that last day—April 17—singing their parts for the programme of the Annual Meeting to begin on the day following. Those hymns were the requiem of a period and regime in the history of the Presbyterian Mission Home, the hours of which were numbered. So much has been written and said about the events that took place on that memorable eighteenth of April and the days following that it seems unnecessary to repeat an account of those occurrences. We only aim to leave a few words of testimony to bear witness in coming years to the kind care of a loving heavenly Father, and also to the unselfish courage displayed by our Chinese girls throughout the terrifying and distressing experiences of the days in which our city and the Home we loved were wiped out of existence.

CHAPTER EIGHT

Upheavals
1906

At 5:12 on the morning of April 18 early risers at the Home looked up at a new moon sailing a clear green sky. At 5:13 Donaldina was hurled from her bed by an upheaval she described as "motions of an angry ocean." She struck a heavy chest of drawers that careened toward her, then jerked back. Scrambling to her feet, she heard the bell of St. Mary's church clang crazily.

It was an earthquake.

She ran to her daughters through fallen plaster, broken furniture, and ornaments littering the floors. Girls shrieked, but none panicked. Lo Mo later told with pride how most of her daughters shed no tears, uttered no complaints, showed no cowardice.

The older girls picked up the little ones to soothe and carry to safety. No one ran to save herself alone. All stood to their duty like little soldiers, a miniature performance of the Birkenhead Drill, for everyone believed her last moment had come. How that five-story brick building on the side of a steep sand hill stood firm while walls of brick and wood around caved and crumbled is little short of marvelous. The first great shock over, we thanked God for having spared our lives, and looked forth to see how others had fared. Already columns of smoke were rising like signals of alarm; but so great was the relief of present deliverance no dread of another form of danger troubled us at that early hour. To calm the frightened children and see that they were dressed, to reduce in some measure the chaos of our Home again to a semblance of order, were our first cares. Then the problem of breakfast for so large a family in a chimneyless house had to be faced for the usual rice could not be cooked. This last perplexity was promptly solved by our efficient matron, Miss Ferree, who

almost before the bricks stopped falling had managed to secure from
a nearby bakery a large basket of bread. This, with some apples and
a kettle of tea sent in by our neighbor, Mrs. Ng Poon Chew, was the
last meal eaten in the hospitable dining-room of '920'. Our girls
gathered round the little white tables, sang as usual the morning
hymn, then repeated the Twenty-third Psalm with more feeling and
a deeper realization of its unfailing promises than ever before. The
simple meal was not finished when another severe shock startled all
from their places. We hurried to the upper floor. Opening an eastern
window and looking across the city, our anxiety became a certainty
of approaching danger. The small wreaths of smoke had rapidly
changed into dark ominous clouds, hiding in places the bright waters
of the bay. As we gazed with feelings of indefinable dread over the
blocks below, there passed at full gallop a company of United States
cavalry. The city was under martial law.[1]

Donaldina was glad to find several Board members at her
elbow. Mrs. P. D. Browne and Miss Meyers, a field secretary, had
spent the night at "920," and Mrs. C. S. Wright, president, Mrs.
E. V. Robbins, historian and columnist, and Mrs. L. A. Kelley
had made their way to the Home after the earthquake. The
women talked over possible plans and decided the Mission's inmates must try to reach the First Presbyterian Church, eight
long blocks up Sacramento Street at Van Ness Avenue. It was
the nearest haven and it would be outside Chinatown. Already
a double danger existed. The streets were choked with refugees
and curious onlookers climbing the hill for a view of the fire.
By noon Donaldina recognized slave owners milling through
the crowds. She warned,

. . . even in the midst of the general calamity the ever vigilant highbinder was on the watch for his prey.

To have our Chinese girls on the streets among these crowds after
nightfall was a danger too great to risk. As hastily, therefore, as we
could work amidst the confusion and excitement, we gathered some
bedding, a little food, and a few garments together and the last of the
girls left the Mission Home. They tramped the long distance to Van
Ness Avenue, carrying what they could.

. . . the small children and babies were carefully cared for through
all the excitement. There were three babies—the tiny Ah Ping, not a

[1] Not officially declared.

The old Presbyterian Mission Home for Chinese Girls at 920 Sacramento Street, as Donaldina knew it from 1895 to 1906.

month old, had to be tenderly carried by the girls; her poor little mother (a rescued slave) was too feeble and helpless to aid much. Hatsu had her wee baby, only three months old, and little Ah Ching, eighteen months, was equally helpless.

Collecting all the defenseless ones in a tight knot, Donaldina, Miss Ferree, and the older girls surrounded them like troopers, their eyes darting warily toward every stranger who pressed near them. The procession picked its way up Sacramento Street past ruined mansions on Nob Hill, their brick and stone grandeur rubble in the street, and trudged on to the First Presbyterian Church. The girls collected pew cushions and carried them to the basement for pallets.

During the night a nagging anxiety woke Donaldina. In the bustle of leaving the Home she had forgotten one important thing—records of her daughters' identity and their guardianship papers. If fire consumed the building, all would be destroyed. Her enemies would be quick to guess that she had lost the proof that gave her the right to hold their chattels. If they challenged her in court, she would lose some of her girls.

She was on her feet. She must go back to "920." She did not weigh her decision. The faith of a lifetime assured her that God had warned her of danger. He was directing her steps. She saw what she must do. She went about it, knowing the risks as fully as she recognized her inner leading. She did not doubt that the sleeping flock would be protected in the church and that the Lord would bring her safely back to them.

On dark Van Ness Avenue, refugees had thinned to a few stragglers. On Sacramento Street no civilians were abroad. Troops stood guard around the great houses; she was stopped, but explained her errand so convincingly that she was allowed to go on.

Once she heard a voice bark, "Get out!" and saw a soldier stab his bayonet at a shadowy figure. A man screamed, clutched his side, and ran.

Looters, Donaldina thought. But why such violent reprisal? A breeze blew smoke up the hill. It billowed around her, cutting off the view. She was near Powell Street before she could make out the dome of "920," silhouetted against flames a few blocks

April 18, 1906. After the earthquake the chimneyless Mission stood. (Photo courtesy California Historical Society)

below it. The dear Home still stood. She hurried down the last half block and started to climb the steps.

A harsh voice shouted, "Halt!"

Donaldina turned to look into a soldier's cold eyes.

"You can't go in."

"I am Miss Cameron."

"You can't go in!"

She faced him. "This is the Mission Home for rescued slave girls. I am its director. I must get my girls' records to protect them from the highbinders." She moved up a step.

The guard raised his gun. "I have orders to shoot anyone who tries to enter a building."

"Shoot then!" The granite appeared in Donaldina's face. She ran up the steps, and thrust open the door. She heard the guard's footfalls follow, then stop. She rushed on through the entry and hall and into her office.

The guard's rough voice shouted, "Hurry!"

The glare of the burning city lit up the room. For an instant she took in each familiar object, reliving the happiness she had shared with Miss Culbertson beside this very desk. She gathered records and a few valuables. A terrific explosion rocked the building. Plaster fell. Glass clattered to the floor.

The guard called, "They're dynamiting in the next block. Come out!"

She snatched up the old ledger and hurried out through the hall, now strewn with personal belongings and treasures her girls had tried to carry but had been forced to leave behind. She took a last look through the rooms, dear to her, but already turning strange in the eerie glow of flame.

She whispered, "Good-night, dear Home," as if parting from a warm friend, and carrying her life-saving papers under her coat she sped into the street.

The guard gave her a grim smile. Taking her arm he hurried her along the desolate pavement. She began the hard climb up Sacramento Street, murmuring farewells to the mansions she knew were doomed. She passed a few scattered troops moving up the hill ahead of the dynamiting. Ash and cinders swirled on the wind. Rats darted along the curb, some, she was to learn, fresh from gnawing the crushed bodies of Chinese caught in falling masonry. She made her way to the church, where she breathed a prayer of thankfulness to find her family still safe and for the precious documents she carried to protect their future.

By dawn, two hours later, the household was astir. Donaldina said, ". . . the little band were hurriedly preparing for another march, the shelter of the night being no longer secure. Fire menaced from three directions. What tragedy, what pathos, and what comedy too, were crowded into our lives these two days!"

Thirteen Board members had been burned out of their homes. Some escaped with their families by ferrying across the Bay both north to Marin County and east to Oakland. Their own losses made them keenly aware of Donaldina's plight. As they sought refuge for themselves, they told everyone they met about the Mission's need for shelter. One plea evoked response. Soon after Donaldina returned to the church from her salvage trip to "920," a messenger brought her word that friends in San Anselmo, north across the Golden Gate in Marin County, had found a barn as temporary refuge for her family.

How wonderful, she found time to reply, that her Board had reached out to loyal friends who succored them and to brave friends who carried messages across the chaos in The City. They now helped her plan a circuitous route to avoid the fires. Could her girls trek a difficult four miles? In answer she began to organize her family. Many objects brought this far must be abandoned, but much remained to take along. How could it best be carried? The girls devised a Chinese solution. With a twinkle in her eye Donaldina recalled the funny interlude.

Sheets were torn up for ropes and broom handles served for bamboo poles. Laughing in spite of their distress, the girls tried the vegetable pedlar's scheme with their bundles, and it worked well, for two bundles could thus be carried by one person. All had a load, not even little five-year-old Hung Mooie[2] being exempt. She tearfully consented to carry two dozen eggs in the hope of having some to eat by and by. An older maiden, whose name I forebear to mention, added not a little to her own load by carrying in her bundle a large box containing the voluminous correspondence of a devoted suitor!

[2] Another spelling of Hung Mui.

Her look of genuine distress when advised to abandon the precious box was so appealing we had to save it. Poor old Sing Ho just out of the City and County Hospital, who had recently lost the sight of an eye, staggered bravely along under a huge bundle of bedding and all her earthly possessions, which she cheerfully rolled down steep hills, and dragged up others. Two young mothers tied their tiny babies on their backs while others helped carry their bedding. As tears would not avail (the hour for weeping had not yet come), laughter was the tonic which stimulated that weary, unwashed, and uncombed procession on the long tramp through stifling, crowded streets. . . .

Other Chinese women and children, made homeless by the quake and wanting protection, attached themselves to Donaldina's procession, which now numbered sixty-seven. When they finally reached the Embarcadero, they saw the spired Ferry Building standing like a pillar of security. Winds from the sea pushed smoke back against the land, and they watched an empty ferry boat churn through the blue water into its slip. To enter the building, the pilgrims had to circle around dead cattle sprawled in the street. Inside, by some near miracle, the constant crowd of the past two days had thinned. The Mission daughters boarded the boat at once.

It was a thankful, though a completely exhausted company that sank down amid bundles and babies on the lower deck of the steamer, too weary to walk to the saloon.
. . . But tired and homeless, knowing not where that night we were to lay our heads, our only feeling was one of gratitude for deliverance as we looked over the group of more than sixty young faces and realized how God had cared for His Children.

In Sausalito, Lo Mo and her family were met by friends who took them to San Anselmo. The barn was drafty and uncomfortable. They had scanty bedding and little food with them. Table service consisted of one tin dipper and a dozen tablespoons and plates. A newly formed Relief Committee from the area provided food, "Manna" Donaldina called it, "mostly in the form of boiled red beans!" The Presbyterian orphanage nearby shared its meager bedding and some clothing. Donaldina and Miss Ferree, who possessed only what they wore, borrowed a few garments for themselves.

A week, made miserable by rain, went by in the makeshift shelter. The children got runny noses from exposure to the cold and growling stomachs from hunger. Members of churches nearby heard of the refugees. Some resented the intrusion of Chinese; others were compassionate. In defiance of prejudice, friends brought food. In San Rafael they located a house big enough to shelter Lo Mo's family—the greatest blessing of all, for two days earlier highbinders had located Fahn Quai's retreat.

Donaldina gave thanks for answered prayers and again her ragged procession set out for sanctuary. Her spirits rose.

Who can describe the Fairy Palace that shabby old-fashioned house appeared to our eyes when we first viewed it at the end of a long drive hedged with roses and acacia, the front almost hidden by two huge sentinel trees of exquisite pink and red hawthorn in full bloom. Tears of grateful joy welled up as we realized that at last the homeless family, cold and hungry, were to be housed, warmed and fed.

Who that saw it could ever forget the ludicrous flitting from the barn refuge at San Anselmo to the newly acquired home at San Rafael! Such an unkempt, rumpled horde our poor girls appeared, with no baggage other than the numerous bundles of ragged bedding, most of which was acquired from the orphanage near by. A few cheap saucepans and tin dishes made up the load. But it did not take long for our good friends to come to our assistance with gifts of all kinds. Among the first to come to our aid was our good friend, Mr. Gail Borden [former neighbor of the Baileys] who came from Southern California laden with gifts like a veritable Santa Claus. There were cases of clothing and bolts of goods. Quantities of nice warm bedding and a fine new sewing machine [a Wilcox Gibbs chain stitcher]. Before Mr. Borden left many more useful and comforting things found their way into the Home, and it was his thoughtful generosity that supplied the fine big tent and desks with which we were enabled to open school on our own grounds.

Donaldina spoke lightly of the hardships during the summer and autumn months in San Rafael, though she admitted finding little time for rest. The danger to the girls in the makeshift Home kept her and Miss Ferree under constant tension, for agents of the slavers had followed them. The girls were warned, and, therefore, watchful. One day, while at play in the yard, a group of them heard the thud of slow-moving footfalls behind a fence too high to see over. One of the girls lobbed a rock in the direction of the sound, while another ran for Lo Mo. Lo Mo raced out and climbed up to look over the fence. There a cow grazed placidly.

Within days after the move to San Rafael Donaldina had resumed her rescue work. After the earthquake much of San Francisco Chinatown had moved to Oakland's Chinese community, which had numbered only 1,000 before their coming. There the slave traffic was easily and vigorously renewed. Highbinders took advantage of new hiding places for girls. Fahn Quai was two hours' travel time from Oakland, and even more from other towns where they concealed their slaves. But Chinese friends spied on their moves and called Donaldina. She ferried across the bay and went by train up and down the coast, finding opportunities for rescue fresh cause to rejoice. The standstill of earlier months was over and the upheavals might be the Lord's opening door. She said, ". . . the outlook was indeed dark but then it was that God made His Goodness to pass before us . . . now . . . our hearts are full to overflowing with gratitude for what is past and with faith and courage for the future."

CHAPTER NINE

God of Love, God of Power
1906-1908

Summer weather allowed the girls more outdoor play, and accelerated Donaldina's pace. As Chinese friends and police learned of slaves' whereabouts, they called, directing her to rescues: in Oroville and Marysville, near Sacramento; in Pacific Grove, a hundred miles down the coast; in Bakersfield three hundred miles through the San Joaquin Valley; in San Francisco and in Oakland.

She brought to San Rafael "a timid woman"; the child of a "poor family who had lost all they possessed in the fire"; the wife of "an utterly bad" husband; "a cruelly treated child"; and a young girl who had taken refuge in jail because her parents tried to force her to marry an old gambler. In Portland a married daughter, "one of the brightest girls of the Home," died, and her husband asked Lo Mo to take their two children while he finished medical school.

These rescues, and provision for her daughters' care, reassured Donaldina that she served a God not only of love but also of power. She exulted, "Temporal losses have been more than compensated for by a deeper trust in Him whose faithfulness has fed us and whose loving wisdom has led us into this quiet haven."

She saw further proof of divine leading. Before the rubble of the old "920" was cleared, her Board planned a new Home. Mrs. C. S. Wright, president, who had hurried to Donaldina's aid the morning of the quake, told of recovery:

. . . everyone is wonderfully courageous. I have not heard a single note of repining. As people meet on the street and grasp each other by the hand, with tears in their eyes they say, "Thank God we are alive!" and in the next breath, "How soon will you begin to build?" . . . Nothing was saved from the Mission House. The records and literature of the Occidental Board, the furniture, everything is gone; only a part of the walls are left standing. Three or four hundred dollars would have covered all the injury done by the earthquake, but the fire completed the ruin. The lot on which the house stood cost eight thousand dollars, the house itself about eighteen thousand, and furniture one thousand, a total of twenty-seven thousand ($27,000) dollars, but we cannot duplicate our property for that, as labor and materials are much higher now.

The Presbyterian Foreign Mission Board allotted $11,000 toward a new building, and Mrs. Wright started a drive for funds and equipment. Donaldina decided to move her girls to Oakland until the new "920" was finished. In July she found a large house, but for months she had to "urge, negotiate and finally plead" with proprietors to rent it to a woman with sixty daughters.

On moving day in mid-November her clean, well-dressed girls clamoring aboard the ferry at Sausalito would never have been recognized as the ragged refugees of six months earlier. The older daughters had sewed a new outfit for each girl and Donaldina had got one tailored suit. She joked over everyone's being spared decisions about what to wear.

The girls ran to the rail to see the wide bay and the churning froth of the boat's wake. They were unaware that some San Franciscans looked askance at industrial Oakland, about one-seventh the size of The City, and lacking cultural centers. As the boat neared shore, the girls saw their new home town, sitting with its heels in the mud, its smokestacks and manufacturing plants glowering down on steep-roofed houses in rows like cabbages. Their roof covered a sturdy old house at 477 East Eleventh Street, in Oakland's Chinatown, looking up to the wooded hills of Piedmont.

The family celebrated Thanksgiving ". . . in the very happiest and most sincere spirit of gratitude. There were plenty of good things to enjoy." Friends from Brooklyn Presbyterian Church in

The old Mission Home after the fire and dynamiting.

Oakland made donations to the Home, and their King's Daughters Society gave $5 and several chickens. From Pleasanton came boxes of treats.

When the last dish from the Thanksgiving feast was dried, the girls began to make plans and presents for Christmas. The treadle of the Wilcox Gibbs sewing machine clattered steadily. Even the smallest children made bright paper ornaments to decorate the tree. Again, friends brought in surprises—candy, fruit, and nuts. The girls, with bright cords plaited into their queues, marched to the little Chinese chapel on Thirteenth Street for a Christmas program. A number sang and recited.

On New Year's Day of 1907 Donaldina took stock of her transplanted life. At the age of thirty-seven she felt like the Old Woman in the Shoe, with her family all but bursting out the windows of the house on Eleventh Street. She had times of nostalgia for old "920," and for personal keepsakes consumed in the fire, especially mementos and correspondence from her world trip. She missed her hats and scarves, and the collection of collars and cuffs she wore to touch up her plain suits. She passed over sentimental losses, turning toward promised gains. Replacement of the Home was assured and San Francisco Chinatown was rebuilding, a matter in doubt following the earthquake.

Because her family had to remain for some time in Oakland, Donaldina explored its expanded Chinese quarter. On a first trip with Captain Peterson of the police force she found a little girl, Ah Yoke, and a slave, Suey Sum, of "peculiar disposition, strong affections and strong jealousies . . . an interesting study . . . and we pray for wisdom and patience to learn her nature."

Apparently the girl felt understood, for she found courage to witness for the United States government's prosecution of her former owner, Woon Ho, one of fifteen women involved in slave trading arrested by a federal secret service agent. During the trial Donaldina made new friends among government authorities, important allies, for Chinese were on the move across country and along the eastern seaboard, where the tongs established depots for slaves. The new underground railroad enlarged slavery, a reversal of the network in the South, which took blacks to freedom. Interrupting transport of girls was, Donaldina said, ". . . a matter of plotting and counterplotting."

Most of her effort centered in the west. In nearly any Chinese hamlet on the coast the underworld learned to dread a visit from her, for in Frenchie's words, she penetrated their hideaways with "the gall of a burglar" and the intuition of a white devil. Donaldina's reputation intimidated some slave owners, such as the Marysville woman who owned a child, N'gun Que, "a pitiful little domestic slave whose mistress treated her with inhuman cruelty!" Her mistress did not resist when Donaldina led the mooie jai down the dusty street one October morning.

Of another girl she reported, with indignation:

Only last week Chow Ha was rescued and she is a truly pathetic object-lesson in what this appalling system of Oriental slavery can bring a young girl to in one or two years. Sorrow and physical suffering combined with the use of opium have made of Chow Ha a pitiful object. Such a sad, hopeless face I have seldom seen. But when she said to me with a glimmer of a smile lighting up her poor pale face, "This is the best day I have had for years (referring to the day she entered the Mission) and soon I will grow strong and well," I knew there was hope for Chow Ha, and when the good Physician lays His healing hand upon her she will be healed in soul and body.

Lo Mo entered sixty new names in the register during her two years in San Rafael and Oakland. She also recorded losses: "We heard of this unfortunate girl . . . we tried to rescue her . . . the owner of the den was warned . . . she had been spirited away and no trace of her could be found. . . . We hope to rescue her later so I have made this entry."

A blank space follows. Several such entries and empty lines occur, speaking of hope, of failure, and of mute grief. When disheartened, Donaldina, like a true Cameron, "bit the bullet," until encouragement came again.

She placed great hope in her married daughters, most of whom made happy homes. A son-in-law in Chicago wrote, "May and I are getting along finely; she is a good girl, so I love her very much indeed."

Some couples proved their stamina by daring to marry. Before the earthquake Lo Mo had slipped a girl away from her

owner, a member of a highbinder tong. A young man paid her
court, but her owner discovered him and demanded $3,000 ran-
som. The suitor refused and Lo Mo helped the pair marry and
find a position in the household of a family in Piedmont, near
Oakland. They had been entirely cut off from their San Francisco friends, and when the Home moved to the East Bay, they
were happy to visit Lo Mo again. But the tong man learned their
whereabouts and offered several hundred dollars to anyone who
would shoot the young husband. To avoid vengeance the couple
sailed for China.

Lo Mo exclaimed, "It means something to marry a slave girl!"

Like many of her contemporaries, Donaldina believed that
Christianizing the Chinese, the most populous nationality on
earth, was the key to world salvation. She expected her daughters to further that cause. Of those in American and Chinese
cities as brides and teachers she said,

They are the first Christianized and educated women to enter the
Chinese communities in these places, so there are great opportunities
for them to scatter the good seed they carry with them from the
Home. . . . In their lives are the words fulfilled, "I will sow them
among the heathen and they shall remember me in far countries."

But, in early 1908, Donaldina looked toward immediate fulfillment for her younger daughters, and heaped appreciation on
the friends and colleagues who worked on their behalf: honest
judges and lawyers who secured justice, often at the expense of
their own popularity: Oakland ministers, the Rev. Mr. Sanborne
and the Rev. Mr. Yip Wan Shang, Bible teacher; her instructors,
Miss Gertrude Humphrey, Miss Pratt, Miss Russell, Miss Ada
Overstreet; a new matron, Mrs. Kindleberger, and Ah Tye, "a
remarkably bright lovable child," now in her teens, who read
the Chinese Bible and the hymns and planned all the Chinese
meals, keeping expenses to a minimum.

Together Lo Mo, her daughters and co-workers looked forward to life in the new Home at "920," to which they were to
return soon.

*   *   *   *   *

On moving day, March 28, 1908, birdsong wakened Donaldina. Dressing quickly, she tiptoed outside. What a morning to
go up in the Wright Brothers new flying machine and get God's
view of this wonderful spot! From above it must look like a
cupped hand, palm cradling the Bay, fingers of land curving
about it, thumb humped into Mount Diablo and Mount
Hamilton.

"I will lift up mine eyes unto the hills," she murmured,
". . . my help cometh from the Lord, which maketh heaven and
earth."

She heard alarms jangle. The household roused and prepared
to go home.

With recurring gratitude Donaldina thought of her helpers:
Mrs. Kindleberger, new assistant matron, and precious Alice, the
cook, big and black and good-natured; her older daughters and
her quartet of singers—Ah Tye, a direct answer to prayer when
she needed an interpreter; Lonnie, so quick to take responsibility; Margaret, a bright sensible girl; and Ah Ching, delighting
in little children.

Lo Mo smiled, rueful. Her quartet knew one of her afflictions.
After performances, when she had been long on her feet, they
would insist that she sit down, let them take off her shoes and
loosen her stockings to ease her burning feet. She pressed a hand
to her cheek. Her jaw throbbed. She must get to her dentist,
though she begrudged the time and dreaded his scraping to fore-
stall pyorrhea.

Her family had dwindled, some earthquake refugees having
returned to friends and relatives. But when thirty-five chattering girls departed, packed into a street car, Chinatown took note.

Men rubbed their palms together in satisfaction. The White
Devil was leaving. But others saw Donaldina as Koon Yum, the
Goddess of Mercy, who possessed a thousand ministering arms.

At the ferry landing she piloted her charges through one of
the peaked sheds to the San Francisco gate. She scanned other
passengers, watching for enemies. A little girl pressed close.

"You're like Moses leading us to the promised land, aren't
you, Lo Mo? Will the new Home be as nice as the old one?"

Donaldina laughed and looked out across the wheat-gold

grasses that furred mud flats behind the pier. She answered the second question.

"Our new '920' is not as beautiful, dear, but a big good house. We will make it a happy home."

"Will you stay with us there?"

"Yes, child."

"Then I will be happy."

Donaldina took the child's hand. The approaching boat made its slip, the barrier chain clanked on deck, and she hurried her brood aboard. They stayed together in a tight knot, making their way forward to a glassed-in section of benches. Mrs. Kindleberger brought up the rear, as wary of strangers as Donaldina.

Would her daughters' lives brighten or dim in the days ahead? Her lips seamed. She had been allowed little voice in designing the new Home on the hill. It must be truly a home for a big family, she had directed the contractor. A fellow Scot, accustomed to building offices and institutions, he charged off her wishes to female foolishness. Home-like atmosphere! he had snorted. Wasn't this an orphanage? He took orders from sensible men. And Donaldina had known better than to argue with the sensible men who were monied husbands of her board members.

Well, her office and those for the denomination's use on the first floor were satisfactory, and she could make do with the kitchens, dining room, and school room in the basement. But on the two upper stories, how could she help her daughters create pleasant bedrooms out of skinny cells stretching from narrow halls to single windows in each room? And she had so longed for a cozy parlor, with a fireplace, where she might gather her Chinese daughters around a hearth like that of her childhood.

But things were as they were. And what a lovely day to be going home. On the Bay, wind fingered blue water into dark troughs and pale crests. Distance and a thin curtain of fog diminished building cranes into grasshopper legs. Skeletons of tall office buildings became spider webs anchored to toy houses and shops edging shoulder to shoulder down the hills. Barely visible was the dome of City Hall, its spire pointing heavenward like a temple spared from the earthquake. Would that The City's government were fit for a temple!

What could emerge from the current wrangling and violence and the grand jury's indictment of Mayor Schmitz and political boss Abe Ruef? Apparently politicians had slyly rifled The City's coffers for years. More openly, they had blackmailed Chinese for protection monies. After the earthquake and fire gobbled up Chinatown, a committee on relocating the Chinese, chaired by Ruef, who as a young lawyer had defended Margaret Culbertson's girls, had tried to prevent "the yellow peril" from reclaiming their expensive real estate situated at the edge of the financial district. Chinatown's ashes had been ransacked for valuables, first by National Guardsmen and then by white looters. Complaints of the Chinese consul general in San Francisco, Chiang Pao Hai, were ignored. But Chinese controlled a third of the land in Chinatown, and absentee landlords let them have the other two-thirds, sure of high rents. While The City's moguls bickered, the Chinese quietly returned to their quarter.

When cinders and ash had been shoveled into the Bay, a horror lay uncovered. Like festered wounds in the earth lay the underground caverns where slave girls had been stabled. Dripping passways, some too low for upright posture, from ladder to tunnel to cave, burrowed into the earth as deep as three stories.

Within weeks the quarter, like a phoenix, had begun to flutter up from the ruin. But Donaldina knew that from both sides of her city the race to mine gold out of Chinatown was on. And what easier way than through the persons of defenseless slave girls?

Riding through the noise of traffic and carpenters' hammers, Donaldina thanked God her daughters did not realize the awful dangers so near them. Scrambling happily up the steps of new "920," the girls were too excited to be afraid. They noticed no lack of grace in the structure, a knobby cube built of klinker brick salvaged from the old home after the fire, with more than a hundred narrow windows girdling its three stories and the double basement on the hill's downgrade.

An article in the magazine, "Woman's Work," described the interior.

The whole furnishing of the Home is eloquent with love. The

handsome bead portieres in the Hall are from Mrs. Sharrocks' little
girls; the furnishing of the hall, from the In His Name Society. . . .
Each dormitory is a memorial gift either to the memory of those
"gone before," or to the zeal and love of auxiliaries and young
people's societies. Chinese friends have lavished bronzes, brass ornaments, embroideries, carvings; and there are the comfortable chairs
for the kind ladies' which Chico's self denial has purchased.

The article continues,

Oh, that dear friends everywhere might catch an echo of the
laughter and song that floated down the halls, or see the happy faces
of these jewels of great price rescued from the filth of sin! Then
would you know that your gifts have not been in vain.

The girls explored every corner of the Home, beginning with
the huge bouquet in a wok on a porcelain elephant in the entry,
and from sub-basement to top story. Lo Mo let them select their
own rooms. Nothing in their experience compared with that
freedom. The older girls sprinted to the third floor, where by
unspoken respect, the quartet got "first dibs." Tiny and Lonnie
chose the "best room," which adjoined the "outside room," an
open alcove with a view of the Ferry Building, later called the
roof garden. Ah Ching and Margaret claimed the "next best"
room, beside Tiny's and Lonnie's. After all were settled, they
helped their younger sisters.

Scents of new pine and calcimine inspired the girls to nest-
making. They stored treasures neatly in drawers, hung their
clothes, and made up narrow mattresses on iron bedsteads. They
drew long breaths of the salt-sweet smell of clean sheets dried in
the sun and whipped smooth by wind off the Bay.

Donaldina remarked to Mrs. Kelley, on hand to help, "Usually
they would prefer to sew a fine seam all day rather than do a
half hour of housework. May their industry and joy be part of
your reward for providing this new Home."

Two weeks remained to prepare for Dedication Day, April 14,
and the Annual Meeting following it. The family made curtains
and cushions, cooked delicacies, and garlanded the meeting room
on the first floor, called The Chapel and later renamed "Culbertson Hall," as for a wedding; they stepped softly on the new rug

The new "920," the Occidental Board Mission House, completed in 1908.

bought from a bequest of Mrs. Mills, co-founder of Mills College in Oakland.

Arnold Genthe, a famous photographer, made observations about the Home and its director:

I got to know Miss Cameron quite well, and she let me come to the Mission to take pictures of her protégées—lovely little creatures poetically named Tea Rose, Apple Blossom, Plum Blossom. Miss Cameron was not a tight-lipped reformer who wished to make the world over into a monotone. She had respect and admiration for the art and literature of China and she saw that the girls she had taken under her wing were educated in its tradition. When I first went to the Mission the walls were decorated with commonplace lithographs and posters. After I became more at home I told her I thought it was too bad that her pupils, who knew something of the value of their native fine sculpture and painting, were learning nothing of what the art of the Occident had to give them. She had the same thought, but there was no money with which to do something about it. Through the generosity of two or three of the San Francisco art dealers I secured some good photographs and reproductions in color of old masters. The girls were delighted and they had Tea Rose write me a letter which I have kept for the poetry of its style and sentiment.

Early on Dedication Day a Western Union messenger parked his bike at the curb and delivered the first yellow envelope. From New York the National Missions Board had telegraphed, "Board sends congratulations. May the memory of this latter house be greater than of the former. A. W. Halsey."

Mrs. P. L. King wired from San Diego, "My greeting clossans [Colossians] second chapter verse five." Donaldina read the reference aloud, "For though I be absent in the flesh, yet am I with you in the spirit, joying and beholding your order, and the steadfastness of your faith in Christ."

Dwight E. Potter's message read, "Congratulations Rejoicing with you. Phillipians one three to six. Absence unavoidable."

Lo Mo placed the telegram and a Bible opened to the verses, where her guests could read, "I thank my God upon every remembrance of you./ Always in every prayer of mine for you all making request with joy,/ For your fellowship in the gospel from the first day until now;/ Being confident of this very thing, that he which hath begun a good work in you will perform it until the day of Jesus Christ."

Though long, the dedication ceremony in the afternoon seemed to please everyone. The room overflowed. Men and women sat on the staircase; they crowded the entry until velvet hatbrims brushed flowers in the wok; they sang and prayed and listened to speeches. Mrs. Pinney, president of the Board, was assisted by Mrs. P. D. Browne, honorary president; Edward Robeson Taylor, Mayor of San Francisco; Dr. Fisher, Moderator of Synod; Mr. Dollar, and Mrs. Goddard. Recognition was made of notables: Dr. I. M. Condit and Mrs. Condit, a founder of the Home's original Board, and the Chinese and Japanese consuls. The Chinese consul and the Rev. Ng Poon Chew, Bible teacher in the Home and editor of a Chinese newspaper, "Chung Sai Yut Po," spoke.

The mission magazine, "Woman's Work," tells of the event.

[The Rev. Ng Poon Chew] . . . one of the first fruits of Chinese mission work on this coast, rejoiced in the new day that has dawned for Chinese women in their own country and assured us that China had never loved her daughters less but her sons more. . . . The Chinese Consul manifested great delight as the Chinese girls sang their sweet songs, and his address expressed appreciation, his hopes for the future and his promises of hearty support.

The quartet sang Lo Mo's two favorites, "Just One Touch" and "That Man of Calvary." With the motto for the day, "O, Sing unto the Lord a new song, for he hath done marvelous things," echoing in her mind, Donaldina responded, "As we begin to enumerate our blessings they appear to multiply. There are so many bright and hopeful things in this work we should never be discouraged. . . . With God all things are possible. . . ."

Throughout the party that followed guests reminded one another of their superintendent's wisdom, that this very building gave proof of God's possibilities. Yet Lo Mo felt a premonition that her confident words would be challenged.

CHAPTER TEN

Challenges
1908-1910

The celebration over, Donaldina forgot her disquieting premonition. She appreciated the congeniality of colleagues in offices near hers on the first floor: the Rev. E. F. Hall, of the Board of Foreign Missions; Miss Carrie Morton, Secretary of Books for Study Classes; and Miss Belle Garrette, Occidental Board secretary. Then too, she could easily attend lectures, illustrated by pictures from the modern Baloptican lantern.

For weeks visitors clamored through the building. Visiting her sisters in Oakland, Donaldina confided that reporters proved a downright nuisance. Nonetheless, everyone was received with courtesy. If the superintendent's time or privacy was invaded, she pleaded "previous engagement." Her daughters took priority. She must keep each one busy, happy, and learning. Training her girls remained the core of her mission. A girl with idle hands and mind could be lost. Older ones, newly rescued from the paths of evil, must be won from vulgar ways and heathen beliefs. And for the small mooie jais, "what a joy to lift these wearers of the thorn crown out of their hopeless, cheerless lives, and in the years of childhood which should be innocent to surround them with a few of life's simple delights."

Knowing only the law of fear, a girl of any age could not at first appreciate the higher law of love, Donaldina explained.

With unbridled passions, anger, hate, superstition and deceit at war within her nature, it is difficult for one of Christian parentage and training to realize the struggle which goes on in the recreation of this little rescued alien. Yet slowly, there takes place a marvelous change. The cheerful wholesome life of the Mission Home transforms body and soul. Family prayers are conducted in the pleasant dining-room, where the large family gather around light, clean, white breakfast tables. The young voices sound very sweet as they join in the morning hymns, "Father, we thank Thee" and "May Jesus Christ be praised." The music floats through open windows down the hillside, falling like a benediction on the ears of poor heathen Chinatown, just below. "Break Thou the bread of life," is sung over their simple meal, which is cooked and served by the Chinese girls. After breakfast come regular household duties. Older members of the family care for the little ones, washing, ironing and sewing for them.

At nine o'clock two schools open: A primary school under the Woman's Board . . . an advanced school, maintained by the Board of Public Education. Each day is well filled with lessons, housework, sewing, music and some recreation. Prayer services are held in the evening; the little ones meet with the matron in their nursery, the older girls with the superintendent in the schoolroom. Between nine and half past, the family retire each to her own clean, white bed.

Lo Mo's elder daughters helped anywhere they were needed. Ah Tye, who still managed the Chinese kitchen, laid in supplies, and after Dedication Day Ah Ching took her turn as helper to Alice in the teachers' kitchen. Of slight build, the girl seemed little more than a child, though she was now in her teens. Working with jolly Alice was fun.

In her soft voice Alice would say, "Run up stairs and bring me my sweater, honey, and I'll dance at your wedding." Ah Ching giggled, and on completing her errand, accepted bits of pastry Alice saved for her.

Her first day on duty, as she was washing dishes, Ah Ching recognized the quick footsteps approaching. From the doorway Lo Mo spoke abruptly,

"Ah Ching, come upstairs immediately. You are going out with me."

Ah Ching dried her hands on her apron as she ran. She and Lo Mo left by the side door, hurried along Joice Street and then Clay, and on to the Bing Goon Tong Headquarters on Waverly Place. They scarcely noticed the new herb shop or the strong smells—fresh fish, dried duck, and incense mingling in the restored Chinatown as they had in the old. They drew their skirts

close to avoid bumping chrysanthemums off sidewalk stalls. Lo
Mo explained their errand.

A girl, Sai Mui, recently imported from China and forced into
prostitution, had sent for them. Horrified by her assignments,
she had run away from highbinders in May Fong Alley to an
innocent-looking lodging place, only to find herself trapped by
rival tong men. Her owner traced her and demanded that she
return. Sai Mui refused. Her owner dared not use force, but
offered to settle his claim if her new-found friends would pay his
price. A meeting to fix the ransom was now in progress. While
the tong men haggled, a friend of Sai Mui's had brought word to
the Mission, and Lo Mo had alerted police. She was thankful
that The City had decided to rebuild the Hall of Justice at
Washington and Kearny Streets, only a few blocks away.

The next step was to get into the tong meeting room and take
Sai Mui. Three policemen met Lo Mo and Ah Ching, and the
five rescuers quietly climbed two flights of stairs to the top floor,
where a heavily bolted door barred the way. Ah Ching spoke a
few Chinese words; unsuspecting, the old doorkeeper slid back
the bolts, and the party surged down a long passage toward a
room from which issued the sound of a girl's pleadings. Recovering himself, the guard cried alarm, and as Donaldina touched
the door, it was slammed and noisily bolted from the inside.

Quiet prevailed for a few stunned moments; then a commotion began upstairs: crashing of glass, muffled voices, running
footsteps. Donaldina urged the police to force an entrance. An
officer beat on the door, bellowing a familiar challenge.

"Are you going to open up, or shall I break down this door?"

Bolts slid back and the door swung open. Lo Mo's party rushed
into a sparsely furnished room where some twenty Chinese men
sat, stolid.

"Where is the slave girl?" Donaldina demanded.

"You come to wrong place for slave girls," replied a serene
elder.

Seconds were precious. Donaldina rushed to an open window
and leaned out, thinking she might find a fire escape. A workman
called: "They pulled her through the skylight; she's in the next
house."

Donaldina whirled. "Next door," she commanded her party. Outside a crowd had gathered, but police held them back.

Next door the guard backed off from the searchers, who ran upstairs into the apartment. They found no one. Donaldina insisted they look again. The rooms seemed empty.

"Let's go," the sergeant said.

"I cannot leave without Sai Mui," Donaldina said. "We must search more carefully."

Leaving the officers to guard the door, Lo Mo, with Ah Ching close as a shadow, scanned every object in each room. Suddenly she shot forward, pointing to a cupboard barely angled from the wall. She pulled at the heavy piece. Behind it a girl crouched.

"Come, child," Donaldina said.

Ah Ching murmured a few persuasive words in Chinese. A girl wearing a wrinkled blouse slid from her cramped hiding place and stood trembling, her frightened glance darting about the room. Donaldina steadied her on one side, Ah Ching on the other, and the three hurried downstairs. Police closed in behind Lo Mo and the girls and followed them outside. There the tong men and a chattering crowd waited. The men stared, expressionless, as the street people cheered. Sai Mui clung to Ah Ching, and Donaldina smiled and waved to the crowd.

How could she ever again harbor a thought of defeat!

Back in the Home she hurried upstairs to look in on two sick girls. Dinner could wait. The feverish children pushing at cold compresses on their foreheads needed to be told a story before they tried to sleep.

When she finally retired to her own room, the exhilaration of victory had begun to fade. She felt tired, and her heart was pounding. A few days ago a doctor who was attending sick children had insisted on checking her blood pressure. It was high. She must slow down. A woman nearly forty could not afford to run up hills all day and bend over sickbeds half the night.

But, she responded, she *must* answer the desperate summons, and her daughters were entitled to a mother's attention. Yet tired times let in doubts. When she compared successes like today's rescue with failures, when she dared imagine how many girls in their teens were right now treated no better than animals and would die in a few years without help, she had to press on.

As always, she woke early. Her head no longer throbbed, though her body felt heavy. She began to pray. More and more she relied on spiritual resources. She called upon her memory for Bible verses and the lovely poetry of her youth. She opened her eyes. Fog pressed against the window, yellow in the dawn light. It would soon burn off.

The day brimmed with duties—God's new opportunities. She reminded herself that this was not her work; it was His. Hundreds of lives had been delivered into her care in these thirteen years. She had cause to rejoice, wherever He led.

Since the earthquake she often traveled up and down the thousand miles of the West Coast or across country. Along all routes she was met by friends, frequently influential sons-in-law. They paid her respect by offering information and protection. She followed every reasonable instruction she received, by messenger or telephone, whether or not she identified its source. Recently, as she had searched for a hidden girl, they had helped her play fox and hound from San Francisco to Portland, to Victoria, B.C., and back to Seattle again, where she hustled her fugitive on board a southbound freighter. Lo Mo covered her own identity by signing herself D. Mackenzie on this last leg of a strange journey.

She was also strengthened by

the very friendly attitude of the Chinese Press, which now plays quite an important part in moulding Chinese public opinion. . . . "Ching Sai Yut Bo" is edited by a clever, educated Christian man, Rev. Ng Poon Chew. Having for his wife a former interpreter of the Mission Home, we are always sure of Mr. Chew's fullest sympathy and interest. Other Chinese papers, though edited by non-Christian men, speak good words for the rescue work.

She admired the industry of Chinese printers, for she knew it took eight men a twelve-hour-day to set up four pages of newsprint.

Publicity favorable to the Mission created "a more tolerant and friendly feeling among all classes of Chinese and an encouraging spirit of self-enlightenment [which] has led many to visit our new Home and there learn for themselves the work that is being done for their country women and children."

From the white press, too, came approval. E. French Strothers, of *The California Weekly,* said of his visit to the Home:

> . . . dozens of bright-eyed Chinese girls patter gaily about in their black blouse-and-trouser costumes, playing at housework, or working at their play with childish absorption, laughing, romping, singing, full of the joy of life and the blessing of freedom . . . they are happy. It takes only a few minutes' walk through the Home to see that the Mission's work of rescuing these girls from slavery has lit the light of gratitude in all their eyes, and that they all, who were friendless, have found in Miss Cameron a friend.

Publicity stimulated invitations from churches and clubs, and Donaldina accepted. With her quartet, and, sometimes, girls who put on a skit depicting their rescues, Donaldina drew billing as "A Living Legend."

In the year 1909, seventy-six women and children registered in the Home, nearly a third of them Japanese; Lo Mo pictured them to one of her audiences.

> If they should all file past you now in actual review, as they do before my mental vision, and if I could conjure up for you their pathetic and tragic histories, you would be touched with a deep pity. Here they come, up the steep ascent to the Haven on the Hill, a sad little procession, all ages from dear baby Ah Que in her little mother's arms up to poor old Lee Shee, just over from China to end her days with her only son, and immediately ordered deported by our inexorable Chinese Exclusion Laws. . . . Such heartaches you will find . . . and such peculiarities of character, such different expressions! . . . Some lovable and intelligent, quickly responsive, others dull and repellent. Some trustful and easily guided: others suspicious, with a deep stubbornness bred of gross ignorance and superstitious fear. All, each and every one, driven to the shelter of our home by some deep vital need, such are the ones who seek us and whom we are here to help as best we may. It matters not that they are always ignorant and often bad; of a widely different race, manner and religion, they all come within the wide circle of our Father's light and love.

During the post-earthquake period, surprise came often. About the time Donaldina felt she knew all the highbinders' tricks, she would meet some new abomination. In China several girls were smuggled aboard a Pacific Mail liner, and led into a corner of a coal bunker. Terrified by threats, they huddled, silent, in a bin as rough and unknown as the dark side of the moon, and ate what food was brought by sailors bribed to see that they reached San Francisco alive. At the end of the long voyage, on a black night when the ship rocked at anchor in the bay, sailors hustled the girls out one at a time into a barge and to a waiting rowboat. Men threw tarpaulins around them and pushed them to the bottom of the boat, muttering about taking no chances after all this trouble, and rowed onto the mud flats, where they were ordered out. Ashore, rough hands hurried them to a hiding place in Oakland's Chinatown.

A girl Donaldina rescued had been sold to Dow Pai Tai, a notably cruel woman who merchandised slaves in San Francisco. In spite of her horrible experiences the girl was almost more afraid of Fahn Quai than of her owner. As Donaldina explained to the Occidental Board, her proffered

"Door of Hope" suggested only the dire woes of an inquisition chamber. Girls were cautioned and coached from the time they left China about the designing "Jesus women", the "agents of a great foreign slave market" who . . . with enticing words and false stories beguile young Chinese girls to go with them. These warnings were followed by most improbable and terrifying tales of the fate that overtook the unfortunate and foolish ones who, forsaking their rightful owners, followed the "Foreign Devils". Too ready is the darkened credulous mind of a heathen slave girl to absorb and blindly accept these tales of a foreign country and a strange people.

Terrorizing stolen girls into submission was commonplace. But as the contest raged hotter, Donaldina heard of more savage threats. Importers mentioned "the boot," a diabolical tool that crushed a girl's foot, told how her finger nails were wrenched out, and described tortures with hot oil.

Frightened slaves jeopardized their own rescues. Some were picked up bodily and carried to safety. An hysterical girl was saved thus from a ship by an immigration official and sheltered in the Home, where an interpreter calmed her. Fred Clift appeared as attorney for the girl's owner, and Donaldina and her counsels,

Monroe and Nightingile, parried his devious efforts to establish an impostor as the girl's stepmother. After a week of daily consultations with police and lawyers and appearances in court, Donaldina traced the "relative" to a noted procuress' address in Oakland; then she was awarded temporary guardianship papers.

She was enjoying her lunch when Fred Clift interrupted. He had come, he said, to take the girl on a visit. When Donaldina refused him, Clift angrily promised he would yet return the girl to her "rightful relatives." A protracted legal battle ensued. For more than four months, Lo Mo sat through tense hearings. Harassment seemed endless. Finally, she said in her report, ". . . a full court room heard Judge Graham's final decision, when at the child's earnest request he delivered her into the custody of the Occidental Board." She was radiant.

Lo Mo would have taken every step twice over to see the dull eyes of one daughter shine with hope. But she counted legal custody of a girl but a beginning. She wrote: "The real victory is only won when through the patient gentle ministrations of love and comfort and sympathy, these Chinese girls slowly but surely realize that they are among those who have only their best interests at heart and who seek to cast about them the love and protection of a good safe home."

Her chance to transform lives came under constant challenge. While strong friends championed her, she recognized the existence of powerful enemies. She knew their trade was thriving. A series of failures warned her. The premonition she had felt on Dedication Day took shape.

Donaldina's daughters could tell when she was worried. She expressed less than her usual pleasure in their accomplishments and was more strict. If she smiled rarely and flushed often, they kept their distance. And if that granite look appeared, they took to their heels before she could say, "My dear children!" in a tone that reverberated in any child's conscience.

The quartet, who had accompanied her on raids, understood something of her anxieties. But they could not know the haunting image of a very young girl who pressed her face against the grille of her brothel door, her cheeks puffy, her nose flat, her lips full and pouting—a piggy face, almost animal—except the eyes,

eyes reflecting deep human suffering. Had the child heard of freedom? Or was it that God-given spark that propelled each soul to seek the light? Donaldina would never know her fate. And how many like her had died before they learned to live?

Donaldina answered a call to rescue, but news of her approach had preceded her. The brothel door was barricaded. Through a grilled window Donaldina peered at a cluster of panicked slaves driven against a wall. At the sight of her a girl burst from the group, shrieking for Lo Mo to take her out. Identified as the one who had called Fahn Quai, she was snatched by her hair and dragged away, screaming. The others were herded after her. Donaldina's cries, "Let us in, let us in!" echoed along the alley. The officer's hammers crashing against the door did not budge it, and crowbars failed to rip off window grilles. Defeated, in tears, Donaldina led the way home. Word came later that, as an object lesson, the girl was beaten to death in the presence of her fellow-chattels.

After such tragedies Lo Mo's daughters tried to buoy her up with expressions of love. As Donaldina's birthday approached, Ah Ching, Ah Tye, and Yoke Lon agreed that they would find something nice for the tiny, bare reception room off the entry, furnished with a small desk and several straight chairs, crowded under a drop light from the high ceiling. The girls decided to buy a desk lamp. Lo Mo would look beautiful in its mellow beams, and maybe one of the men who admired her and came there to talk business would ask her to marry him.

Pocketing all their savings, the girls went to a store on Stockton Street, where they chose a Chinese brass lamp.

"How much?" they asked the proprietor.

"Fifteen dollars."

A chorus of disappointed "Oh's."

The man raised his eyebrows. "How much do you have?"

"A dollar and twenty-five cents."

"One dollar and ten cents."

"Seventy-five cents."

"Well," he said cheerfully, "We fix that. I have more lamps." He led them to another room and lifted a small desk light. "Isn't this pretty?"

Three heads shook. "No."

"How about this one?"

Again three firm shakes of heads.

He pointed to a larger lamp with a lantern shade. "Nice?"

"No!"

"What's wrong with it?"

"We like the brass one," Ah Tye said firmly.

"Why are you so stubborn?" the merchant asked. "Why must you have that one?"

"It's for Lo Mo's birthday," said Ah Ching. "She needs a lamp in her private room."

The merchant grimaced. "Lo Mo! Why didn't you tell me it was for her? I'll make her a present myself." He picked up the brass lamp and carried it toward the wrapping desk. The girls hurried after him, alarmed.

"No! No! Lo Mo won't like it. She says we must never hint or beg. We must pay!"

The man eyed them critically. "The price is what you have got."

The three girls solemnly laid their money on the counter, $3.10.

The precious box was carried up the hill, the lamp installed and turned on before Lo Mo got home. They met her at the door.

"Happy Birthday!"

Lo Mo smiled, hugged each girl, and expressed her thanks.

They waved her toward the reception room. "Come in, come in. A present for you. Take a look!"

Lo Mo stepped into the doorway. Her smile disappeared. She stood perfectly still. "My dear children," she began, her voice even.

The girls had scattered like mice. She glanced at her watch. No time to follow them. But they must return that lovely lamp to the store. They could not have had money to pay what it was worth.

At dinner Ah Ching whispered to Lonnie, "I didn't stop running till I got to the basement. Keep out of sight so she can't make us take it back. She's so busy she'll forget."

Lonnie laughed and caught Tiny's eye. They had brought off their scheme. Yes, Lo Mo would look beautiful when she sat at her desk with a golden glow pouring over her. They could see she needed a kind light on her face to soften lines inscribed by a difficult life. But she resisted sympathy and denied hardship. Her path was her privilege.

Fate sometimes furnished encouragement. One day the street car on which she was riding was blocked by a huckster's wagon across the tracks. His horse refused to budge, though the driver beat him unmercifully. Donaldina climbed off the car and went to the horse's head. She petted and reassured him, and led him to the curb, then reprimanded the driver. Back on the street car a gentleman introduced himself as Mr. Ralston, a businessman, and praised her courage. Later he presented her with a beautifully bound Bible and became a supporter of her work.

During 1909 and 1910 sickness invaded the Home. Donaldina spent unaccustomed time indoors, but "kept busy at my desk." Perhaps the need to keep busy spurred her to start the only diary of her career.

Donaldina doctored herself only when she could not handle her symptoms by will power. For a scalp condition she allowed Miss Andrea to give her treatments. If she could not throw off a cold or sinus headache, she let Dr. White advise, though she hated to take so much as an aspirin, prescribed or not.

During a wet spring the girls traded mumps and measles. Donaldina told stories, played games, and read to them. On Easter it rained and she held Sunday School at home, employing flowers to symbolize new life and resurrection.

In mid-September several children developed fevers and sore throats. San Francisco's chill, overcast summer had kept them pale and prone to colds, but these attacks seemed different. When Baby Ah Yoke and Ah Leen broke out with a rash, Lo Mo took them to Dr. Cheney's office; he could not identify it, but promised to send Dr. Langley Porter. Two days passed before that busy man appeared, diagnosed scarlet fever, and referred the matter to the Board of Health.

Scarlet fever alarmed Donaldina. The disease could spread. She knew of no medicine to prevent its dangerous after-effects.

She appealed to the Board of Health for guidance but a peculiar lack of response kept her on tenterhooks for days. She "rang up" Dr. La Fontaine; she "rang up" the Board of Health; she "rang up" the physicians assigned to the Home, Drs. Muller, Morrow, and O'Neil. Miss Kersell, the nurse, and more girls came down with the disease. A week after Donaldina's first appeal, three doctors arrived, and agreed that the Home was overtaken by scarlet fever! They declared quarantine.

Because few girls occupied the rooms called the Japanese flat, Lo Mo and Alice converted them into a hospital. By nightfall Donaldina herself felt wretched and could not speak. Dr. Luttrell, Miss Kersell's physician, sent her to bed, but she looked in on the sick children before staggering to her own room.

Next morning, Donaldina admitted to Dr. Luttrell, "I did not sleep one moment all night, and I cannot raise my head this morning without getting dizzy." She willingly took the draughts he prescribed and slept until sunset. The next day she remained in bed, and spent another in her room. But she answered the telephone fourteen times, and wrote a letter on behalf of little Mah Ho Ti. On the fourth day she declared she had been imprisoned long enough. Though shaky, she helped nurse the sick children.

By October first, eighteen patients were ill and needed care—ice bags for sore throats and swollen glands, quieting medicines, and a mother's comfort. Outside the quarantine area the tempo of Donaldina's affairs had returned to normal. Visitors flocked in and out. A few hours without callers were noteworthy, "A quiet forenoon. I tidied my room and then repaired my clothes. No callers." Later she entertained a luncheon guest, went shopping to buy a hat at Brownlees, to the bank to cash some checks, and met the steamer "Queen" at the Broadway Dock. Immigration authorities did not clear two girls for landing as she had expected. She feared they would be returned to China, perhaps be waylaid, smuggled into the Straits Settlement, and sold into hopeless slavery.

When wounded by failure, Donaldina sometimes retreated to Paicines, about a hundred miles south of The City, where Allan had moved his family and sisters. Visits from friends also cheered her. She noted in her diary that George Sargent, whom she had planned to marry at nineteen, took lunch with her. He had remained a close friend of the Camerons. Looking into his weathered face, and eyes that still held mischief, she felt no regrets. He was married to the right woman, and she would have missed her wonderful Chinese family, had she made a different decision.

She went south to the wedding of Jennie Bazata, sister of her former fiancé, Charles. In the church Donaldina knew so well, banked with flowers and filled with romantic music, she remembered how she had dreamed of marrying Charles here. Thoughts of Charles turned her heart a little. Yes, they would have made a good life, but, and she drew an inward sigh, doubtless each of them had been led in the right way.

Still, there were times, now that her sisters were growing older, when she wished she had the love and comfort of a husband. Dear Annie was nearing sixty and Helen and Kathie following close. Loyal brother Allan should not be asked to support two families. Sometimes Donaldina was tempted to worry. She must have more faith. A God who had been so merciful to her daughters would not forsake her or her family.

After a drab summer, golden autumn helped restore her confidence. Gentle winds drew back fog curtains, revealing buildings chalked against a sky blue as a Chinese bowl; sea tang flavored the air. But mid-October brought storm. Donaldina felt depressed. In her diary she wrote,

A cold showery day. Mrs. Sing of Los Angeles came to see Margaret. Dr. Muller called. Mrs. Newhall, Mr. Chesney called. Wing and his friend called. Ah Tye & Miss C. [Cameron] took N'Gun Que to get her things on Spofford Alley. Had Chinese lunch with Mrs. Sing and the girls. Lai Kum and Jim met here to discuss their plans. Bok Yan called. Man to see N'Gun Que. A busy rather profitless day.

But next day, Donaldina woke to "a lovely brilliant morning. . . . All quite peaceful at the Home. God seems to bless and fill all things with His Presence today."

Though she had to deal with uncertainty and conflict, she maintained harmony in the Home. Her daughters absorbed her happy ways, and helped draw frightened newcomers into their circle. Rarely had a rescued slave known anyone who cared about her welfare. She had to learn to trust someone who did care. And who could understand as fully as one who had herself experienced slavery?

A daughter confided to Lo Mo how she had won the trust of a new girl, her roommate. Though Mei Ling came willingly to the Home, she found it peculiar. Chinese homes were furnished with mats and low tables and occupied by small families. But she confronted many chattering girls in a big house with dining tables, stiff chairs, and high beds. Lo Mo had seemed kind, but her few Chinese words were hard to understand, and the crowd of daughters overpowered Mei Ling. But her roommate had been friendly. She turned back soft covers on the bed, talking in Cantonese about an unseen Father who cared for this house.

The new refugee was apprehensive. Could the terrible tales be true after all? Did spirits roam here? She stopped her ears against her roommate's words. Still, she read kindness in her eyes and happiness in her face. The girl laid out a clean white nightgown for Mei Ling and put on her own.

"Do not be afraid," she said. "I, too, was a slave. But it will be as if it never happened after you are here for a time."

Mei Ling began to tremble. Her roommate put her arms around her.

"Was it very bad?"

Mei Ling sat down on the bed and the words tumbled out.

Yes, it had been very bad for all of two years in the "City of Pekin" on Jackson Street. Then one of her customers had felt sorry for her, saying that so young and graceful a girl need not wear out her life. He tore a white handkerchief in two, gave her one half and told her he would send a rescuer who would carry the other half.

"The City of Pekin has many girls," she explained. "Men play fan tan at tables. When my friend returned with Lo Mo I could not get to the door. The girls saw her and began to cry and run about, and the men ran after them cursing. I was too frightened." She shuddered.

"Then two men grabbed me and took me to an inner room; they tried to make the trap door open. But it stuck shut. Then your Lo Mo followed, waving the half of my handkerchief, and her Chinese companion called, 'Come, Mei Ling! We are here to help you!' I broke away, but more men tried to stop us. Then policemen came."

Mei Ling no longer trembled. "And now I am here. I think my life will change."

"You will be my sister and you will have many sisters. Lo Mo will be your mother too. Lo Mo says it was not 'by chance' that she was able to save you."

Mei Ling's face glowed. Then she looked troubled. "But what did you mean about a father in this Home?"

Smiling, the other girl reached for her Bible. "Tomorrow I will read to you about Him, and about a man named Jesus who is like an elder brother. Don't worry."

A girl of responsive temperament, Mei Ling fit into the family, as did two other refugees whom Lo Mo said were "among the loveliest characters who have entered our Home for many years . . . gentle, naturally refined and very studious." Mrs. Fong, with her two little daughters, did not adapt so quickly. Crippled by tiny, distorted feet, she had barely escaped being murdered by her husband because she bore him no son. He quite forgot her extra value, her feet, the yellow lilies that fit into teacups.

Donaldina gave personal attention to such women, and to girls "hardened by backgrounds of complete ignorance and dire poverty, too frequently in surroundings of vice, with absolutely nothing pure or true on which to fix their faith or love." In sorrow she admitted that certain of these unfortunates could not accept kindness. They sometimes chose to return to the debased life to which they were, in some degree, inured.

Among those taking refuge in the Home during the year were twenty-one Japanese women and children. A rescued slave, Haru Nme, mother of a tiny baby boy whom she adored, had to send him to his grandmother in Japan because she had no means of supporting him. The annual report carried the comment:

The Japanese department of our work could be made much more effective if the additional expense of a Japanese interpreter and bible woman could be provided for. As the work is now carried on, we must depend for assistance largely on the Japanese Association of San Francisco . . . the Secretary . . . [of many years] helps in adjusting the cases of women and girls who come to the Home for protection. This is not at all a satisfactory expedient. Our hearts often ache for the helpless, often cruelly wronged little women who submit to the decision of purely secular judgment upon the merits of their case.

Donaldina could not reconcile herself to anyone's loss of freedom, or to their loss of a moment's happiness. Between rescue attempts she plucked brief joys, like the wild flowers of her childhood, for herself and her daughters: a weekend's visit from Caroline; a trip to the Emporium to buy Ping Leen her first pair of American shoes; a day in Pleasanton when she and Ah Tye came home laden with blossoms; an overnight visit from faithful Mrs. Browne.

Then she again gave chase to the enemy. After the earthquake, brothels and dens built sophisticated escapes and hideaways for slaves. Donaldina sharpened her perceptions. Was it a faint outcry of pain her sensitive ears caught? Or a little spring in floor boards underfoot, a loose panel in the walls? Or was it prescience, God's leading, that guided her to ingenious prisons?

Lo Mo once confounded her enemies by rolling up linoleum from an innocent-looking floor to expose a trap door, under which four girls, valued at $12,000, stood in a suspended box. The cache served as a haunting reminder of girls she could never save, whole fields white with harvest and no means for garnering.

But early in 1910 she felt greatly encouraged. New immigration laws were passed providing for the arrest and deportation of foreign women brought into the United States for immoral purposes. The statute prescribed arrest and punishment of anyone engaged in the traffic.

Simultaneously, vigilante committees, both national and international, sprang up and launched a campaign to dislodge yellow slavery.

"Tardy attention!" she flung after them. How few of the new crusaders recognized that the Presbyterian Missionary Society and her Occidental Board had fought almost alone for thirty-eight years! They had reason to cherish pardonable pride!

But in spite of her rebuke Donaldina rejoiced. More gain seemed imminent, and she fell in step with all those with whom she held common cause.

CHAPTER ELEVEN

Season of Promise
1910-1912

In October of 1910 the Synod of California, Utah, and Nevada held its annual meeting in Fresno. Some delegates, including denomination leaders from New York, visited "920" on their way home, and attended a Board program. The Tookers, often guests over the past seven years, were among them.

Donaldina had decided to appeal boldly for a nationwide campaign to give slavery the *coup de grace*. As long as she quoted scripture and described the domesticity of her girls, she could expect approval. But how would her hearers, especially the men, react when she asked them to urge enforcement of the new immigration law against immoral traffic? And to press for further changes in the law of the land? Congress had acted, public opinion was aroused. Now was the time for the church to speak!

When Donaldina stepped to the lectern murmurs of anticipation ran through the Chapel. Trim in her blue-grey suit of British cut and a white blouse with an Eton collar, she looked out over the room and noted an unusual number of men from the community mingled with her out-of-town visitors. Nathaniel Tooker sat in the front row. The pockets of his well-tailored Prince Albert coat bulged, making his short, dignified figure appear oval. With amusement she remembered the day he had pulled out of his pocket a newspaper-wrapped package of his favorite codfish, telling her, "Get it yourself. Then you know it's fresh."

From the audience he smiled at her. She took courage. Though she knew her speech, she gripped her notes for extra certainty.

"What is this Home that you have so generously provided?" she began. "A plain, substantial brick building that stands here on the steep hillside overlooking Chinatown, where we listen to the mysterious sounds and sights that go to make up this miniature Oriental City. As one of our early missionaries said of work in Chinatown: 'We go to it as the pioneer Californian went into the mines, where, with every stroke of his pick he expected to turn up a shovelful of gold sand.' To us it is a mine; we have struck gold there."

She laid down her notes. Her voice grew rich with enthusiasm. She sensed her hearers' response. "That mine has proved an inexhaustible vein. It yields far richer and more enduring treasures than any Bonanza of the Golden West. The treasures stored up are not all visible to human eyes, but known to Him who seeth not as man sees. But let me tell you of some of our treasures, the endearing children and women who have come to us recently."

Donaldina bent toward her audience, as she described a family from Portland, Oregon—five little sisters, none of whom had spent a day in school. She told of the wedding of one of her girls, saved four years earlier. Her rescuers had searched through three buildings for six hours to find her, and pulled her out from under a heap of rice bags, mats, and boxes, where she had nearly smothered. Then there was a boy, winsome Woo Doon, nursed after surgery for trachoma; and a gentle old Chinese lady who wanted to study to become a Christian, and inquired if she might "take a little wine occasionally and play dominoes, but not for money."

"One story suggests another," Donaldina continued. "I must tell you of little Chin Ah Ho. Only the dear Lord who watches over the uncertain destiny of such waifs as she, knows her real name. This weird little Chinese domestic slave child was not prepossessing, very small, very frightened, densely ignorant and unbeautiful. But well for the tiny unwelcome alien that the Hon. H. H. North, Commissioner of Immigration combined two fine characteristics—loyalty to the laws he was sworn to enforce and a tender heart that could pity! Somewhat rare characteristics in a government official." Donaldina smiled ruefully.

Children whose mother sought refuge for them and herself in the Home.

"The child was denied entrance, but Commissioner North appealed all the way to Washington, D.C. to protect her and place her in our custody. She came to us with all her worldly possessions tied in a bandana handkerchief. Today you would never recognize in that dull, bewildered child the bright little girl who joyously sings with her little comrades. Oh, the blessedness of love and care for such waifs as she!"

Donaldina paused, "Now these are stories with a cheerful climax, but we know too many others that do not end on such a happy note. Christians! Today our country is ringing from shore to shore a clarion call to men and women to unite in a determined effort to suppress the slave traffic! That great evil even now threatens to keep a foothold in this country."

Donaldina reviewed the Oriental Exclusion Acts, their effects, and other legal injustices. For example, a Chinese could not testify on his own behalf in American courts; he could not own property; he was often barred by law from living outside his quarter except as a servant. Near Sacramento, where the Chinese population was ten percent of the whole, one half the arrests made were of Chinese suspects—and they a notably law-abiding people! A qualified Chinese was barred from many schools and professions. The inequities, the impositions, the crying need for new laws to bring justice and mercy!

"Now, when United States Federal authorities are deeply aroused by the gravity of the situation, lend your strength to your government and to your Chinese brothers and sisters in Christ. Let us set in motion a vast machine to abolish prejudice and enforce laws for the well-being of the Chinese. Do not fear to sink the best of your intellect, your time and talent in this effort. It will repay you a hundredfold."

When Donaldina finished speaking, her Board members applauded with their usual enthusiasm. But some of her visitors remained strangely silent. The Board president thanked Miss Cameron warmly. Donaldina bowed and went to sit beside Nathaniel. She longed to fan her hot face and slip out of her jacket. Though her mind churned, she held herself erect and quiet. Had Lincoln felt this awful tension there on the old battlefield after his Gettysburg Address? (Would that her remarks had made a fraction of the impact that his did!) What did the stillness of her guests mean? They had been too attentive to be indifferent. Were they challenged to help the work? Or antagonized?

As the meeting broke up, she found herself circled by men. Was not the *salvation* of these girls her mission? Let lawyers take care of the *law*. Did she not understand that church and state must be kept separate? Politics was not her business. Competent professional men would handle worldly problems!

At lunch Donaldina was grateful for Nathaniel Tooker's approval. A few others congratulated her for her courage. Fewer still asked questions. She was dismayed. Apparently most of the visitors had chosen to ignore her plea. Where might she recruit support? She must wait for guidance, but suspense tried the soul, even when waiting was on the Lord!

So many uncertainties dogged her. She worried about Sister Jessie, though her health seemed better since her family's move north. Thank goodness she had her husband, Charlie, to care for her, and dear daughter, Caroline, to love. How Jessie must miss Caroline while she was attending Mills Seminary, though those high school years were nearly over.

And it was increasingly clear that the older sisters would have to rely on Dolly, at a time not too far away. She must not dwell on that, but count her blessings, and do the things at hand. Some path would open.

Her mind returned to the work. Her words and those of her faithful Board might fall on stony hearts—a slow erosion until they reached people's sympathies. Well, they would persist! She frequently appeared before clubs and on church programs, and Mrs. Robbins' column in the bi-monthly magazine, "Woman's Work," kept the Home's achievements before the eyes of missionary-minded people. Surely a surge of power must come. She did not try to deny discouraging facts. China still sold her women. Some ships' crews smuggled girls out of the Orient and into the Americas. Too many immigration officials took bribes; and on The City police force the saying went, "If you are sick financially get on the Chinatown Squad and you'll get well quick."

But until the Lord led her elsewhere she would "keep the spence."[1]

A few weeks later Donaldina was planning to attend a New York meeting. She had been invited to stay with the Tookers in East Orange, New Jersey. Jessie, who was visiting Donaldina, helped her shop for the trip. At Jessie's insistence she tried on a softly fashioned blue dress.

"Dolly!" her sister exclaimed, "You are prettier than when you were a girl. With your white hair and your cheeks still rosy, you'll look so stylish!"

"A missionary doesn't need style," Donaldina said dryly, "and I can't afford this." She hung the dress back.

But Jessie was not to be put off. "Remember Paul," she countered, " 'When in Rome, do as the Romans. . . .' "

Donaldina thought it over. She would not want to embarrass her cordial host. "Very well," she agreed.

As always, she felt at home when Nathaniel drove her to Evergreen Place, his two-story frame house on a street lined with ancient trees. Bright autumn leaves drifted down, birds whirred from boughs to roofs with bustling confidence in a long-settled neighborhood. Houses built on rock, Donaldina thought, and their occupants as well grounded. Christian people, steeped in the Puritan ethic. People to count on. Interesting, too.

Over the past seven years she had visited many famous missionaries here, friends of Nathaniel Tooker: Dr. Wilfred Grenfell, a quiet "knight errant of the North," who doctored the Eskimos of Labrador and Newfoundland and helped them set up community service centers; John R. Mott, international Y.M.C.A. secretary; Dr. James C. R. Ewing, President of Forman College of India; Dr. Samuel Zwemer, missionary to the Moslems; the socially gracious Dr. James Walter Lowrie, Chairman of the China Council of Presbyterian Missions; and Sherwood Eddy, author and National Secretary of the Y.M.C.A. in India.

Donaldina "feasted" on her visits with these dedicated men and their wives. And she learned to appreciate the bright mind

[1] A Scottish phrase, literally, "Take care of the pantry, or buttery." More freely interpreted it means, "Be faithful to the job at hand."

of her host. He told her of his early days working in a sugar factory, how he had watched the coarse sugar crystals separated for granulation and the rich bronze molasses poured out as waste. That waste tantalized his imagination. He developed a process to extract remaining sugar from it, a process that had revolutionized the refining industry and made him wealthy. One of his sons had joined him in the business at home, and his son's Princeton roommate, Chester Marquis, was put in charge of Cuban interests.

Donaldina, Nathaniel, and his daughters attended a large denominational meeting in New York. In a party mood she wore her new dress. As Nathaniel escorted her down the aisle of the church, she glanced at him. He carried himself erect, his head proud, and tugged at the lapel of his Prince Albert coat with his free hand. She could imagine how the long coat must be swaying as he strode along beside her. He placed his hand over hers for an instant before she entered the pew.

Toward the end of the program the moderator said, "We have an unusual honor tonight. Miss Donaldina Cameron from the Mission Home in San Francisco is among us. Miss Cameron, will you come to the platform and say a few words?"

Startled, Donaldina whispered to Nathaniel, "I didn't expect to speak. What shall I say?"

"You'll know," he assured her.

Donaldina took her hearers across the miles and years to The City by the Golden Gate. She repeated the story of Old and New "920," "a plain, substantial brick building that has stood on a hillside overlooking Chinatown. . . ." Her words carried more than their usual alchemy that evening. She translated both her "miniature Oriental City" and the lives of her beloved girls into pictures that warmed these New Yorkers' imaginations.

Their enthusiasm cheered her. What good fortune to share her message with these important people! Perhaps their influence would bear fruit. Lighthearted, she and the three Tookers started home in Nathaniel's Columbia automobile.

"A wonderful machine man has made," Donaldina commented. Nathaniel nodded. "Here to stay, and improving all the time. The 1903 model had fourteen horsepower and could go forty-five miles an hour. The 1907 was forty-eight horse-power. . . ." He interrupted himself. "We'll be at the ferry before you know it."

From the back seat Mary responded. "It's lovely, but I do wish we could drive to church on Sundays."

"It would be nice," Gertrude agreed.

"By no means!" Nathaniel said, "Driving a car is labor, and I do not labor on the Sabbath. Those of my house will take the street car to church."

"Yes, Papa," his daughters murmured.

Donaldina smiled to herself. She wondered if Nathaniel had thought of the street car conductor as a working man. But the city's lights reflecting on the Hudson River soon crowded other thoughts out of her mind. They glittered and streaked on paths of the current.

Nathaniel drove onto the ferry. When the boat began to back slowly from the oily water of the slip, they left their seats and stood at the rail. After the evening's exhilaration they were full of talk. But as the long whistle sounded and the ferry slid westward, Nathaniel drew Donaldina's hand through his arm and led her aside. Tonight, seeing her so beautiful in that blue dress as she poured out her heart, he repeated thoughts she had known for some time. He loved her; he wanted her to be the lady of his home. They shared great interest in missions. He could offer her friends and travel and security.

Looking into his earnest face, Donaldina felt gratitude and affection. They were so nearly of a height that their gaze met. They might look at life eye to eye, she thought with an inner chuckle. But, more soberly, perhaps the time had come to think of matrimony. This could be a marriage of mutual respect, a joyful sharing in great concerns of the Lord's work. Nathaniel was many years older than she. His daughters were close to her age. Yet, was this God's leading? Was this His plan for her sisters' needs? And what of the Home? She had left its affairs to the capable management of Nora Bankes. Perhaps Nora was sent at this hour to take over the reins from her tired hands. She was indeed weary. She had realized Nathaniel's devotion to her, and been dimly aware that she must have an answer for him. And now the time had come. Was her feeling of impending good during Nathaniel's West Coast visit a true leading?

Marriage to Nathaniel was a clear and natural step, surely of the Lord's doing. Many needs would be answered, much opportunity opened. Next day, when they were alone, she told him her decision. Overjoyed, he drew her into his arms. What a life they were to share! He would take her to the Orient for a honeymoon. Would she set a date for the wedding?

Donaldina demurred. How would his daughters feel?

"You will see," he said. He summoned them. "Mary, Gertrude, we have a surprise for you. Miss Cameron has honored me by accepting my proposal of marriage."

Gertrude ran to them, her arms open. "You were right, Mary. Oh, I'm so glad!"

"I'd hoped for this," Mary said. She kissed her father and then Donaldina.

"My dears! How did *you* know?" Donaldina said.

Mary smiled. "I can't think of anything more suitable."

Though the Tookers urged her to lengthen her visit, and she was tempted, she felt she must begin to set her affairs in order at "920." Reluctantly, Nathaniel put her on the train, with a promise to visit her soon in San Francisco.

Though she had crossed the continent many times, Donaldina thought the autumn "woods and templed hills" had never looked lovelier. Brilliant colors spilled down their forested sides; in the valleys leaves fell in yellow pools beneath fruit trees. Apples hung like flame pendants. Across the plains the harvested fields lay resting, with here and there baled hay and huge stacks towering in farmyards. Seeding of winter wheat had begun, and Donaldina drew a parallel. Was she not replanting her life with fresh promise for another spring? She knew contentment, tranquillity in "the everlasting arms."

When the train reached Oakland, she stepped into Indian summer, warm and golden. Annie waited on the platform, her brown eyes sparkling with pleasure. She had come from Paicines to share the hour and a half's train ride from Oakland.

"Well, Dolly, the East did you good. You look bonnie," she said, embracing her sister. Donaldina, laughing, tucked her arm through Annie's and the two walked toward the depot.

"Does it show so clearly? Geography is not responsible for my looks."

Annie's eyebrows lifted. "And what is this?"

"I can't wait to tell you, my dear, darling sister. I am to be a bride after all."

Annie stopped short, and turned Dolly toward her. "What is this?" she repeated.

"I have decided to marry Mr. Tooker. Let's talk on the way home."

Annie said dryly, "Well, I think we need to! I can see my fine lemon pie will not be the first topic of conversation."

Next day in the Home Donaldina found all well, the little girls excited over her presents for them, and Nora Bankes welcoming a new refugee. A sulky-faced young woman in an elegant silk sahm, she shrank from Donaldina's outstretched hand and lowered her eyelids.

A hard soul to reach, Donaldina thought. But Nora dealt well with her. Yes, Nora was a natural successor to the superintendency. After clearing the heap of letters and bills accumulated during her absence, she would reveal her plans. But right now she must ring up Mrs. Young Yee Goo, who taught Chinese in the Home and English to new wards. Mrs. Young, with her good, firm Christian approach, might reach Nora's rebel. As Donaldina picked up the phone, she thought back to the time of her arrival in San Francisco fifteen years ago. The telephone company did not list numbers in Chinatown. A caller asked for his party by name and address. Each remarkable operator memorized those facts and spoke the five dialects then in use. In New Jersey an indifferent "central" merely rang one's number. She would have adjustments to make in the East.

After talking with Mrs. Young, Donaldina walked to the open window and looked up at blue sky and wisps of fog. A cable car rumbled up the hill, and the brakeman sang out, "Pow-ell Street next." That call came as regularly as the musical ring of St. Mary's bells through the day and into the night. Children's voices from the play yard reached her. Recess time. A draft from the hall wafted the tantalizing smell of baking bread.

In Nathaniel's home what would punctuate and savor her days? The West had been in her blood for forty years, and her natural family and Chinese daughters composed her close circles. How strange, and wonderful, to anticipate a husband and a home of her own at last.

But practical demands clamored for attention, leaving her little time to dream. Rescues proved strenuous and, too often, frustrating. Twice she had hurried to Oakland to save two young girls held by a cruel mistress, but so closely were they guarded that both attempts failed. Sleuthing revealed that the girls were taken outdoors for exercise in the evenings. Donaldina, accompanied by her interpreter, an Oakland minister, the Rev. Mr. Ecclestone, and a friend of his, tried again.

Hiding in a dark doorway, Donaldina felt her heart pound. Her palms grew wet. She and her three conspirators crouched like jungle cats as they heard the swish of slippered feet approaching. When figures moved before them, they sprang. Each grasped the arm of a girl and ran with her. The keeper screamed, and Chinese men spilled out of houses, furious at the sight of whites making off with Chinese girls. Had Donaldina not waved down a taxi, the slaves could have been lost a third time.

The strain of physical struggles and the tedium of investigation and court proceedings exhausted Donaldina. In the case of Sue Mui she had little to go on except that the girl's parents in China wrote of their daughter's disappearance, and their fear that she had been kidnapped for San Francisco's market block. Through her Chinese informers Donaldina turned up Sue Mui's hiding place and stole her from Wu Gee Quan, who had purchased her for $3,300. The well-educated girl explained that in China, as she had walked near her home, she had been overpowered by sailors and, disguised in men's clothing, put aboard the steamer "Manchuria." Her owner did not surrender a $3,300 property easily, but the girl's intelligence and Lo Mo's reputation persuaded the judge to free her. Donaldina booked her passage to China in the company of a missionary.

After stress Donaldina experienced unsteadiness new to her, more a nervous quaking than visible trembling. Secretly, she worried, and withdrew to regain her equilibrium, pleading headaches or the need to catch up on her work. She sometimes wondered if she were able, or if she had the right, to marry Nathaniel. He came to see her, and though she longed to give him much time, rescues called her away, distinguished visitors arrived, her daughters needed attention. Nathaniel was amused and awed by what he called the orderly chaos of the Home.

"You are the eye of a hurricane," he said.

Donaldina laughed. How fine a compliment! "My dear Nathaniel, you're recognizing my attempt to live in Him who is the calm in the midst of the world's turmoil. It pleases me that you see it."

After Nathaniel left, Donaldina told Mrs. Pinney, president of the board, and Mrs. Kelley of her engagement. Driving herself on nerve, she put her ship in order. Now that Nora Bankes, a woman the Board trusted and the girls loved, seemed destined to become superintendent, she must be briefed on business matters and given the combinations of the two safes, one in her first floor office and the larger one in the basement. Mrs. Carr was a good matron. As for the day schools, they were fully staffed, and Donaldina was comfortable about the Bible classes taught by Mr. Hamlin, a student from the San Anselmo seminary, by Mrs. Fenn, and by the good, gentle Rev. Ng T'sun Sam. Faithful Tien, finishing her schooling in the East, insisted she would return to "920" within the next few months.

Good people filled every niche, though the Home had lost some of its lively and reliable daughters, launched on their own. How she missed Ah Ching, who had sailed a few months ago for China with Miss Grace Barnard after gaining reluctant consent of the Mission Board. No single Chinese woman, and certainly no American-trained kindergarten teacher, had ever before represented the Board. Donaldina reread a letter from Mrs. Fitch, principal of the Shanghai school in which Ah Ching had begun her career.

I have had a long talk with your dear Ching . . . whom I love more and more every time I see her. . . . She has been so very sweet ever since she came, taking an inferior position under a teacher who knows very little, but being willing to do this because she has not been able to speak the Shanghai dialect.

Next Monday the kindergarten opens again after the Chinese New Year vacation, and she will begin to be in charge for about half the session each day. She has such love and tact and gets on beautifully with everybody. I know she will do good work if she has any chance at all.

A letter from Kum Yoke's husband, in honor of Lo Mo's last birthday, was one of her best gifts:

I must write to you to ask you to pardon me because I haven't write you for so long. I am very busy and work hard to hold two jobs to support my family. I am going to tell you about your daughter Kum Yoke. Since we are married seems to me she is a whole hearted Christian. Sometime ago I bought her a sewing machine, so she learn how to make all plain clothes. Also I bought her a piano; she able to play all hymns.

June 28th God give as a great blessing, give us a boy. I give his name, Phillip Moy.

Truly, Donaldina mused, "The entrance of His word giveth light."

She read over one more message in which Mrs. Bigelow, visiting in Canton with Dr. Mary Niles, told of a daughter from "920."

She was from San Francisco, and upon inquiry I found she was none other than your beloved Suey Seen. Her face lighted so beautifully when I spoke of the Home. She is, indeed, a lovely character. It would do your heart good to see her among the blind girls; she is so tender and motherly and so efficient. She is eager for a school in her native village; says they are anxious now to be taught; would provide room and books if only the means to pay a teacher were forthcoming—only three or four dollars a month. It seems such an opportunity.

Donaldina replaced her correspondence. To watch her daughters begin fruitful careers climaxed her work. With Nathaniel she was about to enter a new season. Perhaps they could respond to fresh opportunities. She voiced that thought in the final paragraph of her annual report to the Occidental Board.

Our talents are diverse, our opportunities differ, our pathways in life diverge, but our Master's call to service is the same to all, "Sow beside all waters." All fields are His and the promise is unfailing as the command is explicit. "He that goeth forth bearing precious seed shall come again rejoicing bringing his sheaves with him."

The year had been eventful, after all, not as she had expected, but with possibilities beyond the limits of her human vision.

*   *   *   *   *

The annual meeting of April 1911 came and went, and Donaldina knew special joy and sadness in her final attendance as superintendent of "920." In June Caroline graduated from Mills Seminary, and received flowers from Nathaniel.

Donaldina had set her wedding date for late summer, and as July 26, her birthday, approached, her anticipation mounted. Her simple wardrobe was ready and she felt stronger. Nathaniel was much in her thoughts. He and his daughters were to go to Japan and she would meet them there for the wedding. Then the newlyweds would tour China.

One July afternoon Donaldina received a telegram. She opened it and read, "Lean hard and take courage. Father died today." It was signed "Mary Tooker."

Donaldina did not know how she got to her room. Her mind refused to accept the message. Not Nathaniel. Not dear Nathaniel. Why had she been led into this promise only to have it broken?

She had reset her entire life. There hung her trousseau to prove it. It would be easier if she could go East. His death would seem more real. She could do something in Nathaniel's honor. But she could not afford the trip; so she poured out her sympathy and her own bereavement in letters to Mary and Gertrude.

Mary wrote that Nathaniel had not suffered. He had died suddenly while on an errand downtown. The police identified him by papers in his pockets—those big, stuffed pockets of his. Oh! He had died among strangers. Memories of his dear idiosyncrasies rose like a presence.

Because only two of her associates had known her plans to marry, she felt she could not show her grief openly. Her self-control was taxed beyond bearing, for tears came easily. In August she asked her Board for six months' leave, which was granted. Several ladies expressed concern for her welfare.

"You are too thin, dear Miss Cameron," said an anxious little woman. "I hope you will go up to the country with Mrs. Bailey and get some flesh on your bones."

A hearty woman counseled, "Take care of yourself. Rest those nerves. We need you to come back to us well and strong."

Out of weakness and gratitude Donaldina wept. How kind the ladies of her Board were. She felt loved and cared for. Fortunately, her plans for the Home were in order so she could leave in good conscience.

Dear Tien Fu Wuh had returned from the six years of schooling given her by "my American father," Mr. Coleman, whose family called her "one of us." She had lived with the friendly family of Dr. and Mrs. Frost while attending a four-year preparatory school in Germantown, Pennsylvania, and then for two years studied in the Bible Training School at Toronto, Canada.

The little girl who had promised, "Don't worry, Lo Mo, I grow up and help you," had become the beautiful young woman who said now in her melodious voice, "I owe everything to Miss Cameron. Now I come back and help in the Home."

Tien, high-spirited and sagacious, was a godsend, fostering discipline and enthusiasm. And she could deal with unwelcome callers. "I tell them," she announced. "You stay here, Lo Mo!" And in a few minutes Lo Mo heard the outer door close and an unruffled Tien returned to her.

Tien assigned household chores, listing the girls' turns in a ledger which the girls dubbed "The Book of Lamentations." She was strict about duties but still full of fun and able to find time to play games.

Yes, Donaldina thought, blessings dovetailed with needs in a wonderful way. She packed, told her daughters goodby, and took the Stockton street car.

Dear old Yee Hoy Bok (Uncle) had come to see her off. Dressed in his immaculate suit and derby hat, he faithfully guarded the girls to and from church and was on hand for welcomings and God-speedings. She tried to make conversation, but the world seemed leaden at that moment, fog obscuring the sun and her own plans lumped in a colorless heap.

It was good to be with her sisters and Al's lively family of boys at Paicines, in the San Benito Valley. She loved the seclusion of their country home, calling it "just an oak-covered hill, not a ranch. To approach it toward sunset with its crown of trees silhouetted against the soft colors of the evening sky was like entering another world after the crowded streets of the city I had left."[2]

Donaldina divided her time between the ranch and the Baileys' Grass Valley home. Except for a two-week rest at a health springs resort with Jessie, however, she remained on call to anyone who needed her. In Grass Valley the Chinese cook at the mine asked her to bring him a wife from "920." By telephone she was consulted about problems in the Home. When a girl needed rescue in the East Bay or Fresno or Sacramento, Donaldina was easy to reach. She could not bring herself to say "No" to anyone. Depleted by overwork, grief, and demands, she had not regained her strength at the end of six months. Reluctantly, she secured an extension of her leave.

Caroline had been promised a trip to the Hawaiian Islands upon her graduation from Mills Seminary, and her parents, Charlie and Jessie, urged Donaldina to accompany her. She agreed. Family and friends saw them off on the "Mongolia." The Cameron sisters, the Baileys, Eleanor Olney Babcock, Evelyn Browne Keck, and the staff of "920" filled the stateroom with flowers and gifts. Donaldina's love of celebrations raised her spirits and she was able to join in the holiday fun as they sailed.

In the stateroom Caroline cried out in shock. A frightened Chinese girl crouched behind a steamer trunk. Hurriedly closing the stateroom door, Donaldina comforted the girl, and explained to her niece. This child had been rescued shortly before the ship was to sail, and with cooperation from both immigration and the ship's officials, Donaldina had brought her aboard.

"*You* stowed her away, Aunt Dolly?" Caroline asked.

Donaldina laughed. "Well, yes."

[2] Carol Green Wilson, *Chinatown Quest* (Palo Alto: Stanford University Press, 1931, 1950).

When the ship had cleared dock, and the danger of abduction at the wharf ended, the girl traveled with other Chinese aboard.

At last the vacation could begin. For Caroline there was dancing with other young travelers and the ship's officers. Aunt Dolly was too ill to enjoy interesting people or good meals. But she was grateful for freedom from responsibility and Caroline's kindness.

When they arrived in Honolulu, a pilot boat met them, bringing word of the sinking of the *"Titanic"* during her maiden voyage. Donaldina's fellow passengers, Dr. Hall and Dr. Webster, Presbyterian officials from New York, worried about friends who had taken passage on the vessel. On the island dock former daughters greeted Donaldina and Caroline. But Lo Mo first had to arrange for missionaries going to China to accompany her stowaway, and send cables to Shanghai friends to meet the ship. That accomplished, she was ready to visit. Seeing the active witness of her daughters in their communities, she realized how far the Mission reached. But illness overtook her; she could not participate in festivities, and took a room by herself in an old-time boarding house on King Street, not far from Waikiki Beach. The rest and tropic warmth restored her.

She and Caroline sailed the rough passages to the islands of Kauai and to Maui on a windjammer loaded with nitroglycerine. One barrel broke loose and some of the passengers panicked. Donaldina was preoccupied with seasickness. She drank stale beer and ate raw codfish as a cure. It worked. Though her Scottish family had taken drinking for granted, Donaldina had joined the temperance movement and pledged total abstinence. But she was permitted the use of alcohol as medicine.

On Maui Caroline was welcomed as a granddaughter of the Bailey missionary family, and as a daughter of the man who introduced polo to the Islands. At a "Cousins' reunion," she met the music teacher of Makawao Seminary, where her mother, Jessie, had taught and where her parents had met. Caroline stayed on in the Islands for a longer visit, but Donaldina sailed for home, more rested than she had been in years and recovered from depression and grief.

Before returning to "920," she felt led to make two decisions.

The work of the Mission was her life's portion, her total commitment. She must have faith that the Lord would provide for her sisters. And because doors had three times closed on marriage, she would never again consider it. Because she enjoyed men, she would love them in a way never to make their wives jealous.

When coastal heights rose from the water and she could see the two arms of land that reached out to form the Golden Gate, she yearned to be home. The dear familiar hills would be toasted brown this time of year, and her good grey city brisk and cool under an umbrella of fog.

As the steamer passed through the Gate, Donaldina thought of the welcoming faces she would meet. Those of three members of her quartet would not be among them: Ah Ching, teaching kindergarten in China, Margaret Woo, attending the University of Arizona in Tucson and Lonnie Lee, training to become the first Chinese nurse, after being admitted to Presbyterian Hospital, Philadelphia. "Tiny" she would see more often, for the immigration officials had appointed her as Chinese matron on Angel Island.

But what other wonderful people and opportunities might the Lord have in store for her as she entered the dear Home again?

CHAPTER TWELVE

From Broken and Empty Vessels
1912-1915

Of her daughters' exuberant welcome home Donaldina said, "I believe the Chinese, more than any other race, never forget a kindness." She shed quick tears when a young woman who had spurned her touch offered an exquisitely embroidered collar she had made. A former rebel insisted on serving Lo Mo's dinner. She did so with grace, and told Lo Mo she had learned to sing. Could she perform at meetings?

And the little girls drew Lo Mo from looking back to Nathaniel and toward their future. Old dreams must fade and new ones replace them. How could she best nurture these little ones?

Practicality indicated a direction. Some seventy residents crowded the Home, which was intended to house fifty. And during the difficult adjustment of newly rescued girls, the younger children often were exposed to violence and vulgarity that were not good for them.

Donaldina presented the need to her Board, but kindled little sympathy. They could see only good things happening in the Home. Look at Tien Wu, Ida Lee, Ah Ching, Ah Lon, and Margaret, who had spent their formative years here. Were they not evidence of splendid training?

Yes, the superintendent conceded, but remember how baby Yoke Lon had shocked them by lisping Chinese swear words? Young children should not hear tales out of the mouths of sing-song girls from cribs and parlor houses! And little girls needed to play outdoors on God's good earth, not behind bricks and bars!

Seventeen reasons Donaldina wanted a separate home for younger children, 1916.

Another day must come! Meantime some interests were advancing. The day schools were in good hands again, with Miss Nancy Chew teaching at the seminary level, Ida Lee in the Home School, and Minnie Chan in charge of the kindergarteners. Miss Harris gave the girls physical training, and Mrs. Gilchrist and Mrs. Cannon were the souls of constancy with their Sabbath School class. Devoted Mrs. Fenn, who came all the way from Lindsay, in the southern San Joaquin Valley, to keep the wheels of the Industrial Department going, had stimulated the girls' interest in hand work. Many a newly rescued slave stilled her nervousness over a knitting needle, crochet hook, or tatting shuttle or at a loom. How proud they were of their contributions to the Annual Bazaar! Proceeds of their needlework had paid for three new sewing machines, equipment so prized that a bride might prefer one to a diamond ring.

Donaldina encouraged broadening of the school curriculum. The California State Series of textbooks were faithfully covered in both the Home School and the Occidental School, thus qualifying graduates to go on to high school, though few possessed the means or the drive to do so. Lo Mo approved new emphasis on literature and listened to her daughters recite "Spring" by Browning; "Love" by Coleridge; "Light" with its lovely line, "The night has a thousand eyes," by Bourdillon; and selections from Tennyson, Whittier, the Careys, and Sir Walter Scott. A volunteer art teacher, Mrs. Woods, taught the girls to make hand-painted place cards, silhouettes, and displays for an exposition. Evelyn Browne Keck instructed them in music. At graduation pupils presented recitations, read original compositions, and sang. Afterward, Donaldina's praise boosted everyone's satisfaction.

Of course contentment did not always prevail; congestion provoked the girls to compete. They did their personal laundry on Saturdays, four at a time, using the round galvanized washtubs in the basement, and jockeyed for early turns. One morning before the allowed rising time four girls tiptoed into the hall, carrying their soiled clothes. They had barely made the landing below Donaldina's room when her door opened. She came into the hall in her long nightdress. Her eyes blazed.

The Industrial Department in the early 1920's.

"Girls! Don't you know what time it is?"

The four girls nodded and crept back up the stairs.

Inside her room Hung Mui said, "Lo Mo was indignant." She stared at the clock. "We have to wait another hour."

"Her eyes were madder than her voice," her roommate replied, and with a sigh climbed into bed.

The months after her sabbatical, Donaldina wrote in her report, "were crammed full of rescue work" and a subsequent spate of court appearances. The case of Yoke Wan and her unrelenting effort to regain her baby, Choy Toon, seemed one of the most frustrating in Donaldina's twenty years of legal battles. In the spring of 1914, after forty-three appearances in five courts, over a period of eleven months, poor Yoke Wan still waited in suspense for a final decision.

Uncertainty and change pervaded Chinatown. In 1912 China had ordered the cutting of queues, and her sons all over the world had obeyed. If only the Celestial Kingdom would act on behalf of her daughters. Rumor said that Sun Yat-sen and his supporters had designed an idealistic new government in the Flatiron Building on Market Street a few blocks away. But idealism had not triumphed thus far.

Meantime, in the Home, rescues caused more crowding. To reduce friction Donaldina arranged outings and vacations. The older girls went on short camping trips when the Board could afford to send them. Donaldina and Tien, now called "Auntie," arranged picnics for the little girls, and the middle group visited nearby church meetings, sometimes staying overnight in members' homes.

Lo Mo could not forget her wish to give her babies a separate home. Again, she pleaded with her Board. With a little girl clinging to each hand, she said:

Children are of paramount importance, always. The rescue work has been unusually satisfactory because of the large proportion of little children and very young girls saved before they are sold into lives of sin. Among the latest additions to our nursery family are these two happy little girls, Ah Yoke and Ah Oie. They sleep side by side to the left of the nursery door. You have heard them singing together today,

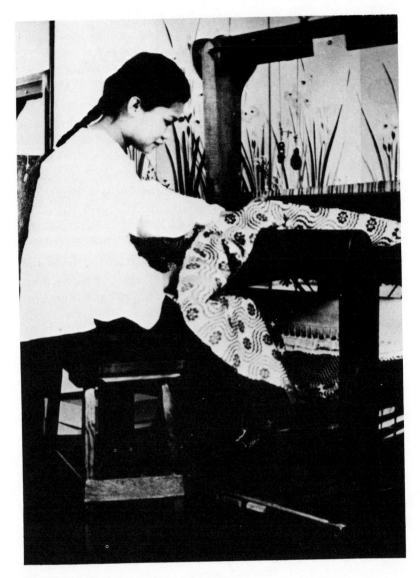

A foster daughter weaving a table runner.

> *Two little eyes to look to God*
> *Two little ears to hear his word.*

A picture of their early homes may shock your sensibilities, yet I want you to realize the life from which our innocents come. Ah Yoke's home in Chinatown was a house of vice on Spofford Alley. Her mistress, Foon Ying, one of the cruelest, most depraved women of the underworld, vented her anger on this helpless child every time her evil nature asserted itself.

She held up Ah Yoke's arm, covered with black and blue patches. The ladies of the Board gasped their horror.

As they quieted, Donaldina went on, "When Foon Ying heard the Mission Home was about to seize Ah Yoke, she tried to sell her. Unable to get her price she took the child to Marysville and hid her in a vegetable garden. Eight months later we found little Ah Yoke in a condition of filth and neglect that was indescribable. Ah Oie came out of similar plight."

Tien Wu led the two little girls away. Donaldina finished her remarks. "God 'setteth the solitary in families and bringeth out those who are bound with chains.' I assure you that God is using the Mission Home of the Occidental Board to fulfill His promises."

Soon thereafter Donaldina went east, and visited the Tooker sisters. In their comfortable old home, which she had so nearly shared with them, the three women dear to Nathaniel talked of his favorite theme, missions. Donaldina told her dream for her youngest daughters. Sympathetic, Mary and Gertrude Tooker offered $2,000.

On Donaldina's return to San Francisco her Board informed her they had given second and favorable thought to her project. They had done their best to raise funds, but a new home remained out of reach. Mrs. F. H. R. Robinson, a Berkeley woman, refused to accept defeat. Having educated her own three daughters, she was now giving a home to two girls from "920" while they finished their training. She rose to speak.

"There are ways we know not of," she said. "If this thing is meant to be, let us cease our striving, and wait on our knees."

The ladies dealt with other business. Minutes later a letter from Mary Tooker was handed to Donaldina. Mary wrote that

The girls studied Chinese and the various subjects prescribed in California public schools.

she and Gertrude had advised their banker to forward to Donaldina another $5,000.

The new home was assured and the meeting broke up with applause and a flurry of excited embraces. Mrs. Robinson beamed, "They that wait upon the Lord shall renew their strength."

Donaldina began to search for a house in Oakland, which would be safer than The City. And property there was cheaper. A few blocks from their former earthquake refuge, at 953 East Eleventh Street, she discovered a roomy Victorian home with a big fenced play yard. The Board purchased the place and it was named "Tooker Memorial Home," in honor of Nathaniel. Miss Nora Bankes became its director and musical Ida Lee, now in her late teens, her assistant.

Donaldina moved thirty-two children. The parting proved difficult, for she had delighted in her youngest. She decided to send fourteen-year-old Hung Mui Chew, who, as a baby, had considered life "a big joke." As a reliable five-year-old she had been entrusted to carry eggs from the earthquake-stricken home. Hung Mui had learned efficiency when a little girl, tagging after the kindly Miss Thompson so much that she had been called the housekeeper's shadow. And now, happy and even-tempered, she had become almost as much Lo Mo's daughter as if she had been born to her.

At Tooker she was assigned the care of nine younger children in the hours before and after school. At first, she confided, she did wonder why she had been sent away from "920." But she came to realize her advantages; she could finish the eight grades in Franklin grammar school, and, later, go to Oakland's high school. Further, the danger of kidnapping from Tooker was slight; she, as one of the trusted girls, was free to come and go. She taught herself to follow Lo Mo's admonitions, "Make progress, dear Hung Mui. Be happy."

Girls from Tooker Home were brought to San Francisco to appear at each Occidental Board meeting. Dressed in pink sahms and foos (tops and pants), they sang and recited. Sometimes it seemed to the children a long time to stay on stage. Pretty Helen

Wong, exceptionally tiny even among her small sisters, could rattle off all the books of the Bible. Her inability to pronounce Leviticus and Deuteronomy added to her charms. At a performance a dignified lady asked, "Will you say a verse for me?"

Helen smiled, guileless, "Be sure your sins will find you out." The ladies gasped, and Donaldina rose to introduce the next number.

Later Helen caught scarlet fever, but Lo Mo refused to take her to quarantine in the county hospital. She hurried to Oakland, rented a house, and hired a nurse to tend the sick child. As Helen got better and grew restless, her Tooker sisters serenaded her.

At the year's end Donaldina composed her annual report, which she was to read to the Occidental Board.

Only fifteen minutes! How can I begin to tell the story of nearly nine thousand hours—a whole year's history of more than a hundred souls! . . .

Here is a long list of names enrolled this year, each representing a different individual created in our Father's own image, each given the precious opportunities of life, yet handicapped from the very start: . . .

She copied thirty-seven names, the youngest, baby Howard; there were women and children from Los Angeles, Oakland, Red Bluff, and Santa Barbara. She wrote further:

From within the very shadow of the Statue of Liberty . . . comes this cry for succor on behalf of a little Chinese slave girl. We give it translated as it came to us some months ago:

New York, June 1915

Leung Kai Ming came back from Hong Kong last year bought girl from Haw Yow, name Ah Ying. Claimed to be his own daughter.

January married to somebody; but does not know the name of man.

April 25, Sunday, Leung Kai Ming took this girl to some place; but does not know what place.

When I saw this I followed them to depot. The child cried all the way. Leung Kai Ming bought ticket. I asked child what was the mat-

Donaldina missed her little ones when they were moved to Oakland, 1925.

ter but she cried so she could not answer. When I saw her it made me want to weep. She is *so little,* and does not know a word of English.

When Leung Kai Ming put her on the train it was like pulling a dog onto the train. When I investigated I found that Leung Kai Ming took her south and sold her to be a slave. I feared to help this girl because Leung Kai Ming is head of highbinder society.

I thought the Mission could help because you always help the girls who are in trouble.

If you want to help this girl you must get her picture at Seattle, perhaps the police can help.

Although this girl is married she is so little, only three feet.

Please teacher try to find some way to help this girl.

WONG SOW
[An informant]

Donaldina told the Board of a search for the child whose traces led:

From Seattle to New York, then to Boston and south to Florida, west again to the slave market in San Francisco,—for like the quest of Evangeline there were but faint clues to guide, yet eagerly we followed them. Sold by Leung Kai Ming for $3,400.00, held fast by three owners, who could hope to find a little slave girl like Ah Ying in the vortex of San Francisco's great Chinatown? . . . On the side of her oppressors were the allied powers of evil, but on her behalf the "Comforter" came with mightier power—the strength of truth and justice.

One peaceful Sabbath evening not long since, while the Mission Home family were at church, there came a mysterious telephone message. Ah Ying, the little slave girl long sought, was that night at the Ga Bun House, a low resort in Chinatown . . . in room three. Quickly a messenger ran to call . . . our young Chinese assistant. A good detective was summoned. . . . Concealed in a closed carriage an eager rescue party was soon speeding through startled groups of Sunday night street loungers to the very spot where Providence had placed the long sought child . . . within our reach.

Guarded by her mistress, she stood ready, decked for the night's orgie, when an assuring arm passed over her shoulder and a persuasive voice whispered, "Come a home, friends and love are waiting just over the way. Come with us Ah Ying." She turned a child-like face, smiled on the new friends, and with them stepped over the threshold of that house of gloom into light, liberty and a new life.

A few hours later Ah Ying, through an interpreter, beseeched Donaldina to save King Seen, a dear friend left behind. Donaldina secured a warrant and followed with Ah Ying, disguised in American clothes:

Up the stairway of the notorious Yutton hotel, through winding passages, then down again by a back stairway, into a deep basement to room 29. To the dismay of our little guide the room was found to be empty,—no King Seen could be found, upstairs or down, and the discouraged rescue party returned slowly home.

After holding earnest council it was decided to visit the Chinese theatre where a very popular play had just opened. . . .

A ripple of excitement ran through the theatre as Miss Wu and little Ah Ying with their foreign chaperon walked down the aisle and took seats in the middle of the house. Two good officers remained on guard at the rear entrance. The large audience was carefully scanned, but no King Seen was there. Nearly half an hour passed when suddenly there entered through a side door (under guard of course) a tall, attractive Chinese girl, bearing the unmistakable stamp of that tragic life which spells death.

Ah Ying almost sprang from her seat. "King Seen, King Seen!" she ejaculated. "Take her, take her *now!*" Quickly one of those human vultures who are always hovering near their prey, sprang from her seat nearby and hastened to where the unsuspecting girl was sitting. There was no time to lose. Miss Wu, always alert and fearless, rose quickly to warn our officers that the moment had arrived for them to act.

In a moment the attention of that large Chinese audience was diverted from the garish, "make-believe" scene on stage, to a far more realistic, vital drama in real life.

Quickly and decisively our detective and federal officer closed in upon the young slave girl and her guard. They were led down the aisle, followed by Ah Ying, now a very exultant little person, with her friends from the Mission Home.

Later as Detective Barron escorted King Seen and her rescuer home he quietly remarked, "It were well worth all the work of the Mission, if only to rescue one such little girl as this."

There! The story was on record the way it really happened. Perhaps she could head off imaginative reporters from embroidering this into another legend, as they had her rescue of Sai Mui. All that nonsense about her leaping through skylights!

Now to finish her report with a ringing challenge:

Are you who read this message today willing to assume some share in the responsibility which this work . . . places upon us?

Let us help now, lest through our delay they [young girls and children] fall beneath their burden, and so fail to reach the Heavenly goal, and the King shall call us to account because we helped them not by the way.

Donaldina had regained her footing. But fate was balancing another shattering blow.

CHAPTER THIRTEEN

Ordering the Tumult
1915-1919

One morning as Donaldina worked at her office desk, she heard a rattle at the open door. A small girl, her eyes downcast, played with the door knob.

"What is it, dear?" Donaldina asked.

The child stuck two fingers in her mouth and smiled.

Donaldina held out her arms. "Umm, I think I smell spice cookies baking," she said. "Let's go see, Suey N'gun."

This little thing had slipped away again to be with her first friend. A mooie jai at five, she had served as personal maid to an unusually harsh and unfeeling woman in Los Angeles. She had been treated as a convenience, a comfort like a footwarmer, and taught to ease the muscle cramps of her "small-footed" mistress by beating her fists up and down the woman's spine. Since her rescue the child had insisted on giving Donaldina the only gift she could offer—rhythmic pounding of tiny fists on a tired back. She was to Lo Mo "one of the most lovable, intelligent, original child natures it has been my privilege to see unfold."

Now, finding cookies cooling on fresh towels, Donaldina put several on a plate. "We'll have a tea party," she said.

As they reached the entry hall, a visitor, Miss Ethel Higgins, was announced. Donaldina invited her to join them.

Dr. Laughlin, pastor of the Chinatown Church, and Director of Oriental Missions, had discovered Miss Higgins, a singer, and a woman of happy disposition, sagacity, and dedication, and referred her to Donaldina. Later, after Ethel joined the staff, she confessed that a woman who would take time from her crowded day for a party with a troubled child had won her.

With Ethel as well as Tien at "920," Donaldina spent more time at the Tooker Home. Occasionally she brought a little child to "920" for a weekend.

One baby had been a favorite from the first. "She dropped from the clouds," Lo Mo had told her visitors, leading them upstairs to peer over the edge of a large telescope basket at a wee doll-like face. When the baby smiled, one cheek dimpled and her bead-black eyes sparkled.

Lo Mo had asked, "Who can fathom the possibilities concealed in so small a form?"

Often, as she grew, this child came to visit. If no beds were free, Lo Mo set up a cot in her own room. If all cots were in use, the little one shared her bed. Early in the morning she waked and tweaked Donaldina's nose, which "put Lo Mo in a jolly mood."

Older daughters used the little girl to wangle special favors. One evening they sent her to Lo Mo, who was working at her desk.

The child stood quietly in the doorway. Lo Mo asked, "What is it, dear?"

"I'm hungry."

"Didn't you eat your dinner?"

"Yes, but I'm still hungry."

"Would you like some bread and butter?"

"No. I want to phone for a snack."

Lo Mo considered this request. She realized the child had been "put up to it" to try for a special Chinatown treat.

"Very well," Lo Mo replied, "You may have snacks if you get them here by nine o'clock."

The child disappeared, and Donaldina chuckled as she heard a rush of feet toward the telephone.

Donaldina developed favorites among adults too. She met newcomers Helen and Andrew Wu, who lived in a flat near the Home, at a Christian Endeavor meeting in the Chinese Church on Stockton Street, where she had escorted some of the older girls. She was attracted to the serene and intelligent bride and invited her to visit "920" lest she be lonesome in a strange city. Soon it was Donaldina who found herself befriended.

"Come in, come in," she always welcomed Helen Wu.

"I only dropped by to say 'hello,' " Helen invariably responded.

"By all means sit down a while. You are just what I need," Lo Mo urged, putting an arm around the young woman and leading her to the cubbyhole off the lobby, still called her "private room." With the door closed, Donaldina felt free to speak to her guest. One day she was especially harried.

"Oh, my dear," she said, "I put so much time into saving these girls and getting them husbands. And only today word came that another of them has gone back to her old ways." She could not restrain tears. "Sometimes I wonder if this work is worth it. The girls are so *bad*. I wonder if they are even worth crying over. To think they are willing to sin to get silk dresses and fine food!" Donaldina dried her eyes and answered her own outburst. "Of course they are worth it! You do me so much good, Helen. You are like having a family of my own to confide in."

She spoke of love and support by countless friends and professionals, among them "Dr. Elizabeth Keyes, Dr. Peter H. Luttrell, the Drs. Green and Dr. Susan Lamb [to whom] we are indebted for the faithful care they have freely given our large family." She spoke often of "Mr. Henry E. Monroe, our loyal devoted attorney. For more than twenty years this wonderful friend has graciously laid upon the altar of the rescue work for Chinese slave girls the splendid offering of a deep and tender sympathy along with an exceptionally gifted legal mind. Only by this generous free-will offering from Mr. Monroe is it possible to carry on this difficult rescue work with its truly wonderful results."

She hoped recent investigation of immigration scandals might hasten reforms. She had long deplored the complicity of American officials with Chinese who tried to enter the country illegally. So, on November 1, 1915, she was not entirely surprised to see headlines in the *San Francisco Examiner*, "Federal Officials Bribed by Chinese Is Charge," and sub-heads: "86 Celestials Caught on Liner Mongolia; Stowed Away for Purpose of Being

Smuggled Into Port of San Francisco; U.S. and Steamship Officials Said to Be Mixed in Plot; $100 to $500 for Each Man if He was Landed in This Country; Chinese Are Found Hidden in All Parts of Ship; Will Cost Pacific Mail $6000 to Return Them to Their Homes."

Officials from Washington, D.C. and a federal grand jury explored the shocking situation; indictments were issued; and a general shake-up of the immigration department followed. Authorities did not solve all problems, but Donaldina hoped that soon reasonable immigration laws concerning the Chinese would be enacted. Since the first Exclusion Act in 1882, entry of Chinese had been restricted to a few groups: wives and children of Chinese men in America, Chinese government officials, scholars, and certain classes of merchants. Each person who qualified for these categories established a right of entry commonly called a "slot." But the importers of human flesh sometimes contrived to bring in substitutes for legitimate entries. They also devised fictitious "slots" and filled them. Men were wanted as cheap labor and women for another kind of servitude.

The government's action to stop these illegal entries attracted public approval. All key posts in the Home were filled again. Donaldina felt that she and her quest were on a singularly even keel, at least as nearly as her hectic life could ever be even.

Then, without warning, word came that her brother Allan was desperately ill. Dolly rushed to his home in the San Benito Valley. A well-known surgeon performed an emergency operation, and discovered an undiagnosed ulcer. But Allan could not rally; three days later he died.

How often she had found contentment and direction, only to have both interrupted by death or separation from men dear to her.

Now Charles Bailey remained the only man of the family, a stalwart to whom all turned: his wife and daughter; Allan's widow, Lucy, and her three young sons; and the Cameron sisters.

After Allan's funeral, Donaldina and Annie walked out together to watch the sunset. "Love never dies," Annie comforted. She unfolded a yellowed letter. "Dolly, here is the letter Grandpapa wrote me after our mamma died. We can take hold of the same faith." Donaldina read:

Balnabeen
21 July 1874

My dear Annie,

Your mournful letter anent the sad, sad event of your dear Mother's death was such a shock to my feelings that I do not expect to get over it ever. Since I received your Father's intimation of that event I look upon the world a wilderness. My dear Isabella was my first born. I loved her with more than ordinary parental affection. Perhaps too much so, and is now made to suffer for my idolatry; but your Mother was no ordinary person possessed no ordinary talents and active courage to go on through with her plans, and a warm heart full of love and affection, attentive to her domestic duties and devoted to her family. I never knew a woman in her sphere who filled so great a space in society as your lamented Mother did. But she is gone, we do fondly hope to happier Regions where sin and sorrow never enter—*God is love* and a heart so full of love as that of your dear Mother will never be cast away.

And now, my dear Annie, that you are in God's providence deprived of a dear and excellent Mother when at a time of life that you stood most in need of her wise counsel and guidance, may it be the means of leading you to place your trust and confidence in God; read the 27th Psalm and remember the Godly upbringing of your young sisters and only brother devolves in a great measure on you. It is a heavy burden and solemn responsibility, but God will give you grace to bear it if asked, and oh, He is worthy of being trusted for His guidance.

Your Mother's death was and is a great event, and God must have some important design to bring about by such sore affliction on your family. He can bring good out of apparent evil. And this may be the method He took to bring some of you into close union with Himself. And remember, the Judge of all the earth can do nothing wrong, for what we know not now we shall know hereafter—our duty now is simply to pray for submission to His will and rejoice that He Reigns.

Oh, my dear Annie, may He grant each of us grace to say from the heart—"Thy will be done", and that may the Lord bless each and all of you is the constant prayer of your,

Affectionate Grandpapa

P.S. Please tell Papa that I will write soon.

Be sure and write often, as your dear Mama used to do, answer—
1. How are the children off for school?
2. Can Luty [Allan] read and write?
3. How far is my own Jessie on in school?
Bella[1] is coming tomorrow from the Nairn Boarding School

D. McK—

All here desire to be remembered to you. Papa, Helen, Catherine, Jessie, Luty. And tell what is little Dolly like and how old is she?

D. McK—

Aunt Annie is to write you soon and your sister, Bella, is come home improved very much and is very like her late lamented Mother except her eyes are not so large and round as their dear Mama's were.

Adieu   D. McK—

DONALD McKENSIE, Esq.
Balnabeen
Dingwall, Scotland

Yes, God was good. Donaldina knew that, and His love was sufficient for all needs—even now. But oh, the empty yearning for a loved one! It took time for feelings to catch up to knowledge. And she had to make other adjustments. Tien Wu, who had never forgotten the home of her childhood, had finally saved enough from her twenty-five dollar a month salary, and the gifts of friends, to search futilely for her family in China. In October 1916, with Mrs. Young, one of the Home's teachers, who needed to provide for an aged mother still in the Orient, she traveled to China. Yoke Lon Lee (Lonnie), the first Chinese girl to become a graduate nurse, added Tien's duties as housekeeper and interpreter to her nursing. At Tooker Home, Donaldina appointed Mrs. Jennie E. Horsch of Glendale to succeed Miss Smith, who had resigned.

Early in the new year of 1917 her Board gave their weary superintendent a vacation. She accepted an invitation from the Tooker sisters to join them in Florida. After three months she wrote that she was "made over" and longed to be back at her post. In spite of her Board's protest, she returned to "920."

---

[1] Isabella, Donaldina's sister, who remained in Scotland.

The First World War had involved some Americans in Europe for nearly three years. On April 6, 1917, the United States officially joined the Allies. The Home cooperated in "Hooverizing" its food, substituting dark flours for highly refined, and brown sugar and molasses for white sugar. When possible, foods donated to the Home were canned or preserved. The girls knitted socks and scarves for soldiers and worked in the Junior Red Cross. But those offerings seemed meager. Patriotism demanded more.

With men leaving the farms for factories and battlefields, ranchers cried for help. Why not see if her girls could pick fruit? She discovered that Chinese girls from an orphan home did not appeal to the ranchers. Still, she was persuasive. At last a Mrs. Williams of East San Jose, fifty miles south of San Francisco, agreed to try out twenty workers to cut apricots for drying.

Donaldina and Ethel Higgins, nicknamed "Gunny," chose their most trusted older girls, fitted them with overalls, and bought bedding and food for a few meals. The ranch provided harvest hands no quarters and primitive facilities had to be shared with other "fruit tramps," as migratory farm workers were called. A few rusty bedsprings were supplied, but most of the Mission crew rolled up in their blankets on sacks or on the ground. That night it rained, and a bedraggled group of greenhorns, some of whom had never before been outside a city, faced their first day's farm labor.

Lo Mo had appointments in San Francisco and was forced to leave. Ethel Higgins' equanimity, the girls' thirst for adventure, and the warming sunshine carried them through. Though the work was taxing, they enjoyed camping.

When apricot cutting was finished, Donaldina found prune picking for her crew on the Silker ranch, near Los Gatos, a rural town west across the Santa Clara Valley, at the base of the Santa Cruz Mountains. Unseasonal rain pursued them for three days. Fortunately, they could take shelter in packing sheds, where they set up canvas camp cots, a new luxury.

With the last candle blown out, Donaldina lay down on her stiff cot. She listened to the girls' whispers and giggles, like the twitter of sleepy birds, and breathed deeply of the country smells, cool, sweet air, with the fragrance of ripe plums, and now and then a whiff of decaying fruit. Between showers crickets chirruped. A cow bawled and her calf answered. At a distance dogs barked. Donaldina heard rain dripping off eves with a plosh, plosh on the spongy adobe ground. She remembered other ranches, her home in the San Joaquin Valley, the warmth and freedom in her family. Though her daughters' country experience was brief, she hoped it would widen their horizons.

She thought of her children at Tooker. In the back yard each could have her own small plot and a choice of vegetable or flower seeds. That was good, but perhaps she could arrange a trip to the country for them, too. She turned uncomfortably, drawing her blanket under her chin. Her bones were not padded enough for her to enjoy a hard pallet. In the dark she smiled at herself. A woman nearly fifty years old playing harvest hand!

On the fourth day of the new venture the weather reversed itself, turning hot. Fruit had to be picked immediately or it would drop and rot. Though it was Sunday, Donaldina saw the harvest as an "ox in the ditch." Pulling on a pair of overalls, she led her girls into the orchard. As the sun drew up moisture, the air became almost too humid to breathe. Adobe earth, turned to glue by rain, sucked at their shoes. But, working from sun-up until dark, with a mid-day rest, they picked and spread the plums to dry. The crop was saved.

Exhausting though the girls found their work, they came through it without serious mishap. And Lo Mo was proud of their fortitude and of their contribution to the war effort. The girls, too, were proud. They forgot their aches, remembering good times around the campfire at night, and found new excitement in using money of their own. Each worker was able to pay for a year's supply of her own clothing and shoes, and their gifts to the Home totaled $100. If a girl had money left, it was placed in an envelope and secured in the Home's safe, as had been customary with sewing profits. She could withdraw whatever she wanted. At Christmas what a thrill it was to buy gifts in a store!

In the summer of 1918 the Home's crew worked again at the same two ranches and also picked berries in Santa Cruz on the coast. With experience to guide them, they chose better equipment, and camp life rolled more smoothly. Ethel Higgins, Tien Wu, and Lonnie divided management duties and kept the girls' free time lively with games and singing.

When Armistice Day in November of 1918 brought an end to the terrible World War, Donaldina decided to curtail plans for future fruit picking, though she allowed those who elected to cut apricots in San Jose during following summers to do so. The work was not backbreaking, good living quarters were now available in nearby Sunnyvale, and employment outside the Home gave some of her girls a healthy sense of independence.

War, with its tragedies and distractions, had not slowed the rescue work or enrollment in the Oakland or San Francisco Homes, but an epidemic threatened both. In 1918 a pandemic disease named Spanish influenza, highly contagious, killed thousands of people all over the world. In the winter of 1918-19 flu struck thirty of the Tooker youngsters and nearly all of The City's family.

A former helper in the Home wrote, "You are constantly in my thoughts . . . anxious as regards all of you on whom the burden of the nursing falls. . . . Are you wearing a mask and taking precautions? . . . I can see the W.O.B. [Woman's Occidental Board] keeping carefully in the safety of their own homes and phoning you to be sure and disinfect the house thoroughly against the next meeting! !"

So grave were the illnesses that the annual Board meeting was cancelled. Many friends rallied to help care for the little children, jeopardizing their own health, and in some cases, life itself. At last, "two good Scotch nurses" were found to attend "920"'s girls. Of the eighty cases in both homes, not one died. Donaldina asked, "Could we ask greater proof of our Father's care?"

She declared, "God's providences are written in letters of gold across the months, dim sometimes through the mist of tears, but never quite hidden." Deep loss visited the family with the death of Mr. Laughlin, called "Shepherd" by his flock in the Chinatown Church he had pastored for fifteen years, and illness robbed the Home of Alice Lamb, "our loved and greatly valued assistant. . . ."

Mary and Gertrude Tooker had moved to San Francisco for a time and taken an apartment nearby. Mary assumed responsibility for business details at "920" with the title of General Manager. Ida Lee returned from four years' schooling in the east and became an assistant at the Tooker Home. Miss Mills set up a summer vacation Bible school, with Miss Dingley of Oakland's Brooklyn Church, on the Outing Farm in the hills of Saratoga, near San Jose.

No one realized how many hours and days of Donaldina's time went into recruiting new workers and initiating them into the routines of her scattered homes. For all who contributed services, she fed rivers of praise into letters and reports, and expressed her gratitude to each giver.

In 1918, Miss Wong Chi Oie, with Hung Mui, did a fine job teaching the Chinese and English classes; when Miss Wong left, a former missionary, Mrs. O. F. Wisner, replaced her; and Miss Katherine Hazeltine of San Jose aided in teaching English. The Home at "920" had welcomed back Mrs. Lai Qui, a good helper of former years, now widowed and seeking comfort and employment to support her little daughter. Miss Bertha Blount, who had proved "an earnest and competent teacher," was reassigned to the Mission in Siam.

A new housekeeper, Miss Waghorn of Redlands, who had the extra qualification of training in the Bible Institute, relieved Auntie Tien Wu,

. . . ever faithful, and unfailing in loyal service to her Master . . . from household cares, so that she may devote most of her time to talking with, counseling and teaching the Chinese girls in their own language, the truths which she has made her own, and also for the important duties of interpreter and assistant in the rescue work.

At this opportune time, Ethel Higgins and her sister made a gift of a year's salary, $500, for a new teacher of the Industrial Department. When a candidate was located, Donaldina said of her:

God seems to select choice Spirits to do hard tasks, and so He laid it on the heart of Miss Edith Culter to relinquish home, parents and

comparative ease to take up the very strenuous life of teacher and
director of industrial work at the Mission Home . . . Miss Culter
proved herself to be . . . a veritable "Jack-of-all-trades", and Master of
many.

With publicity about the two homes widespread among churches
and clubs, . . . generous donors of gifts, teachers of music, helpers in
the Sabbath school and friends . . . have realized that youth loves play,
and have given their time and thought, as well as money, to give
happiness to the shut-in Chinese girls of the two Mission Homes.

Donaldina lauded the lawyers who continued to contribute
their services without payment: Attorney Henry Monroe, the
girls' "Abraham Lincoln"; his young colleague, Robert Borland;
Ernest Page of Oakland; Richard Belcher of Marysville; and L.
T. Hatfield of Sacramento.

"In season and out . . . faithful and skilled physicians" treated
the girls: Dr. Luttrell of San Francisco and Drs. Green, Hols-
claw, and Swanger of Oakland.

Of Donaldina, Bertha H. Smith wrote in an article published
in *The American Magazine*:

. . . said Miss Cameron . . . "I love these girls. I must go anywhere
when the call comes from one of them who would be free."
A flush of enthusiasm overspread the aristocratic face of the woman, a face far too young for the white that has come into the dark
hair above it. The spark of humor is never long out of her gray-
brown eyes, for Donaldina Cameron is not the ascetic type of missionary. She is keenly alive to the picturesque and dramatic elements
of her work. She sees the comedy as well as the tragedy of it. There
is in her manner so much of her charm and social grace, of pronounced femininity, that she is quite the last woman in the world
one would connect with the raiding of highbinder dens. She is utterly
and delightfully human.

With great support and long gains made in her work, this was
a time for Donaldina to press toward greater fulfillment. Tooker
Home had become overcrowded. Youngsters in desperate need
could not be admitted. At "920" she had again accommodated
a few young children. She could not turn her back on helpless
babies born to her rescued daughters or neglected little boys.
She could not keep them indefinitely, yet she refused to cast

them out on the streets or into an orphan home that scorned Chinese.

Though the Chinese valued their sons more highly than their daughters, a surprising number of boys had no families. For several years she had prayed daily for the Lord to raise up a man who would care enough to *do* something about these boys. The year 1919 held an answer in store. Or so it appeared.

CHAPTER FOURTEEN

New Faces, New Forces
1919-1925

On an unseasonally warm afternoon in March of 1919, Donaldina attended a meeting of Chinatown's religious and social workers. She knew all of them, people from the one Catholic and nine Protestant organizations that served Chinatown. She felt that some plodded along, accomplishing little, interested only in competing to save souls of "heathen Chinee," in Bret Harte's epithet. But others did significant work. The Methodists' Women's Missionary Society of the Pacific Coast had organized about 1870 and established a girls' home, later named Gum Moon, two blocks away from "920" at 940 Washington Street, next door to the Chinese Methodist church. Stalwart Deaconess Drant had sheltered slave girls, but left rescues to the Presbyterians. Donaldina cooperated with her and with her successor, Miss Katherine Maurer, known as the "Angel of Angel Island." Clad in her uniform, a little black bonnet and simple coat, Miss Maurer spent much time at the immigration station on Angel Island trying to raise the morale of Orientals in detention there. She had begun her work with "only her smile, her spirit of kindness and her determination to serve." She had attracted much support.

At this March gathering, Donaldina was greeted on every side. She was introduced to a newcomer, the Rev. Charles Shepherd, a former missionary to China now appointed Director of Chinese Missions in the United States by the American Baptist Home Mission Society.

Donaldina sized him up as a vigorous and attractive young man. "So this is Charles Shepherd," she said, and sensed that he was assessing her, too. With a flicker of humor she went on, "I am glad that you have come to join forces with our assorted denominations. There are plenty of opportunities for service, especially for a man who has lived in China and has a genuine affection for the Chinese people, as I hear you have."

Shepherd's face lighted. "Yes. I hope I can find something different—something that really needs doing here."

Later he described his first impression of Donaldina:

> . . . a woman of medium height, apparently a trifle past middle age, somewhat frail in appearance, but of erect and soldierly bearing. She was dressed simply but in perfect taste; and from beneath a small hat . . . quite the vogue, was revealed an abundance of soft steel-gray hair.
>
> She regarded me appraisingly with eyes that were gray, flecked with gold, clear and steady. Unquestionably sympathetic were those eyes, and yet within their depths shone a gleam of quiet defiance.
>
> Her mouth, which was of generous proportion, firm and resolute, had a slightly downward curve at the corners; but such as indicates determination rather than produces sourness of expression.[1]

Soon afterwards young Shepherd accepted an invitation to call on Donaldina. When she rose from behind her desk, he glanced at her hair as if surprised. The upswept front, entirely white, had not been visible under her hat at their first meeting.

Donaldina opened the conversation. "I asked you to come," she said, "because I want to speak with you about a matter that has been on my heart these many years. Something must be done for the needy small boys of this community. There are so many of them." Her voice was intense. "Orphans, half-orphans, foundlings, and children from broken homes. Already we have five boys right here in this house which is intended only for young women. We have been sheltering them since they were infants, but we cannot keep them much longer. They are nearing the age when an institution like this is no place for them. And then, too, boys need a man's influence. They need a father."

"I am surprised," Shepherd responded. "In China I have seen

---

[1] Charles R. Shepherd, Th.D., *The Story of Chung Mei* (Valley Forge, Pa.: Judson Press, 1938).

the traditional family's high regard for their male children."

"Ah, my dear friend, this is not China. Somehow things are different here. Our Chinese friends have been uprooted from their old civilization and transplanted to an environment that is alien and vitiating. You will find here comparatively little of the wholesome family life with which you have been familiar in China." Donaldina regarded Shepherd. Yes, here was a man with ears to hear.

"Scarcely a week goes by," she continued, "that I do not listen to some new tale that wrings my heart, but I am so helpless to do anything about it. Boys such as Ah Wing are picked up by the police for petty theft. Would you believe there is a man very like Dickens' Fagin of *Oliver Twist* in Chinatown? He teaches boys to steal cigarettes and cigars and rewards them with a pittance."

Shepherd nodded. "I've met some of his trainees. The Chinatown squad picks them up now and then."

"We and our Methodist friends have for years devoted ourselves to caring for needy girls, but no one has ever seemed to think about the boys."

In agitation Shepherd turned in his chair to stare out on Sacramento Street. A cable car clanged up the hill. "Pow-ell Street," the conductor sang out. As though reminded of where he was, he turned back to Donaldina.

"I have been disconsolate about the work in Chinatown, so much duplication. As I told you at our first meeting, I have looked for something different, something that no one else is doing, some great need that has not been met." Shepherd's blue eyes darkened with excitement. "Well, it seems that I've found it. Surely, God has spoken. Something will have to be *done* about it!"

As she said goodbye to him, Donaldina knew Providence had sent another unusual person to Chinatown. It did not occur to her that she would be an instrument to change the direction of this man's life and that of his wife, Esther, his son, and two daughters.

Learning more about Donaldina's rescues, Shepherd offered to go along and supply the muscle she needed. He often could be reached at the Chinese Baptist Church, a block down the hill from "920," and she came to count on his quick response and natural sagacity during a raid.

This new recruit infuriated the tongs' highbinders. Despite friends' warnings, Shepherd continued to aid Donaldina. Yet he was a realist and knew he could become the target of tong hatchetmen. When returning to his Berkeley home late at night, he would get off the "Red Car" and walk up the middle of the street at a fast pace, alert for possible ambush. Later, when she learned he had been endangered, Donaldina was shocked and apologized for having put him in jeopardy.

Shepherd invested four years' work in San Francisco's China-town, much of it pursuing will-o-the-wisp promises of financial support for a home for Chinese boys. Looking for a house, he canvassed the East Bay for the same reasons Donaldina had located the Tooker Home in Oakland: lower prices and more play space. He was defeated by prejudice, fire regulations, building restrictions, and rights of way—but never by despair.

Finally, in 1923, after he had attracted many Chinese as well as Caucasian Baptist supporters, he located a two-story frame building with no restrictions against its use for a children's home. On October 7, 1923, three hundred friends gathered for dedication of the new Chung Mei Home[2] at 3000 Ninth Street, Berkeley.

Wearing a muffin-shaped hat and a grey-blue suit with her customary white-collared blouse, Donaldina went forward to present to the Board of Governors seven little stepsons from "920": George Chow, Adam Wu, Walter Lim, Frank Louie, George Haw, Howard Deah, and Benjie Wu. Though she had no official responsibility for the Home, she continued to regard the Shepherds and their charges as part of her extended family.

Though Donaldina could then refer boys to Chung Mei, facilities for her girls were again overtaxed. When the Tooker Home opened, it filled so quickly that she was forced to rent a smaller house several blocks away on Ninth Street as an annex. The view, near the old Ship's Slough, a burial place for worn-out

2 The word "Chung" means China and "Mei," American.

vessels, was not inspiring, and the smell was unpleasant. But the house sheltered her youngest; it was called "The Baby Cottage."

Donaldina added several new workers: Ann Wharton, a Red Cross nurse, returned from four years' service to China; Pearl Shockley, a trained nurse; Mrs. Szto, a Chinese helper; and later, Lisette Miller, a trained nurse and former missionary to Korea.

Motherly Nora Bankes had made Tooker a real home, and with her special tenderness for all things sick or maimed, she taught the children to be merciful and sympathetic. But failing health forced her to resign. Miss Blackford of San Jose succeeded her for a short period, and she was followed by Emma Mills.

Finding a proper roof for her nursery remained a problem. Who could help? Donaldina, pursuing an impulse, invited a long-time friend of the work, Captain Robert Dollar, owner of the Dollar Steamship Line, to visit the Tooker Home. He spent a morning silently inspecting every detail. Anxious, Donaldina asked for his appraisal.

"That's no place to take care of all those children," the Captain replied. "Tell your Board to go out and find any piece of property they think adaptable and I'll buy it for you. And," he finished crisply, "you'll have to put up a suitable building, too."

Elated, Donaldina reported Captain Dollar's pledge to Mrs. H. B. Pinney, then president of the Occidental Board, who asked a friend, Carrie Judd Montgomery, to explore possible sites with her. Mrs. Montgomery proved a fortunate choice, for she and her husband owned acreage in the Oakland hills near Mills College, which the two women inspected. Four acres, level and wooded, looking across town toward the Bay, appealed to Mrs. Pinney as an ideal spot for a children's home. Was the plot for sale?

"Yes," Mrs. Montgomery replied. "Years ago I walked this piece of land with Mrs. Mills, who owned it then, and she stopped at this very place, saying she would like to dedicate it to service. It has stood idle ever since."

Captain Dollar approved the choice and made out a check to pay for the land. The improbable had been accomplished almost overnight.

Donaldina wondered, "Has that beautiful site been waiting all this time for Tooker's daughters?" She had known the spot

Workers in the Home in the early 1920's. Left to right, standing, Tien Wu, Donaldina Cameron, Emma Quon, an unnamed English teacher, Miss Waghorn, Mrs. Kung Chan; seated, Laura Hughes, Ethel Higgins, Mrs. Fenn, Ann Wharton, Emma Mills.

well, a stretch beyond the Beulah gate, where she had strolled with Caroline when her niece was at Mills Seminary. They had loved that ridge, with its garlands of eucalyptus trees, and a musical stream running through a dell where lilies grew. It was a fitting goal for a modern Christian from *Pilgrim's Progress.* Were not her children waylaid like small pilgrims near the old Ship's Slough, waiting to press on to this bright place?

To thank Captain Dollar, several little girls presented a bouquet and a song to him, and on each of the old gentleman's birthdays thereafter, Donaldina arranged for the pretty ceremony to be repeated.

When construction of a building for her little daughters was delayed, Donaldina secured approval from the Foreign Mission Board in New York to rent an upper flat across the street from the Tooker Home, at the corner of Tenth Avenue and Eleventh Street. It served as a dormitory for the older children.

Admittedly, several locations were makeshift. But she could be patient, knowing her babies were to have a fine new home. She did not have to wait for another excitement to find her, however.

*   *   *   *   *

In March of 1920, Donaldina's grown daughters reminded her that she had served the Home for twenty-five years. Tien Wu had written "the old girls," inviting them to help celebrate, and money poured in from as far away as China. Tien asked Lo Mo what gift she would like. A family party Donaldina could not resist. But a gift? "Nonsense," she said, "I lack nothing. Plow the money along with your beautiful thoughts into the work." She was stern, wringing a promise from Tien not to buy a gift.

Eventually, Tien confessed that she must take back her pledge. The girls insisted, she told Lo Mo, on giving her a present for herself. Looking into this favorite daughter's oval face, at forty still smooth as gold satin, teeth beautifully white and even, and eyes bright with intelligence, Donaldina relented. Very well, then. Set up a scholarship in her name in the school for blind children in Canton, China.

Tien made no promise. Secretly, she, the staff of the Home, and "old" girls nearby decided to refurbish Donaldina's bedroom when she was absent.

A few days before the celebration, Donaldina, with her quartet, left to attend a conference in San Diego. Tien, Ethel Higgins, and their conspirators excitedly moved furnishings from Lo Mo's room into the hall. Light floral paper was hung on the walls. A painter sealed cracked window sills and trim, and enameled the woodwork white. The worn pine floor was replaced with hardwood, a stylish symbol of elegance. In its changed setting the Chinese rug, an earlier gift, took on new beauty, and sheer curtains and a homespun bedspread added the feminine softness that belonged to Lo Mo. Wanting her to be well dressed for her party, Tien had used some of the gift money to buy a length of silk brocade, and had reserved time with Donaldina's dressmaker, Mrs. Koeple, to make the garment.

All was prepared. But a wire from Donaldina stated that she would return just in time for the party, bringing with her Ida Lee, who had been studying at the Bible Institute.

And so, Tien mourned, the brocade could not be made up in time. But Ida, who had not been expected, would add to Lo Mo's happiness. Donaldina arrived the morning of the anniversary celebration. Her taxi discharged the four little girls of the quartet and Ida, who cut short Tien's questions.

"Come quick," she said, "Lo Mo is bringing a very sick girl."

With Tien, she ran back to the taxi, where Donaldina was supporting a bandaged girl too weak to sit up. They half-carried her up the stairs and into the hall. The girl could not stand. When a bandaged wound began to hemorrhage, Ida and Donaldina did what they could for her, while Tien called a doctor. The patient was treated and moved to the infirmary on the third floor.

Donaldina revealed to Tien the story of her trip. Ida Lee had joined the party in Los Angeles. In San Diego, while riding on a streetcar, Lo Mo had felt a strange compulsion to get off before reaching the conference. Directing Ida to see that the quartet appeared on the program, as planned, she followed her hunch. Within a few moments she met a former San Franciscan who had been on the verge of calling her to help a young Chinese couple in desperate trouble. A girl, Suey Seen, had been stolen out of slavery by a man in love with her. Hounded by her owner for money he did not have, and frantic to get fare for escape to China, the young man got a gun and robbed a store. When the store owner also produced a gun, a shooting followed. The store owner was killed and the girl injured. Police had put her lover in jail. She was placed in a hospital and charged with abetting robbery and murder. Suey Seen was not only frightened and hysterical, but also suffering from opium addiction. In the hospital she had tried to kill herself.

Donaldina took charge. The girl was not a "hard case," only a bewildered and abused young woman whose sanity, perhaps her life, was in jeopardy. She must have an immediate advocate. Donaldina was sure divine prompting had led her to Suey Seen. So she phoned the conference, asking that Mrs. Kelley, a capable Board member, speak in her stead. She then spent hours with Suey Seen, soothing her, telling her about the Mission, and gaining first her attention, then her trust. More hours were required to secure her release by the court, and assurance from the doctors that the gunshot wound would not prevent her from traveling.

"And here we are!" Donaldina finished.

"Lo Mo," Tien said, in her excitement lapsing into Pidgin English, "you forget Suey Seen. I take care of her, I let you know how she gets along. You come to your room and unpack so you can have a good time with your visitors." She stayed at the open door only long enough to hear Lo Mo draw in her breath, then fled. Lo Mo should have a moment to herself, she explained to the guests downstairs. Besides, it would do no harm to let her annoyance at the girls' disobedience cool.

To Donaldina the bright room was as refreshing as cool water. April sunshine poured through the airy curtains and lifted the murk of tragedy that had surrounded her. Her loyal daughters! What a beautiful thought! She ran her hands over the smooth enamel, touched the bedspread and the silk cloth. How cheerful and clean! Even the penetrating smell of paint was good. And she could draw the new green blinds to make a quiet retreat, a place where her girls could come with problems or good news. She knelt and murmured a prayer of thanksgiving.

She was tired, but there was no time to rest. At least she could change into a fresh blouse. Opening the closet, she found a rose-colored dress, and below it, a pair of silver slippers. A note was pinned to the dress: "Dolly, will you wear this tonight for your girls, who are disappointed that time will not allow the brocade to be made up? Hope the slippers won't pinch your toes. Eleanor."

She spread the soft skirt. Who would be so loving-kind but Eleanor! Of course, she would wear her beautiful things that night. She bathed and put on a crisp blouse, dismissing a wish to run upstairs to see the sick girl. She must trust Tien. At this moment she belonged to the people awaiting her on the first floor.

She moved through a stirring day, receiving well-wishers, answering a steady stream of telephone calls, and snatching visits with her daughters. When, dressed in rose silk and silver slippers, she came down to dinner, she found her sisters, the Baileys, Eleanor and Evelyn. Evelyn had written verses for Dolly, which were sung by a daughter to the air of "Silver Threads Among the Gold."

In the evening The Chapel was crowded with friends and dignitaries who had come to pay their respects. The Board presented Donaldina with a silver basket of roses. Mrs. Wing's kindergarteners gave her a silver dish, and her daughters a watch inscribed, "From the girls—April 15, 1895 to April 15, 1920."

The children twittered and ran to Lo Mo when she opened a mysterious silver package tied with shiny red ribbon. It held a large album bound in black and gold brocade, the flyleaf dedicating it to her in silver Chinese characters, translated, "Light of Womanhood and Mother of the Flock." On its pages were mounted pictures of people and events spanning the past twenty-five years.

Watching for a private moment, Tien bent over her and slipped an opal ring on her finger. "Suey Seen sent you this," she whispered. "She sends it as her promise to be a good daughter to you, if you will teach her."

After the guests had gone and the excited children were tucked in, Tien told her how the gift had been made. Suffering from her wound and the dreadful anguish of opium hallucinations, Suey Seen had writhed and moaned all day. Now and then, her cries had carried downstairs. Finally, during one of her lucid moments, Tien got the girl's attention. Speaking in Chinese, she explained that today was Lo Mo's anniversary, and that her friends were giving her a party. Suey Seen looked steadily at Tien. She fumbled at the ring and removed it from her finger. "Take this to your Lo Mo," she rasped, and gave her pledge.

Later, as Donaldina leaned over her, the girl roused: her puffy lips tried to smile. Her eyes, under heavy lids, gleamed briefly. Hope? Trust? The lamp caught a flash of fire from the opal. Yes. Lo Mo had been led to this girl. Another life would blossom and bear fruit—in His own good time. Tiptoeing out of the sickroom, she thought how full of such leading had been the first fifty years of her life: Twenty-five with her family, and twenty-five with her Chinese daughters.

In her room, gifts were displayed everywhere. She picked up a beautiful fan, Oriental symbol of happiness, and threw it partly open. The delicate silk was encrusted with gold outlines of Chinese forms portraying calm and violence, with the ribs of the fan separating scenes. Like the fan, her life here had been overlaid by Chinese faces, changing with the years. Astonished, she realized that what she had heard whispered was true—she was loved and hated more fervently than any person who ever braved the sometimes gilded, sometimes sordid, streets of Chinatown. With a thrill of curiosity she opened the fan to its full spread. What would her future hold? Surely work with the Chinese must fill it.

In the following week, from April 20-22, 1920, Presbyterian Women's Boards celebrated a national jubilee at the Mission Home, and among other programs Donaldina took nostalgic pleasure in a drama of the Home's history titled, "The Pictured Years." It was devised and presented by her and her staff.

"The Pictured Years", [says her annual report] showed the Chinese work under that militant Saint, Miss Culbertson, and also under Miss Cameron and Miss Higgins. Realistic scenes of rescue work in the cellars and on the roofs of the Chinese quarter were thrillingly presented; . . . the days of the exodus, after the earthquake and during the great fire of 1906; a prune-picking scene, prettily staged, showing the latest experience of our Chinese girls; and the climax—a tableau of a Christian Chinese family (the wife and mother a former ward of the Board), with the daughter in University cap and gown. . . .

Many of the actresses played their own stories, as did Detectives Barron and Richards and several other members of the Chinatown police squad. Again Inspector Robinson waved the "half a handkerchief" he and Donaldina had used to identify themselves to a slave girl.

Looking backward stimulated Donaldina's curiosity about the future. As she closed the door of her room, she heard a shot ring out a few blocks away. Tong wars had set everyone's nerves on edge. Donaldina knew that upon her future, like much of her past, the shadow of the tongs would fall.

CHAPTER FIFTEEN

Cross-Currents From the Tongs
1920-1925

Workings of the tongs rarely felt the public eye. Disclosure was too risky. Reputation could be lost and life jeopardized. In the early twenties, Charles Shepherd, who founded the home for Chinese boys, sidestepped danger by putting his information into fiction. He told the history of Chinatown's tongs, exposing spectacular tangles of woman stealing, vengeance, and gaudy opulence.

About his novel, *The Ways of Ah Sin,* subtitled "A Composite Narrative of Things as They Are," Shepherd says,

It is not a fairy story. . . . It is founded upon fact. . . . The wily Ah Sin [as served by the tong men] does not represent children of the Middle Kingdom at their best—the intelligent, industrious, high-minded group which are . . . an asset to the land of their adoption. He represents rather, what might be called the unregenerate Chinese. . . . He and his tribe still exist. They have increased in number. They have waxed fat, prosperous and powerful; and in addition to their own native wiles and cunning, have adopted many of the ideas and vices of the lower strata of American society. They constitute to-day the greatest single menace to peace, prosperity and social progress in every Chinese community in the United States; and perhaps Bret Harte did not after all so greatly err in speaking of them as "heathen" and as perpetrators of "ways that are dark and tricks that are vain."

If this story should fall into the hands of any of my many Chinese friends . . . they will understand why I have written these things; for they have suffered much and long at the hands of Ah Sin. They would like to say . . . what I have said . . . ; but as they value their lives they dare not. This being the case I have undertaken to speak for them, as well as for my American friends and colleagues.

The Ways of Ah Sin traces the life of a fourteen-year-old girl in China, who was sold to an American Chinese, who brought her through immigration as his daughter. He glibly promised her education and a rich husband, but instead, for $1500, sold her to become a concubine. The girl located her older brother, who had come to San Francisco some years earlier. But he had become a highbinder. He belonged to the Sing Dong Tong, one of the most powerful in America. His sister's owner was an officer in the same tong. Nevertheless, he decided to rescue his sister, and sent a note to the House on the Hill, addressed to "Misshun Hows."

Lo Mo read, "Misse . . . yu go pletty quik 243 Jos alle 36 Jue yat place cache one small girl all same slave girl me highbinder no can cum yu hows no likee my sistr be such place hully quik."

Lo Mo quoted, " 'Me a highbinder.' So a highbinder has found his own sister ensnared in a net such as he has helped to weave."

Several times she tried in vain to locate the girl. In the meantime, a young opium dealer, member of the Suey Dun Tong, had become infatuated with her and tried to force his attentions upon her. She rebuffed him, but, on the pretense of taking her to a Mission, he lured her into his own quarters. Her owner, infuriated by the theft of his slave, appealed to his tong to get her back. A meeting was called at headquarters, on the fourth floor of an impressive building in Chinatown.

In a large room, members of the tong sat in red-cushioned, straight-backed chairs facing a massive marble-topped table. The hand-carved Chinese blackwood table was inlaid with flowers of mother of pearl. Above it hung electroliers of Oriental design. On one side of the room stood an elaborate shrine, with an altar to the tong's gods, and upon it a beautiful lamp in the shape of a lotus lily. Its fuel was peanut oil on which floated a small, lighted wick. Before the altar were ranged five hand-worked pewter incense holders engraved with Chinese inscriptions, each standing nearly six feet tall.

The Exalted Master took his place at the head of the table, with the girl's owner, the Secretary, on his right, and the Treasurer on his left. Six Honorable Elders filled the remaining chairs.

A ceremony of great solemnity opened the meeting. The Exalted Master commanded an observation of the Three Incense Sticks. Each member received three joss sticks, which he lit in succession:

"Let the first oath be recited," the Master began.

Members: By this incense stick we swear to avenge any wrong committed against any brother of this Tong.

Master: He who violates this oath, let thunder from all points annihilate him.

Members: By this incense stick we swear to resolutely and fearlessly fight the battles of this Tong.

Master: He who violates this oath let him suffer death by a thousand knives.

Members: By this incense stick we swear to kill without mercy all who lift their hands against any member of this Tong.

Master: He who fails to keep this oath shall without fail die at the hands of the salaried assassin.

Some who take oaths are true but others false,
But true brethren are alike the world over.
Those who are true are honoured;
Those who are false die the death.

The ceremony over, the girl's owner presented his case. An Elder was delegated to demand her return through her abductor's tong. Negotiations went on for several days. The girl's captor offered to buy her for $2,000. Her owner refused, indignant. After he turned down $4,000 and then $6,000, his tong was called into special meeting. The owner repudiated all compromise, and the Exalted Master decreed death for the Kidnapper. Because no one was believed to have a personal grudge, lots were about to be drawn, when the girl's brother volunteered to do the deed. His offer was accepted, although his relationship to the girl was not known. Normally a tong member had to defend his "kin." Disguised as an aged "hop-head," the brother gained entry to his sister's hideout. Before her abductor could turn from bolting the door, he had been shot twice through the heart.

Hurrying the girl into a taxi, the brother directed the driver to The House on the Hill. He ran with her up the steps, rang the bell, and pounded. As the door opened, he darted away.

Piece by piece, Lo Mo and her interpreter drew out the girl's story, assuring her of protection.

"Shall I be able to see my brother?" she asked.

"He may come here to see you as often as he wishes to."

"Maybe the highbinders will get him; maybe the police. What do you think, Teacher?"

Lo Mo turned away. She knew what usually happened in such cases. "I hope he will return," she said.

He did not return. He fled to Fresno, but a price had been placed on his head by the murdered man's tong brothers. A Fresno member spotted him soon after he got off the train, and shot him. Police witnessed the killing and arrested the murderer immediately.

Morning papers carried a sensational, if not too accurate, story of the bold murder in San Francisco. By noon a second Chinese murder, in Fresno, made headlines.

At the House on the Hill, Lo Mo grieved with a broken-hearted and lonely girl. "There is something of the best in the worst of us," she said, and quoted, "Greater love hath no man than this, that a man lay down his life for his friends."

Police braced themselves for the usual aftermath of tong killings, a new tong war. These murders involved two powerful tongs. Shepherd cites news stories of what happened:

A fierce Tong War, one of the worst experienced in many years, and one which many think will yet prove to be the most bloody and disastrous in the history of Highbinderism in America, is now in progress throughout the Pacific States. From Seattle to Mexicali, from San Francisco to Ogden, highbinders of the powerful rivals, Sing Dongs and Suey Duns, are on the war path, each seeking to outdo the other in the number of lives taken.

Already the toll in lives has been heavy. Seattle, Los Angeles and Sacramento all report killings. As many as a dozen Chinamen, among them prominent Tong officials, are said to have been slain; and it is thought that a much larger number will be shot down before the bloodlust of these highbinder organizations is satisfied.

The larger Chinese settlements of San Francisco, Los Angeles and Seattle are in the throes of terror. Owing to the fact that many prominent merchants have been forced into hiding, business is practically at a standstill; while the streets, which in times of peace teem with gay and busy celestials, are almost deserted.

As in all other Tong Wars, it is difficult to get at the real root of the trouble. Various conflicting rumours prevail and persist. The San Francisco police declare that the trouble started over the killing of Lum Ming, a wealthy Chinese merchant, who was found dead in his room on Sacramento Street on Friday night, and that the murder was the result of a quarrel over a slave girl. Moreover, the Department claims to have positive proof that the young man who was killed in Fresno early Saturday morning was none other than the slayer of Lum Ming. There are others, however, who scout this idea as being highly improbable.

In the meantime Chinatown squads have been doubled in all coast cities, and the police authorities declare that they are well able to restore order within a short time.

* * * * *

Public interest was short-lived. Accounts of Chinese affairs soon dwindled and slipped into the back pages. Vigorous police action quelled open fighting. But the war went on for nine months. Prowling at night, the Sing Dongs and Suey Duns preyed on one another, killing in a contest to even scores.

San Francisco's Police Chief, Daniel O'Brien, had seen tong wars enough to sicken any law-loving man. He determined to move in on The City's Chinatown.

Though The City had stationed a police force in Chinatown, private justice had always been meted out to Celestials by their own elders. Well, City Hall intimated, as long as the "yellow devils" didn't stir up too much dust, let them take care of their own peculiar quarrels. But matters had gotten entirely out of hand. Six powerful tongs waged a bloody war, fighting over the trade in women and opium, over gambling and political power. Little Cathay reverberated with sounds of gunshots, screams of the victims of hatchetmen, and cries of the oppressed. Chief of Police Daniel O'Brien determined to clean out the quarter. He called in a man he had known since boyhood, John J. Manion, a sharp young sergeant who got things done.

"Jack," he ordered, "pick yourself a squad and take them over to Chinatown. Tong killings and crime must stop. Stay there until you suppress it all."

The tongs passed the word: the new boss of the Chinatown Police Squad was just a poor cop, so it shouldn't take much to sweeten him, a couple of hundred dollars here, a good jewel there. Manion was his name, Sergeant Jack Manion. A big guy, but take a look at his innocent face. An Irishman, which could be good or bad. Anyhow, pay respects.

Donaldina heard of Jack Manion, too, and invited him to tea. On a windy March afternoon he stood in her sitting room, inflexible as a Prussian. Donaldina half expected him to click his heels. She indicated a chair.

"Sergeant Manion, I asked you to come so that I might express our gratitude for all the help your department has given us for twenty-five years. I could not go on a day without it."

"Thank you, Ma'am."

"We offer our full cooperation. I believe our friends can be of value to you."

His eyes distrustful, the sergeant repeated, "Thank you, Ma'am."

The sounds of children at play reached them. "I am rich in daughters," Donaldina said. "I understand you, too, have a daughter?"

The sergeant's face brightened, "A good girl, my Agnes," he replied with a rich Irish brogue. "And two fine boys."

Manion was polite over tea, but Donaldina could elicit no real conversation; the interview was failing. This man, who wielded power for good or ill in Chinatown, had turned a cold shoulder to her. Would he line up with crooked politicians and fill his own pockets? She found it hard to believe. He had an honest face, and he was known as a good Catholic.

As her guest rose to leave, Donaldina heard the bells of Old St. Mary's. She looked out the window. "Sergeant Manion! I want you to see this sight!" She pointed. The last red-gold rays of sunset poured over the church, setting the cross afire. "That cross is the symbol of the One we both love and serve."

Manion stared for a long minute. "It is that," he said softly. "It is that, Miss Cameron." He looked down at her with a genial smile. "And we might be doing a better job of serving if we tackle the heathens of Chinatown together." He held out a big hand.

He later said of her, "Miss Cameron is a handsome woman with fresh, rosy cheeks, and a frank, open face that inspires confidence. . . ."

That Manion had already tackled crime in Chinatown Donaldina soon learned. The new sergeant had opened his campaign with a visit to each tong headquarters.

"Boys," he had said bluntly, "it's all off. There's a new deal. No more killings. No more opium. No more slave girls. Businessmen must be safe. No more shakedowns. Step out of line and you will be arrested and deported."

Strong men of the tongs obediently stashed away their hatchets, tucked their hands up their sleeves—and waited. They could afford to pacify this brash youngster. The heat wave would pass.

When the sergeant requested a peace conference, tong leaders indulged him, and every influential Chinese in the quarter attended. Manion had prepared a treaty for the tongs to ratify. It guaranteed an end to crime and violence in Chinatown. Seeing power returned to their hands, the Chinese, tongue in cheek, put their names to the document. When the last man had signed, the sergeant folded the paper and slid it into his pocket.

"I now have the promises of all officials of all tongs," he said, patting his coat, "which I will give to my chief to keep. This means no more killings, or all tong officials who signed this paper will be deported back to China."

When the news of the treaty-signing reached Donaldina, she laughed aloud, imagining the self-possessed Chinese taken off guard, their bland expressions peeled away to reveal shock—and grudging submission. Manion's treaty put teeth into his threat. No Chinese would be so stupid as to risk being shipped back to China.

Nevertheless, they would be unlikely to abandon their profitable ways, Donaldina reckoned. Cunning could achieve their ends as well as violence. So the contest would go on. But she was glad the new sergeant had proved as adroit as he was vigorous. He was an ally after her own heart, a man her Chinese friends could admire and trust. Report of an encounter soon reached "920."

Manion had decided to break in on a meeting in a house on Ross Alley trafficking in the three evils of Chinatown—slavery, gambling, and narcotics. If police could identify the managers, they could make arrests and crack a ring. Sergeant Manion and Officer John Connolly picked the lock of an outer door, but could not budge the inner door. Though armed with an ax and pick, Manion knew the racket of forcing their way in would warn their quarry and give them time to escape.

While they schemed, a stray cat rubbed at Connolly's ankle.

"John," Manion whispered. "The cat! Grab the cat! Scratch on the door."

Connolly rasped the cat's claws against the oak door. The animal yowled its protest, and the men inside swore at it. Connolly continued to scratch, the cat to squall, and the men inside to grow more nettled, yelling and pounding on the door. Manion leaned forward in readiness. Suddenly the door flew open and a foot kicked at the cat. It barely missed Manion, who ducked and sprawled full length inside the room.

Surprise hushed everyone. Then the Chinese exploded with laughter at the sight of the smart cop flattened on their floor. He laughed with them. Connolly covered the men with his gun until Manion could get up. Then the two herded their captured tong lords into a patrol wagon. Even so, bumping along over the cobbles, the Chinese roared with mirth at memory of the cop's loss of face.

The Chinatown squad, composed mostly of bright young Irishmen, played ingenious games with the Chinese. Each side displayed a long sense of humor. Lottery, a favorite Oriental pastime, violated regulation No. 68 of The City's code. Often officers knew where a drawing was scheduled and contrived to catch the Chinese in possession of their tickets, rice-paper slips written in Chinese characters.

Men from outlying towns were met by police at the ferry, or as they climbed off streetcars, and their tickets confiscated. But local gamblers slipped into dens unnoticed. In one, if officers approached, holders of tickets stuffed them into a mason jar full of black ink, and the owner placidly stirred the ink with a long-handled brush.

Officers John Patrick O'Connor and Horace McGowan tried to outwit the gamblers. They painted a jar black on the inside, surreptitiously switched it for the pot of ink, and placed the brush in the empty jar. At lottery time they "rushed the place."

"You're under arrest," they shouted.

Instantly, men awaiting the drawing dropped their tickets into the jar, and grinned at the officers.

The owner cried, "No can do now!"

O'Connor turned the jar upside down. The tickets fluttered out. "You're under arrest!" he repeated.

The Chinese realized they had been tricked. They broke into laughter, calling, "You fish! You fish!" But sometimes they turned the tables by memorizing their lottery numbers and, unthreatened, did their gambling free of incriminating evidence.

Manion's threat of deportation and his vigorous law enforcement quieted gunfire on the streets; and spectacular raids on brothels and gambling and narcotics dens created a false impression that order and justice had been achieved in Chinatown. But thievery, gambling, violence, and sales of narcotics and girls flourished under cover. While the new police squad chipped away at those adult evils, it also bore down on juvenile delinquency. Having a son sent to reform school brought terrible loss of face to a Chinese family. Manion introduced a homely discipline. When a boy was caught breaking a law, his parents were summoned, and the sergeant ordered the youngster, "Down with your britches!" He then demonstrated the art of an American spanking. Police blotters indicated a sharp decline in juvenile offenses, and Chinese parents adored the man who could set their young people straight.

Sergeant John Manion displaying a cache of confiscated opium and pipes, 1920's. (Photo courtesy San Francisco Chronicle)

"Sargee Minion" and shoe shine boys in Chinatown. (Photo courtesy San Francisco Chronicle)

They needed all the help they could get, for filial respect dwindled in America. When a boy was disobedient, his mother threatened, "I send you down to Minion." Teachers in Commodore Stockton elementary school and sisters from St. Mary's school dispatched boys to "Minion" for bad behavior. After one trip, the culprit usually shaped up. Manion organized a Boy Scout troop for Chinese boys, whether to help the community or to satisfy his own love of children no one was sure.

Gradually the people of Chinatown came to accept him as a confidante. He never betrayed them; he was a square, honest man, "Sargee" was. If an officer on his detail bent a little toward letting crime go by, he was dismissed. "Sargee Minion" often stood at weddings as best man and took his vows as godfather at christenings. Among the newborn boys of the Lees and Wongs and Chans and Youngs, given names of Jack and Manion began to appear almost as frequently as Donalds, Donaldinas, and Camerons.

Whatever Miss Cameron wanted, Manion told his officers, she was to get. One evening O'Connor and McGowan received the order, "Miss Cameron wants to see you at a place on Stockton, between Jackson and Washington."

Officer O'Connor told how they met Miss Cameron, Miss Wu, and Miss Higgins. Donaldina pointed to an upstairs room.

"Get us in."

O'Connor climbed a fire escape and reached the window. By the light of a lamp he could see a young woman in bed and an old lady beside her. Several other people were present. When McGowan pounded on the door, the women jumped up, confused and shrieking. One saw O'Connor at the window and let him in. He unlocked the door for the rescue party. The young woman was in labor, so an ambulance was called, and she reached the hospital in time to be delivered of a baby boy.

Two years later, O'Connor and McGowan were invited to tea at "920," and introduced to a handsome namesake, Horace Patrick Soo Hoo,[1] whose mother they had rescued.

Manion's loyalty and effectiveness rekindled Donaldina's belief that she could rout her mortal enemy—slavery. Importation

---

[1] Killed during the Battle of the Bulge in World War II.

of girls had diminished, the wholesale dealer was no more, and large parlor houses were almost out of business. In 1924 she heard rumors that a place at 654 Jackson Street held a stable of "scarlet women." The owner, Mrs. Chin Bow, had bathed her name in innocence by spreading word that Officer Jack Robinson, known for his honesty, had been godfather and Donaldina godmother to her grown daughter. On Donaldina's tip, Manion said, "Get a warrant, and we'll see what we can find."

Later, Manion, by then promoted to the rank of Inspector, wrote an article for the Presbyterian magazine, "Women and Missions," in which he described the event.

We planned our raid carefully in advance. "But how can we get in without chopping down the doors?" Miss Cameron asked me. An eighteen year old slave girl named Yum Gue was held prisoner, Miss Cameron had heard from a very much frightened little Chinese girl, and she was afraid they would escape by means of some secret exit.

I recalled that there was a skylight in the roof of the house that was left open during the day. I believed that it only dropped closed, and was not locked during night time, so we planned to try to get in through that.

On the rain-lashed morning of Saint Patrick's Day, Inspector Manion led a raid on the Jackson Street place. He wrote:

At five o'clock in the morning we went to the house. It was pitch dark outside. An eerie ghostliness seemed to surround the black grayness of the building. Miss Cameron and her assistants, Miss Wu and Miss Higgins, and Inspector Robinson stayed at a near by street corner. As soon as we whistled they were to come and take charge of the girls.

. . . Tom Cronin and J. Patrick O'Connor . . . [and I] climbed carefully and silently to the roof, taking a piece of stout timber and ropes with us. As I had expected, the skylight was open, not locked. Placing the timber carefully over the open skylight, we fastened the ropes around it. I gently lowered myself into the inky blackness below. Not a sound was heard.

I had lowered myself only a few feet when my leg caught in a small rope. . . . Hanging precariously with one hand, I was able to kick my leg free and continue to lower myself. Finally I got to the bottom. It was all of twenty-five feet. It seemed quite a while as I lowered myself, not knowing whether I would have a Chinese knife put through my back any minute. . . . Next came Pat O'Connor. He also caught

Lo Mo, Ida Lee, an interpreter, and two policemen from the Chinatown Squad rescue a girl from the Siberia [Gambling] Club in Cameron Alley, early 1920's.

The rescue completed, the girl is assisted from the alley. The name of Cameron Alley was changed to Old Chinatown Lane on April 27, 1939.

his foot in the rope, but got loose. Then came Tom Cronin. He too caught his foot in the rope. But this time it broke. He slid quickly down our heavy rope to the floor beside me, but a sound gave us away.

Mrs. Chin Bow came rushing out of her room. We turned our flashlights down the hallways. I noticed that she knocked at certain doors as she ran away from us. One of my men guarded the entrance while the other kept every one in the house in their rooms.

Manion thrust open the street door and whistled. Donaldina, Tien Wu, and Ethel Higgins rushed from their hiding place. Under one arm the Sergeant carried a protesting old Chinese woman, Mrs. Chin Bow, and with the other he held a girl, who stretched out her arms to Donaldina and whimpered, "Missee Cameron."

Manion grinned. "Got four more inside. How about a cup of coffee, Missee Cameron?" He ran back into the building. Half-dressed patrons fled into the street, and a frightened knot of girls emerged.

John Robinson appeared, and Mrs. Chin Bow blazed at him, "Why you do this? You promise to warn us."

"Warn you! What do you mean, warn you?"

"Yick Yee say you promise when he give you my diamond ring."

"Say, tell me, what is all this?" Robinson exploded. "On the other hand, let me tell you. I don't know Yick Yee and he didn't give me a ring. I didn't make a promise." He stared at her. "You've been outsmarted at your own game! And you and your daughter are under arrest."

Thus one of the last of the large brothels was emptied. Most of the captive slaves were deported, but after a long legal battle one girl, Yum Gue, was allowed to remain at "920."

Manion's, "Give Miss Cameron anything she wants," disconcerted some of the young officers on the Chinatown detail. Officer Peter Conroy and his partner were called early on a Sunday morning to meet Miss Cameron at a house on Washington Street. They remember her as "stately, proper, aloof," with a single thought, "Rescue this slave!"

The party was admitted to a Chinese apartment where a pretty girl of about sixteen sat rocking. "Arrest her," Donaldina ordered Conroy.

"But we have no warrant."

"We know she is a slave."

"We have no proof. No crime is being committed now."

Like a stern Mother Superior, Donaldina replied, "Take her into protective custody. I will vouch for your right."

Conroy replied, "I can't, Ma'am. If we're challenged I haven't a leg to stand on. I'll have to check with the Inspector."

Annoyed, Donaldina ran with him out of the house. "Hurry!" she ordered. "We must come back immediately or the girl will be gone!"

Officer Conroy called Manion and to his amazement was instructed, "Give Miss Cameron anything she wants. She'll be proved right."

The party returned to the flat and took their girl. Idealistic young officers fresh from police training school grumbled. All Miss Cameron was interested in was saving souls! She had no sense of police obligation, of their sworn responsibility to all people. Not that there was any question of her judgment. As Inspector Manion said, she never led the police astray. Her underground always brought her accurate word. But what if they were challenged before proof was forthcoming?

Yet, for all the efforts of the Mission and the police, the buying, selling, and enslaving of women did not stop. Manion's clean-up of Chinatown diminished the practice and discouraged a flagrant show of commerce. But old customs died slowly, especially when their demise canceled easy and lucrative revenue. The price of beautiful Chinese girls had crept up, along with other postwar costs, to $6,000 and $7,000.

During the early years of Manion's command, highbinders soft-pedaled their commerce in girls. Interference from The City's police might be short-lived, they consoled one another. But when Lee Young, son of a joss house priest on Spofford Alley, was sentenced to San Quentin for holding a slave, the tongs' complacency was shaken. Their leaders paid lip-service to police, but rewarded their clever members and eliminated the uncooperative or clumsy.

More cross-currents washed over the House on the Hill.

CHAPTER SIXTEEN

Each One and the Many

1923-1926

In her office, early one Saturday morning, as Lo Mo wrapped a birthday doll to take to a child at Tooker Home, she mulled over the tongs' recent assaults against "920." When would the time come that no skulking figures hung around the Home hoping to entice or waylay a rescued daughter? She counted on Providence and Jack Manion to help her disarm the tongs. Her further obligation was to maintain a happy family. A discontented, suspicious state of mind laid a girl open to fear and seduction, while the fruits of the spirit, love, joy, and peace, as daily expressed in the Home, shaped her toward a good life. And what gain was rescue unless a girl came to a spiritual awakening? As someone recently said, if these girls learn allegiance to their Lord, they will be safe whether in America or returned to their native China. Donaldina blessed her childhood family. Was this the thousandth or ten thousandth time she had taken comfort and guidance from her remarkable heritage?

She tied a ribbon on the package and straightened, slowly. The army cot she had slept on last night was no feather bed. For one so thin the taut canvas made her stiff and sore. She had surrendered her room to sick twin babies because the nurse decided burning tincture of benzoate would clear their chest colds, and the infirmary rooms were full. The children were better, and she had enough to do today to limber both back and mind.

Several older girls passed her door on the way to breakfast. She waved to them and called, "Good morning."

Mae Wong ran into her office. "Oh, Lo Mo, see my new dress. Mrs. Stone sent it. I am so proud."

"It's beautiful, dear," Lo Mo responded. "I am proud of *you* and how well you are doing in your studies. It's a joy to have you here this week end."

Here indeed was a girl to joy in, Donaldina told herself. She had found little Mae in the home of a relative when she was fourteen years old. Now, like Hung Mui, she was helping at Tooker Home and going to school. The girl's good family in China had entrusted her to the relative, who had promised their daughter an opportunity to get an education, for which she was eager. Instead she was kept at home, doing housework and caring for children. She was very unhappy. At present, sponsored by a Long Beach club, whose members gave her clothes and presents, Mae was as happy as she was hard-working. Lo Mo expected much of her.

And Yoke Yeen, or Jade, as she was known to her American friends, was sure to distinguish herself. Jade had never been a slave, but had lived with her family in San Francisco as a child, and after her mother's death, with an older sister in a northern California logging camp. In her early teens, when her father decided to take his family back to China, she insisted on remaining at "920." She wanted an education. With Donaldina's help she stood with great courage for the right to make plans of her own. In the end a judge persuaded her father to give over legal custody, and Lo Mo acquired a promising daughter. Beautiful, gracious, and with a fine mind that she knew how to use, Jade won friends among influential Board women, who helped her enroll in Lux, a high school with high scholastic requirements. She had decided to become a doctor. She and Lo Mo had no doubt that a way would open to her.

After breakfast Donaldina looked in on the twins, picked up each of the sturdy year-old boys, cuddling and playing with them. Moments like this were worth a week's loss of sleep.

Returning to her office, Donaldina cleared away correspondence. Some matters had backed up for a month; unless urgent, they did not ruffle her. Surely people must realize her work came first. She wrote a letter of thanks to the Commissioner for granting entry to a legal wife, for whom Donaldina had petitioned, "These young people are my personal friends." She also commended the Commissioner for refusing admission of a tong slave. Would that officials were always so sympathetic and perceptive.

And she encouraged the court to allow a poor fellow confined in San Quentin prison time to attend to personal affairs before deporting him. She wrote the U.S. Department of Labor, confirming the character of a Chinese who was offered a job in Mexico, and guaranteed that he would remove an alien from the Home by marrying her.

With a pang of nostalgia Donaldina filled out annual report forms. All Pacific Coast Chinese work had been transferred gradually from the Woman's Occidental Board and the Board of Foreign Missions, under which the Home had operated for fifty years, to the Board of National Missions, now supervising all stations within the United States.

Monthly meetings of the Occidental Board ladies were no more! Her new advisory board, composed of both women and men, met only on call to establish general policy and to take care of emergencies. Though the changeover had cost her pain, new relationships proved cordial, and her long-time Occidental Board friends remained supportive.

Next she wrote to Miss Grace Abbott. From a news story she had learned that Miss Abbott, head of the Children's Bureau, planned to attend a conference on white slavery, sponsored by the League of Nations, in Geneva, Switzerland. Donaldina's letter was long and emphatic. Among other things she asked,

I wondered, Miss Abbott, as I read of the Conference to be held in Geneva, if there would be any intelligent representative from China who might speak on the almost unlimited and ghastly traffic that is carried on in girls and children all through China and down through the Straits Settlements.

She described the "Door of Hope" in Shanghai, which deserved support as an international, non-sectarian refuge dedicated to rescue and care of former slaves.

Mrs. Linn gives gentle care to the shy ones.

... I really think it is time that some very definite steps were taken to draw public attention to the conditions which exist, not merely in China but right here in our own country. ...

I shall very deeply appreciate ... if you can in some way bring to the attention of the Conference at Geneva the problem of Oriental White slavery. ...

The traffic would never stop unless cut away from both sides of the world. Charles Shepherd's image was apt. A slave girl was like a lamb in the toils of a boa constrictor. Donaldina thought of many girls she had seen face the serpent; some had not escaped. Such memories were hard to live with, and impossible to forget.

She straightened her desk and leafed back through her past week's appointment calendar. Beside the name "President Wilson" she had written "canceled." While she was in New York for meetings, Dr. Halsey had arranged for her to see Woodrow Wilson, his Princeton classmate. But shortly before her appointment, she had received a call from a girl in Chicago on the brink of being sold. Donaldina could reach no one capable of helping her. So she had taken a train to Chicago instead of to Washington, D.C. She wondered if she had made a right choice. Could she have enlisted the President's help in saving many girls? But the Master had gone searching for his one lost sheep.

Later that morning she went with several Board members to the Tooker Home. Emma Mills had arranged a party for a birthday girl, who gleefully blew out her candles and opened her presents. Donaldina was glad her youngest daughters continued to wear sahms and foos, often tiny-checked pink ginghams. Their shining hair, cut in square Dutch bob, was a cute style, but she wished they had kept their pretty queues. And she would have preferred embroidered slippers to the patent leather Mary Janes that made them feel dressed-up.

While the little children napped, Emma Mills gathered her staff and guests for tea. Donaldina sat beside Mrs. Jun Bok Lee, a professor's widow who had come to work for "920" to "do anything just so I can keep my baby." Soft-voiced, beautiful, and refined, she proved a superb cook of Chinese dishes and an excellent teacher of Chinese. Donaldina had placed her in Tooker Home to assure her youngest a good Chinese background. Now,

A foster daughter's wedding party in the elaborately decorated chapel room, 1921.

at tea, Mrs. Lee's baby daughter, who had grown into a lively child, sang for the ladies and danced about happily. With enthusiasm Donaldina complimented Mrs. Lee on her work and her enchanting child.

Flustered, groping for appropriate English, Mrs. Lee dropped her gaze and said abruptly, "Oh, shut up!"

No one moved or spoke. Mrs. Lee glanced about her uncomfortably, then ran upstairs. Emma Mills followed, and found her sitting in a small rocker bent over her sewing.

"What happened?" Emma asked, sympathetically.

"I not know. Miss Cameron say too much. I not so good. I want to be modest—like Chinese good manners. 'Shut up' is what my friend say when he want people to stop talking."

Emma Mills patted her shoulder. "I see," she said. Downstairs she explained to her guests.

" 'Wad some power the giftie gie us,' " Donaldina laughed, and hurried upstairs to Mrs. Lee. Putting her arms around her, she comforted, "I understand; it's all right. Come back downstairs with us."

Miss Ida Lee, a "920" daughter who had been assistant in the Tooker Home since completing her training, joined the Board members' tea. Donaldina was glad to hear her beautiful voice again, be it only in singing, "Happy Birthday."

With romance on her mind, Donaldina asked, "And how is the delightful Mr. Linn, my dear?"

"Very well," Ida replied noncommittally, and after a pause added, drawing her brows down, "He is a very fine man, Lo Mo. It is just that I am so busy. The children—." She lifted her hands and dropped them helplessly.

Donaldina wanted to protest. The years were slipping by for Ida and her suitor. But she kept silent, remembering the tug of her children's needs on her own feelings years before. She turned the conversation. "You will all be glad for the good news that our building on the Mills campus is to become a reality. Best of all, Mrs. Monroe's sister-in-law, Julia Morgan,[1] will design it for us."

---

[1] Architect who designed the Hearst castle at San Simeon, California, and other distinctive buildings and homes around the Bay Area.

Such satisfactions, as well as intervals of pleasure, enabled Donaldina to stand up to contention. In her work contention was commonplace and diabolic surprise all too frequent.

*   *   *   *   *

Donaldina had gone to bed early on the night of May 17, 1925, anxious about the morrow in court, when a hearing would climax a life-and-death struggle for young Sing Choy and her four-year-old son. Three times in four years the Mission had tried to free the girl, and at last she was in its care. Now the director was battling to keep her custody and that of her little boy. Sing Choy seemed well rehearsed for her trial, her fortitude firm; yet bitter experience had taught Donaldina that a girl could turn to putty under cross-examination.

With defenses at lowest ebb, her thoughts wandered to another bitter contest. She and Tien had accompanied a girl to court, confident that she was well schooled. The trembling plaintiff stuck to the truth during badgering by the tong's attorney, and vindicated herself. Then, without warning, she crumpled and pleaded guilty to all the false charges. She later explained that she had caught the eye of her highbinder owner, remembered he was the son of a Taoist priest, and that he undoubtedly would call down upon her the demons of earth, air, and water. The Home could not protect her from devils. She dared not doom herself for eternity, so she lost all in this life.

After the trial Tien had cornered the attorney. Charles Shepherd reported her outburst:

"What kind of a man are you?" she exclaimed. "Either you know nothing of this abominable slave traffic which is such a blight and a curse upon my own people here in America; or, you are one of those contemptible beings, one of those human vultures, who prey upon the misfortunes of their fellow-beings.

"My own people are guilty. They are unspeakably cruel and bad; but to whom shall we Chinese people look for help and uplift if not to the Americans among whom we live in this country? . . . this notorious slave traffic, that ruins lives and degrades my people, is made possible through the selfish and unscrupulous co-operation that American attorneys like yourself extend to the Chinese highbinders and slave importers, thereby making it possible for them—in fact encouraging them and helping—to carry on this traffic.

". . . Furthermore, it is still more outrageous that when respectable Chinese and American women are giving their lives to overcoming this traffic, and saving these helpless girls from slavery, they must be dragged back into it through the efforts of American lawyers, and other white men, who are party to this whole illicit business. I am Chinese myself. I have for many years been assisting the women who carry on the work of this Home; and I know of what I speak."[2]

Donaldina smiled at the memory of Tien's fiery courage, for she was barely half the size of her target. But the tragic verdict had crushed all of them. To assuage that recollection and invite sleep, Donaldina quoted aloud a passage from Longfellow's "Resignation."

> There is no flock, however watched and tended
> But one dead lamb is there!
> There is no fireside, howsoe'er defended,
> But has one vacant chair!
>
> There is no death! What seems so is transition;
> This life of mortal breath
> Is but a suburb of the life elysian,
> Whose portals we call Death.

By morning her hope was restored. Many friends were interested in Sing Choy, whose story had appeared in the *San Francisco Examiner* almost a year before:

A nation-wide search for a Chinese slave girl and her 3-year-old son, conducted by Miss Donaldina Cameron of the Chinese Presbyterian Mission of San Francisco, was brought to a dramatic close in the juvenile court yesterday afternoon when the baby was placed in its mother's arms. . . .

For over a week the San Francisco police have searched the Chinese quarter for some trace of the missing infant. Their efforts proved fruitless until yesterday, when the young mother arrived here with Miss Cameron.

The Chinese girl was able to lead the police of Sergeant Manion's Chinatown squad to a house at 504 Pacific street. Here the little fel-

---

[2] *The Ways of Ah Sin* (Old Tappan, N.J.: Fleming H. Revell, 1923), p. 133.

low was found playing with his purchaser, Lum Lap Lee, said to be a member of the same society as its father. . . .

The little fellow was taken before Judge Murasky on a bench warrant. Policeman Kelly of the Chinatown squad was detailed to accompany Miss Cameron and the boy to court as fear was expressed that tong men might attempt a kidnapping.

Judge Murasky after hearing the case made the boy a ward of the court and placed him in the custody of Miss Cameron . . . extraordinary precautions were taken. . . . A special automobile was provided . . . carefully guarded by Miss Cameron and the police. . . .

Today, May 18, 1925, almost a year later, the court was to appoint the boy's permanent guardian. When Donaldina and Sing Choy reached the courthouse, Mr. Borland, their counsel before Superior Court Judge Graham, awaited them. Sing Choy, he reminded them, must prove that she had not chosen prostitution but was forced into it. Otherwise she would lose her son.

When she took the witness stand, Sing Choy confronted her questioner and the Chinese interpreter without show of emotion. Her responses were clear and forthright. The story was long, brutal, and complex. She was orphaned when one month old, and with her brothers and sisters lived with the family of her brother's god-father. Because his small salary as a village schoolteacher was inadequate, he went to Hong Kong to work, first as a laborer, then in a store.

Lum Quong, a Chinese-American man, had returned to China for a visit, having agreed to bring back a slave girl to a San Francisco dealer, a woman who had paid him in advance. But, in fact, he was looking for a Chinese wife, and married a woman in her native village. The marriage was not a success; he left his wife, and returned to Hong Kong. He saw Sing Choy at her foster father's store, and through a matchmaker proposed marriage.

Sing Choy said, "My foster-mother consented, and while no licee was demanded, Lum Quong sent us the wedding cakes and gave my mother $100. The ceremony was held and the 'three generations papers' executed. Lum Quong did not tell my parents about his previous marriage."

He also failed to mention the fact that he was commissioned and paid to buy a slave. After six months in Hong Kong the couple prepared to return to America. Lum Quong's sister-in-law appeared, asking Sing Choy to send money to her husband's first wife. Shocked and distressed, Sing Choy told her parents about Lum Quong's deception. They questioned him. "He promised," the girl told the court, "that I was to live respectably in America as his wife. . . . My father felt it best not to bring disgrace upon the family by making trouble. . . ." And so the pair sailed on the steamer "Nile."

Sing Choy was detained a month by immigration officials at Angel Island, though Lum Quong, showing native papers, went immediately into San Francisco and took quarters on Grant Avenue. When released by Immigration, she joined him there. After a few days, Lum Quong, weeping, informed her of his promise to buy a slave, said he could not repay the money he had received, and that he was being harassed. He tried to borrow money from a kinsman, but failed.

Painful negotiations with the slave dealer followed in which Lum Quong asked for time, pleading that his wife was pregnant. But the dealer insisted that she be handed over at once, saying, "The girl is pregnant only two or three months and by the time the baby is born I could make a great deal of money."

After they had lived in San Francisco only three months, her husband surrendered Sing Choy to the dealer. The girl was forced into prostitution, bound to work for three years to repay the money her husband had received.

Donaldina learned of her case, secured warrants, and removed her at the end of her first week in servitude. Sing Choy welcomed rescue and wanted to remain in the Home. But, under pressure from the slave dealer, her husband petitioned for and won her legal custody. Before the consulate general of China at San Francisco, in the name of his family association, he made the following pledge, duly signed by his clansmen and members of the Lim family:

This agreement drawn under the auspices of the Consulate General of China at San Francisco—
Witnesseth. That Lum Quong husband of Gum Oye[3] undertakes

---

[3] Gum Oye is another name for Sing Choy.

and agrees that he will not permit allow or persuade the said Gum Oye to lead an immoral life, or to live during the duration of their marriage in any way other than a decent honest and moral way.

And his clansmen represented by [names in Chinese] officially and individually pledge themselves for and on behalf of the said Lum Quong that the above agreement will be fully and in good faith carried out.

It is agreed that Miss Donaldina Cameron shall be at all times allowed to take any step that she may deem advisable to assure herself that the terms of this agreement are fully carried out.

Sing Choy testified that her husband, who had turned tong man, did not keep this agreement. She gave birth to his son, whom he took away from her and sold. He allowed her to be sent to Chicago, where she was again forced into prostitution against her will.

Three years later, Sing Choy said, she served tables at a meeting attended by Thom Yoke Lun, whom she recognized as her cousin. She implored his help. A New York man, Thom mortgaged his business, bought his cousin's release for $6,550, and took her to live with his family. But within a week the powerful On Leung tong notified him he must pay $5,000 more or return her to Chicago. Failure to do so meant death. The young man had no other funds.

Thom returned his cousin to Chicago, tried to negotiate further, but failed. He was forced to leave Sing Choy, but on her urging came to "920" asking Donaldina's help. The Mission responded and rescued her from Chicago.

Sing Choy's witness completed, Donaldina took the stand, erect in her witness chair. Calm, her expression determined, she corroborated Sing Choy's story. The girl had married in her teens, and been betrayed into abject slavery. Her husband, given a second chance to care for her, had violated his contract with the consulate general. He had sold his own son, Stewart Milton Lum. He had not honored his pledge to allow Miss Cameron's supervision.

Donaldina described the first search for Sing Choy in Chicago. When Lum Quong discovered she was in town, he had taken his wife on a midnight train to Jackson, Michigan, and brought her back to Chicago the following week. Still fearful that Sing

This agreement drawn under the auspices of the Consulate General of China at San Francisco —

Witnesseth. That Lum Quong husband of Gum Oye undertakes and agrees that he will not permit allow or persuade the said Gum Oye to lead an immoral life, or to live during the duration of their marriage in any way other than a decent, honest and moral way —

And his clansmen represented by 林西河堂 林九 林賀 officially and individually pledge themselves for and on behalf of the said Lum Quong that the above agreement will be fully

Lum Quong's unkept pledge before the Consulate General of China in San Francisco, written in English, agreeing he will not permit, allow, and in good faith carried out.

It is agreed that Miss Donaldina Cameron shall be at all times allowed to take any step that she may deem advisable to assure herself that the terms of this agreement are fully carried out

林燦

林

九正金山埠

林家公所

(Room 15)
710 Sacramento Street, San Francisco

143 Grant Ave, San Francisco

Witness to signatures and stamp
of the Lim Family of San Francisco.

or persuade his pregnant wife, Gum Oye (Sing Choy) to lead an immoral life, after her rescue from prostitution by Donaldina Cameron.

立約人林廣願領回其妻金愛同居此後

不舟強迫伊妻有不正當之行為并不得

苛待恭有伊叔林九并林家西河堂林賀為

擔保立約人蓋先 Miss Cameron 隨时可到

伊家看視他日如有事為擔保人是向特

此在金山中國搭領事館立此為擦

林賀
林九

金山
正埠 林家公所

The same pledge in Chinese. Sing Choy's odyssey of marriage in China and then slavery and rescues covered San Francisco, Chicago, New York City, Chicago again, Jackson, Michigan, and finally back to San Francisco as a court case.

Choy would be found, he would not permit her to go to her own room, telling her it was being painted.

When Sing Choy's cousin revealed her plight to the Home, Ethel Higgins immediately went to Chicago for a second attempt at rescue. Donaldina made arrangements to cover her arrival. So important did she regard anonymity that she advised Ethel by a telegram, which she presented to the court, handwritten in its original manuscript:

MAY 26, 1924

MISS ETHEL V. HIGGINS
CARE PULLMAN CONDUCTOR CAR 27
UNION PACIFIC NO. 2
TREMAN, NEBRASKA

MRS. WELLS OR FRIEND WILL MEET YOU. I FEARED TELEGRAPH DR. GLOVER. YOU BETTER TELEGRAPH HIM MEET YOU MOODY BIBLE INSTITUTE TUESDAY MORNING. LOVE,

DONALD MACKENZIE

Ethel replied by night letter, a copy of which was entered in evidence:

CHICAGO ILL   1243P   MAY 27, 1924

GIRL SAFELY FOUND AND AM NOW ARRANGING RETURN TRIP WILL WIRE DETAILS LATER SHE WISHES TO RECOVER BABY BOY WHO IS IN CUSTODY OF LUM LAP LEE IN HOM YICK LUNG STORES ON GRANT AVENUE AM THINKING MUCH OF YOU LOVE TO ALL INCLUDING SISTER

ETHEL HIGGINS

Donaldina answered:

IN CARE OF THE
PULLMAN CONDUCTOR TRAIN #21, WESTBOUND
DUE 359PM, KRAMER, CALIFORNIA

DEEPLY THANKFUL REJOICING WITH YOU
MEET YOU SUNDAY MORNING LOVE

DONALDINA CAMERON . . . . . . 302 PM . . . . F

To protect Ethel and her charge on the way home, Donaldina sought the cooperation of a railroad agent in Los Angeles. He arranged for the travelers to change cars at a small valley town, Clovis. If tong men met the train in San Francisco, a slight delay in locating their victim might allow time for Mission friends to spirit her away. The ruse worked.

Meanwhile, Sergeant Manion had located Sing Choy's son.

And finally, the tong had agreed to terms between Sing Choy's husband and her cousin. Though the terms were registered in a spine-chilling bill of sale[4] published for all to see, at least the affair was closed, and Sing Choy was free, as long, Donaldina thought grimly, as she was rigorously protected. Judge Graham appointed Miss Donaldina Cameron guardian of four-year-old Stewart Milton Lum, and allowed Sing Choy to remain as her ward.

And so it was over. Now Donaldina faced the next problems: the brick-and-mortar plans for her younger children.

---

[4] From the *San Francisco Chronicle*, May 19, 1925:

CONTRACT BARES BARTER OF YOUNG CHINESE GIRL

THE CONTRACT between Lim Se Quong, who claimed to own the Chinese slave girl known both as Chan Kum Leen and Sing Choy, and Tom Yok Lin, a first cousin of the girl, who paid $6650 to secure her freedom, translated reads as follows:

"This document is to certify that the following facts and agreement are recognized by the Ong Leung Labor and Commercial Association:

"That prior to the drawing of this agreement, a girl (or young woman) Sing Choy by name, was the property of Lim Se Quong;

"That the girl had (more than once) asked her master for her freedom;

"That the Ong Leung Labor and Commercial Association, representing Tom Yok Lin, honorable member of the said association, has agreed to pay Lim Se Quong the sum of $6650 for her possession; that the girl, Sing Choy, is now the property of her former master, Lim Se Quong; that her former master waives all right to her;

"Lim Se Quong, himself, picked up the brush and wrote this contract.

"Witnesses—Mue Jung Yin, Yung Woey Fong.

"Honorable members of the Ong Leung Labor and Commercial Association,

"x   x

 x   x   This is Sing Choy's thumb print.

"Chinese Republic, 12th year, 8th mo. 3rd day."

CHAPTER SEVENTEEN

Roofs Over Their Heads

1924-1931

During 1924 and 1925 Donaldina enjoyed consulting with Julia Morgan about the new home for younger girls. Miss Morgan sensed the practical needs of a large family, and knew how to incorporate Oriental grace and spaciousness in her design. Contractor D. B. Farquharson brought the plans to reality.

On Saturday, December 12, 1925, the new building at 3671 McClellan Street in Oakland was dedicated as "Ming Quong," meaning "radiant light."[1] Eleanor Preston Watkins, a member of the Advisory Committee for the Presbyterian Chinese Mission Homes, described the event:

. . . we shall not soon forget her [Lo Mo's] radiant face as she watched the little Chinese orphan girls marching into the beautiful chapel of the Ming Quong Home—sleek black heads, small pink coats and trousers, happy faces turned to their beloved "Lo Mo," happy voices singing:

> *Thou didst leave Thy throne and Thy kingly crown*
> *When thou camest to earth for me.*
> *O! come to my heart, Lord Jesus.*
> *There is room in my heart for Thee.*

[1] Among those listed as special guests with Donaldina were Mrs. Lynn White and Miss Edna R. Voss of the Board of National Missions; Miss Emma Mills, Miss Tien Fuh Wu, Miss Ida Allen Lee, of Lo Mo's staff; Chinese ministers, the Rev. Lee Yick Soo, the Rev. Tse Kei Yuen, the Rev. Ng Poon Chew (who gave the dedicatory address), the Rev. R. E. Cooper; the Hon. Kolian Yip, the Chinese consul general; Captain Robert Dollar, donor of the ground; Mrs. H. B. Pinney, former president of the Occidental Board; Miss Julia Morgan, architect; and D. B. Farquharson, the contractor.

Ida Lee and children in the courtyard of the new Ming Quong home in Oakland, about 1925.

. . . Miss Julia Morgan dreamed the plan of a concrete, fireproof building whose wings reach out like welcoming arms on either side of a gracious entrance-court. The walls are the soft color of apricot blossoms, the tiles of the roof are weathered like smoky jade. One enters the courtyard through an oriental archway which suggests a mission compound, and on the top steps sits, on either hand, a gorgeous blue Chinese dog, a royal bit of color. They were the gift of Miss Morgan, the architect. When someone protested that the babies would surely ride the dogs and break them she said, "Let them ride! When these are broken, I will give you others."

Gifts of elegant teakwood furniture lent the glassed-in lanai and large living room the air of a well-appointed Chinese home. Bedroom and dormitory chairs, beds, and chests had been scaled to the size of little girls, who could spread out their treasures, parade doll families, and tuck rag or bisque babies into small cradles. On the grounds the children had space to play and trees to climb and a stream to wade in.

Now her daughters could invite friends and brothers from Chung Mei, a few miles away in Berkeley. Boys and girls should share the same home, Donaldina believed, but as long as that was impossible, visiting between the two Chinese institutions would keep pleasant boy-girl ties.

Donaldina confessed one discontent. Eleven infants remained in the rundown baby cottage in East Oakland, and no funds were available to build an addition to Ming Quong or a separate home for them. She had been fortunate, though, in the workers who cared for her babies. In 1926 efficient young Lisette Miller, a graduate of Mount Holyoke Seminary, as were Emma Mills and Ethel Higgins, joined her staff. Lisette, preoccupied with making a hard decision, talked with Donaldina one moonlit evening as they sat on the wooden steps of the Baby Cottage. Lisette had trained for missionary work and had fallen in love with a man who shared her ambition, but whose health was not good enough for him to go abroad. Lisette had to choose between the mission field and marriage.

Donaldina knew all too well the conflicts of such loyalties and the routes to decision. From her the young woman drew power to find her own way, and decided to marry. "Miss Cameron is a rare person," she told a friend. "She gives so much love, and I can see it grows because she lets us give love back to her. As Macaulay said of Boswell, "she is great because she sees greatness in others."

Counseling with her grown daughters and members of the staff afforded Donaldina great satisfaction. When Hung Mui Chew finished high school in Oakland, she encouraged her to attend the Los Angeles Bible Institute and then the Santa Barbara Normal School. Many daughters took American names when they left the Home, but when Hung Mui asked, "What name shall I use?" Donaldina advised, "Be Miss Chew." This intelligent girl would do her race credit. Later, with her training complete, Hung Mui wanted to use her skills wherever the Mission needed her. "You took care of me when I was little. You educated me," she said. Though she had worked for her room and board, she reminded Donaldina of the $10 a month she had received from her and Tien throughout her years of study. "Where would I be without you?" And so she had become a mother to the little girls in Tooker Home and in Ming Quong.

Theological differences among staff members sometimes required counseling. On one occasion the director of the Baby Cottage objected to a nurse's reading *The Meaning of Prayer*, by Harry Emerson Fosdick, a minister hailed by some adherents as a great revealer of new insights, and scorned by others as an unacceptable "modernist."

Donaldina asked the accused woman why she read Fosdick's controversial books. The nurse replied, "It helps me to be a better Christian."

Donaldina smiled. "My dear, if Dr. Fosdick helps you to be a better Christian, I see no reason to ask you not to read his works."

Donaldina's efforts brought public recognition. On June 6, 1926 the *San Francisco Chronicle* reported that Miss Cameron,

. . . veteran worker against the Chinese girl slave traffic in San Francisco will be named as the woman who has rendered the most distinguished achievement in the country in 1926, if California women have anything to say. A movement has been started and presented to City and County Federation. $5000 prize is offered by a national magazine.

Mrs. D. E. F. Easton, Mrs. Annie Little Barry and Mrs. Edward Dexter Knight, are among a long list of California women who will sign their names advocating the recognition.

Mrs. Easton said, "We women feel that such recognition would be the least California could give to one who has played a hard and often losing game and has had the spirit to keep on with her job."

Donaldina expressed gratitude, but no further mention of the award appeared. She gave passing notice to personal honors, but money always seemed to be needed for the work. She had discovered that turtle men and women were setting up a brothel on the small lot across Joice Street from the Mission. Outraged by the slavers' audacity, she had gone to court, secured restraints against what she considered trespassing, and used hoarded funds to purchase the lot, eventually used as a parking area.

During the building of Ming Quong Home, she had tried to raise funds for a new home for babies born to rescued slave girls, and those abandoned or orphaned. Unable to do so, she could no longer allow the staff of the Baby Cottage to make shift in the old rented house. The infants were moved into the Ming Quong infirmary. Even so, good environment and good nursing were not always enough to make healthy children. After months of tender encouragement a poor little "impossible," as the nurses called him, remained blind, paralyzed, and without response. Donaldina had no alternative but to let him be assigned to a state hospital. Little Connie died of pneumonia. More happily, Billy, whose "Chinese chuckle" had delighted his nurse and visitors, was adopted.

Giving adequate care to infants at "920" was out of the question, and Donaldina clung stubbornly to her dream of building a separate home. If only she could show all San Francisco the newborn babe found in a suitcase in the Stockton tunnel! Or let them open the bundle left on a church pew and see a tiny face screwed up against the light.

Postwar prosperity led her to expect increased support. But the stock market crash in 1929 and the terrible depression that followed splintered many hopes, among them that of building a new Baby Cottage. By 1931 Donaldina was hard-pressed to make ends meet on a "shaved budget" in Ming Quong and "920."

Clearly, omens did not favor new campaigns, but Donaldina chose to believe President Hoover's slogan, "Prosperity is just around the corner." Regardless of worldly affairs, the affairs of the Kingdom must go on. In May she wrote a supplicating letter to Mrs. Bennett of the Board of National Missions, touching

> . . . some of the difficulties we face. . . . Many times . . . I have longed with all my heart for your clear vision and constructive mind to help those of us who live too near the problem to have a true perspective. . . .
>
> It seems "a large order" dear Mrs. Bennett to suggest that as busy and necessary a person as you are . . . would come all the way to California to help solve our local Chinese problems! But the fact is that our Chinese work has such almost limitless implications, it's lines go out, if not "into all the earth", at least half way around it, and we do want to strengthen our end here in the Mission Home. Come over and help us if you can dear Mrs. Bennett, I verily believe that I could get a pass from Chicago—perhaps! And if you could put up with our simple bed and board we would love to have you at 920. Much love from; Donaldina Cameron

Apparently her persuasion failed, for no further correspondence followed. So in June she dispatched Tien Wu to the General Assembly in the East, where the National Board of Missions also met. Tien attended as a representative of "920" and went armed with a formidable agenda:

GENERAL TOPICS FOR DISCUSSION WITH BOARD

What steps can be taken about Establishing a Home in China?

Refer this to Foreign Board.
If any Mission already established in South China will take our girls what financial provision can we offer for their support for a period long enough to get them trained for self support.

How shall we finance their return trip to China? Must have some this July. Frequently Missionaries who will protect them on return voyage do not sail on same line by which government must send them back, then we have to pay expense of trip.

Also we must pay difference between steerage and second cabin.

Can Mrs. Mills of Washington D.C. legacy be used, at least the interest on the five thousand dollars she gave, for Rescue Work.

Suggest that we get our married girls interested in helping with this fund.

Mrs. Wilson will help us start our Bi-Monthly Paper to help launch our former pupils organization this year.

Discuss plans for some segregation of our different groups here in the Home, if we must stay here in our present location may we use some of the money that was to prepare for Day Nursery in this building to make some internal changes, and prepare rear lot for recreation purposes. Also change roof garden, putting laundry all in basement.

What is to be the Boards final decision about care of homeless babies?

Under what conditions would the Board consent to allow the eleven thousand dollars already given for care of homeless Chinese babies to be used for erecting a building for that purpose?

As Donaldina kissed Tien goodbye, she thought how incredible it was that the once-rebellious girl was rounding off twenty years as a staff member of the Home.

Articulate Tien did justice to her agenda, but reported that the Board had its hands tied by lack of funds. Nonetheless, Donaldina decided to keep up a courteous agitation in regard to the Mission's compelling needs, ranging from "920" to China, and back again. Dr. Hassler of the Health Department, urged that a new home for babies and little children be erected, but that was impossible. Because of the depression, some young children were allowed to remain in "920," but The City required that a new fire escape be installed, which would cost $520. Donaldina also saw good reason to do minor remodeling on the twenty-year-old building, entailing an outlay of about $145 or $150. Her funds would not stretch that far. She wrote Miss Voss, Secretary of the Board of National Missions, for money to install the required fire escape and added:

After much thought and deliberation on the part of our American and Chinese staff members, we have decided to unite our three dining rooms, having the entire staff take their meals together . . . with our Chinese family in this large basement room. I feel sure, Miss Voss, that this plan will result in benefit to the Chinese girls as well as to the staff, drawing us all more closely together in a united family.

We would hardly have had courage to decide upon this step, perhaps, had it not been for a generous fine gift from a group of friends, in Fresno....

The friends raised a memorial fund to Mrs. Austin, Bible teacher and president of the California Synodical, to buy a "bright cheerful linoleum" to cover what Donaldina described as a "floor which long ago was oiled leaving it very dark and impossible to keep clean looking." She elucidated further:

We are anxious to get the dining room ready before time for our annual fall bazaar as we have decided to serve Chinese luncheons and dinners on the two days of the bazaar to help swell our industrial department funds. Times are so hard that it is difficult to sell things that are not necessities but people will pay for meals and our family and married girls can prepare nice Chinese food very inexpensively.

Letter after letter went back and forth, counting the saving of $25 as significant, before the fire escape was installed and the remodeled dining room completed. She felt like the Biblical petitioner who importuned his indifferent neighbor.

Yet she knew her board was sympathetic when she pleaded for a sister agency in China:

I am sure Miss Wu has helped to make clear to you and the other members of our Board in New York, Miss Voss, why we have now definitely arrived at the conclusion that only through the cooperating organization doing protective and rescue work in South China, can we hope to entirely suppress the slave traffic.

And she subtly reminded Miss Voss of the Board's responsibility to nudge New York immigration authorities on her behalf:

Yesterday I had another urgent appeal supposedly from the same Chinese slave girl for whom Miss Wu has been seeking. This last letter was sent to the care of our Chinese Christian newspaper, Chung Sai Yut Po, but addressed to me in Chinese. I trust the Immigration Department in New York will be successful in locating this girl.

Having set all possible wheels to turning toward reaching her larger and more remote goals, Donaldina plunged again into solving the problems on her doorstep.

*   *   *   *   *

The Home sheltered three strangers awaiting deportation. Always, a girl traveling alone faced the danger of seizure en route to China. Furthermore, if she possessed no family, only rarely could she support herself by honorable work, even if she did reach her homeland safely.

Donaldina undertook protection of every girl in the Home, however brief her stay. If a girl had to return to China by herself, Donaldina paid the difference in fare between steerage, which the government provided, and third class, where a chaperone was sometimes enlisted. And she planned for the traveler to be met and escorted to a family or to a Christian school which could shelter and train her until she was equipped to take care of herself.

All those arrangements called for money, scant in 1931. Donaldina asked for $150 from a bequest made to the Board of National Missions, to return a girl to China. The fund held $227.23, and she was granted the $150, with the precaution, "If you use as much as this for one girl there will, of course, not be sufficient to provide for all three who are under consideration."

For the Board to refuse any request of its devoted, but sometimes imperious, superintendent seemed impossible. When restraints were attempted, Donaldina pursued other resources. Within the year she maneuvered to return the other two girls to China, and was assured of their care through the help of Miss Amy Law and Mr. and Mrs. H. P. Hinkey in Wuchow, Kwan-Si. She had met Miss Law, a Chinese teacher known as the "most spiritual woman in South China," and head of her own mission school, during her round-the-world trip in 1905. Miss Law formed a strong link to the Orient, and her influence bore directly upon one of Donaldina's long-time adversaries, Ah Peen (Opium) Amy.

For years Donaldina had clashed with Ah Peen Amy, a beautiful courtesan, "the toast of Chinatown," who had bought her own freedom by peddling opium, and then became part-owner of other girls. A personal power struggle developed between her and Donaldina. Therefore, when Ah Peen Amy sent word asking rescue, Donaldina suspected treachery. She would not refuse a call, but she asked Charles Shepherd to accompany her and Lonnie. Ah Peen Amy explained that she had been double-crossed and that her erstwhile partner was planning to sell her. She clung to Donaldina, pleading remorse for her evil ways and asking to go to "920."

Donaldina had problems enough without adding an underhanded dealer in opium and slaves to her household. Still, Amy seemed sincere, and man's extremity *was* God's opportunity. Laying down rigid restrictions, Donaldina led her home. As a test of her tractability, she locked her into a small room.

Soon afterward, Miss Amy Law arrived from China. When she heard Ah Peen Amy's story, she asked permission to talk with her. That conversation of the two Amys in their native tongue stimulated many more. Miss Law convinced Donaldina that Ah Peen Amy had renounced her past life and become a Christian. Donaldina welcomed her into the household, and in due time put her in charge of the kitchen. Amy, as her name was shortened, proved faithful.

But she harbored one obsessive longing. In her teens she had borne a child who had died. Now she wanted to adopt a baby. Donaldina demurred, insisting that Amy must prove herself further. Early one morning Amy heard a mewing, opened the door, and discovered on the doorstep not a kitten but a baby boy. The arrival seemed providential, and with joy Donaldina allowed Amy to adopt their foundling.

Later, to make the story even more fabulous, an admirer, a farmer from a valley town, wooed and married Amy. Her Christian conscience grew. She wished to clear all debts incurred before her conversion. She earned money cooking for her husband's harvesters, and gradually paid off all she owed except one hundred dollars to a Chinatown merchant. With the final sum in hand she returned to the Home and asked that the merchant be sent for. He refused the money, saying the debt had been canceled years earlier at a Chinese New Year celebration. In her book, *Chinatown Quest,* Carol Green Wilson adds to the story:

It was hard for . . . Amy to face him. She had seen none of her old associates since she had left Chinatown. But she came down and held out the hundred dollars.

"I am a Christian now. I owe the money. You must take it."

He rose with a low bow, unprecedented for a merchant of his class before a woman such as she had been, and accepted the currency with all the courtesy that those who know these gentlemen behind counters of Chinatown love and respect.

"If that is what your religion teaches, I want to know more of it."

Donaldina was touched. A miracle the Lord had wrought. She was in need of more miracles and dared to hope the Lord and His servants like Amy Law might raise them up. Perhaps He would help find a way to establish more mission schools in China, to receive unprotected girls in Shanghai and Hong Kong, which still supported prosperous slave clearing houses. The selling price in the United States for a teen-aged Chinese girl had risen to between $6,000 and $10,000 in gold.

The advancing market was due in part to tightened immigration supervision at American ports and borders. Donaldina applauded, though it worked a hardship on her temporary wards. Without legal entry papers they had to be deported unless someone could show good cause for delay. She devised good causes: a girl's papers would be provided later, she promised; or a child was too frail to travel alone just at the time of a ship's departure; or her family might be located in China were Donaldina given only a little more time to inquire.

Even a slight extension of parole might enable a girl to get enough education to support herself. China needed teachers and housekeepers. Let her prepare these girls, she pleaded. The United States could be proud of its democratic contribution. She could show an impressive list of daughters who were successful in their native land.

While jockeying for time, Donaldina sweetened life for her

short-time daughters. Evelyn Browne Bancroft, Donaldina's life-long friend, observed the effects on one young life:

> A darling little girl, looking about thirteen years old waited upon us at table. She was bright eyed, pretty and smiling. She was well trained and careful. I thought surely this must be one who was saved before she was old enough to be forced into the terrible bondage. Presently I heard Lo Mo in her soft sweet voice saying "Betty Dear, will you please bring some more muffins." Then it flashed over me that this innocent child had been through these terrible experiences and pollution but because Christ died for her and His witnesses had been faithful in making Him known, she stood there washed spotless of it all and face shining with hope and love. . . .

Donaldina counted each girl's conversion as crucial:

> Almost without exception the Chinese girls and women who are sent from Angel Island to the Mission Home on parole remain with us until they either definitely accept Christianity or become sufficiently interested so that they wish to be sent back in the care of Christian friends to some Mission School when they are returned to their own country. One case almost invariably leads to another and so it is more or less of a continuous chain, starting in China, touching Angel Island, then the mainland through the Mission Home, and then back again with new and stronger links that anchor each life to higher goals in their own country.

All girls captured Donaldina's interest; some played on her sympathies:

> [Gum Ying's] gentle, wistful face . . . haunts us as we see her going quietly about her allotted household duties or sitting in the school room trying to master her first lessons in the Chinese written language. Always her eyes hold the anxious question "What will become of me when parole days in this safe home are ended?" We can only answer with the inward prayer that God will in some way provide in the near future a Christian Home in South China.

Good medical care was contributed to "920" by several of The City's young physicians. Though few serious illnesses occurred, Dr. Milton Hall, a young Chinese, came to check heavy colds to be sure no complications were developing, and left directions for bed rest, aspirin, and fluids. One of his cases was serious, a girl who had tried suicide. Held for weeks in the austere Immigration detention buildings, the despairing girl had jumped from an upper-story window. Though she had failed to kill herself, she had broken a leg and was hospitalized. Donaldina paid her bill and brought her to "920," hoping to restore her shattered faith in this new land. Dr. Hall's skill and the atmosphere of the Home produced good results. Thankfully, he noted, Chinatown was spared danger from typhoid or other waterborne diseases, for the Chinese drank only tea made from boiled water.

Another young doctor, Helen B. Pryor, a pediatrician in practice with Dr. William Palmer Lucas, at prestigious 490 Post Street, and formerly a Methodist missionary to China until expelled by the Chinese communists, regularly looked in on the younger children. She discovered that the "Mother of Chinatown" knew and cared for her children individually. After a house call when she had not found Lo Mo in the Home, she wrote:

My dear Miss Cameron:

In regard to the babies at the orphanage little Wing Chen is greatly in need of a tonsilectomy. Could she be brought up to Children's Hospital or wherever else you wish to have it done in the near future?

Little Joyce Yuen probably belongs at Pacific Colony or some other institution for feeble minded children. I feel that it is bad mental hygiene to keep a child like that in daily contact with normal children. . . .

Yours very sincerely,

HELEN B. PRYOR, M.D.

Now and then Donaldina found a moment between crises to mull over the state of affairs in her kingdom. All Gaul may have been divided into three parts, but *her* complicated life had at least five clear layers, or rainbow colors, that paralleled one another:

First, she never lost sight of the goal of her long crusade—the defeat of slavery. Second, individual rescues whittled down the awful toll in wrecked lives. Third, those rescues took her into another sphere, the courts. Fourth, her wards in the homes engrossed her, and, fifth, her three maiden sisters across the Bay laid claim to her time. Plans must be made for their future; all were over the age of seventy. Faith would find a way.

She did not credit her own human efforts in the establishment of all the Mission homes, or for Chung Mei, as Charles Shepherd insisted she should. All came out of her faith. Ultimate victory over slavery could not be too far in the future.

She had to trust that her strength would be sustained to finish her work, for of late she found it necessary to excuse herself from trips and surprise visitors. In an emergency, however, she could move as swiftly as ever. The week before, when she and Mae Wong were on a hurried errand, she had stepped into an elevator, pressed the button, and turned in time to see Mae's startled face beyond the closing doors. The young woman had then run upstairs where Donaldina waited impatiently. "Why are you so slow!" she reproached. Mae wondered at her sharpness, for Lo Mo often complimented her for speed.

The gift of a large Studebaker automobile to the Home facilitated rescues. A young college man who drove for Donaldina reported her swift covering of an exchange of passengers at the Berkeley depot. He pulled the car to the curb, where a disguised slave girl waited with a friend. Two women, Donaldina and Tien, stepped out of the car, and visited with the pair on the platform a moment. Then two slid into the back seat, but not the same two. Donaldina comforted a frightened new passenger, and the driver, watching through the rear-view mirror, made sure no one followed them. Tien, substituting for the rescued girl, was on her way with a friend.

Once in Sacramento on a rescue Donaldina knew the Studebaker had been recognized and went home by train. Her driver was intercepted on the highway but not detained. As a ruse she sometimes rented a strange car.

Dear Tien poured her whole life into the Mission. She had turned down several suitors, and now, nearing fifty, followed in Donaldina's footsteps. Daughters like Tien and Mae multiplied her strength. Mae had set the Industrial Department humming as never before, and filled in anywhere. But the time had come to hire another professional aide. The National Board held a firm, if absurd, rule that staff must retire at the age of sixty-five. When Donaldina turned sixty-two on July 26, 1931, she felt a little like Elijah charged to locate a modern Elisha to inherit her cloak.

By the end of the year she had screened a number of applicants. In the process she discovered that hard times had turned job-hunting young people toward the mission field, some of whom possessed neither aptitude nor dedication for their work. Finding the right assistant was critical, for hard times also widened the needs in Chinatown. People in deep trouble sought sympathy and counsel. The Mission was called on for community help—food, housing, health care.

On a friend's recommendation Donaldina interviewed Lorna Logan, a 25-year-old Seattle journalist. She was strongly attracted to her and wanted to urge her to come to "920," but the matter was too sensitive, too crucial. Miss Logan must follow her own inner voice.

Highly intelligent and beautiful, with wavy dark hair and sparkling brown eyes, Lorna could have chosen from several futures, but, drawn by the warm and regal director, she decided a career at the Mission Home was what she wanted. She signed a contract for three years, as required by the Board of Missions. Her salary was $600 per annum.

Donaldina smiled to herself. Limitless futures were known to grow out of limited commitments.

CHAPTER EIGHTEEN

The Gospel of Giving
1932-1934

On New Year's Eve, 1932, the household at "920" buzzed with more than holiday excitement. A new member of the family, Miss Lorna Logan, was coming. A room on the second floor was ready for her; the little girls were primed to present flowers, and a chorus had practiced to serenade her with a hymn when she arrived.

Donaldina met the train at the Oakland mole. No matter how often she crossed the Bay at night, she thrilled to the salt smell of the sea and lights glittering across the waves. Learning that the train was hours late, she stretched out on a bench near the Cascade arrival gate, and fell asleep. About midnight when Lorna arrived, Donaldina bounded up, apologetic, but enthusiastic in her welcome.

The girls at the Home had been sent to bed, but in the morning their greeting and performance charmed Lorna. Her modest acceptance and her ready laugh immediately endeared her to them. As time passed, Donaldina observed a rapport developing between Lorna and Tien and with Mae, who was almost Lorna's age.

The next two years became as productive as their events were hectic. Donaldina led Lorna into every area of the work, and found her remarkably adept. She nicknamed her Jehu, after the charioteer, because she drove the Home's Studebaker so rapidly and well. Though a journalist herself, Lorna understood Donaldina's sometime unwillingness to talk to the press. Her new boss hated the reporters' habit of romanticizing misery and making heroines of the women who fought it. The two enjoyed a fast pace, and shared the same kind of humor. And Donaldina appreciated her young assistant's gift for taking hold.

During the depressed 1930's, needs in the three homes increased and community involvement expanded. While the Chinese quarter retained old customs, young people looked for a bridge from Chinese tradition to Western culture. Hard times accentuated differences between parents and children.

Donaldina encouraged "920"'s staff to offer guidelines for families to blend old and new ways. Four clubs within the Home attracted Chinese people. Auntie Wu (Tien) sponsored a group of business girls who worked outside the Home. Mrs. Robinson and Mrs. Thom brought the newly rescued and paroled girls together socially; Mae and Mrs. Garten formed a children's group; and Miss Barrell, a secretary, and Grace Chan, a rescued daughter who had become an ardent Christian, organized activities for mature women in Chinatown.

Donaldina felt a special satisfaction in the Friday morning Bible class, which drew both young men and women from the community. She saw it as a nucleus for growth toward her most cherished goal, the greatest harmonizer, an ingathering of the Chinese community to her faith. Older daughters were encouraged to participate in the Christian Endeavor Society of the church, with Mrs. Andrew Wu, Donaldina's long-time friend, as advisor. Some of them sang at the "great C. E. Chorus" of the International Christian Endeavor Convention, which met in The City.

As always, Donaldina expressed Christian principles. The true way to happiness was to be found in a gospel of giving, she told her daughters, and knowing they could not learn by mere cerebration, she encouraged them to offer gifts for the benefit of their fellows. At her Board's request, she tallied money contributed by individual girls or through organizations:

$ 59.50 for local church repairs
$100.00 to the Board of National Missions
$ 11.40 to the Ming Sam School in China
$ 84.35 for Famine Relief
$ 2.00 for Leper Work in The City
$ 9.25 for poor children in Chinatown
$ 30.00 for War relief work (in China)

Mae Wong teaching at "920," 1932-33. "Lo Mo needed me."

The clubs gave $108.05 to the Industrial Department, and business girls undertook support of an orphan child in the "Door of Hope" in Shanghai.

Sales from the annual bazaar continued as the main source of earnings, older girls contributing articles produced in the Industrial Department, and the children making candy to sell.

The busy spring of 1932 had been interrupted by an epidemic of serious flu, and illness among the babies brought an ultimatum from a pediatrician who donated his services to the Home: separate housing for infants and tiny children must be arranged! Donaldina had long recognized the need, but money had been, and continued to be, non-existent. However, what must be could be!

She and Lorna Logan drew together an interracial board of responsible men and women from the community and its churches. They began a drive for funds and a search for a home. They raised enough money to operate on a shoestring and located an old, rundown house near the railroad tracks in San Mateo. Staff members of "920" and friends repaired and scrubbed the place to make it livable. But when neighbors heard of its intended use, they objected with such vigor that the new Board was forced to look elsewhere. They found an old home in Atherton on Middlefield Road. Later a friend in Menlo Park offered a house on Santa Cruz Avenue, next door to the little white-spired Presbyterian church. It was named "Gabriel Cottage."

Moving the babies coincided with another happy event. Daughter Jade came home with her M.D. degree from the Women's Medical College in Philadelphia. Jade had finished Lux High School in The City and, with the help of Mrs. Pinney and Mrs. Wright, former presidents of the Occidental Board, had graduated from San Mateo Junior College and Stanford University. To satisfy her sponsors, she had also studied at the Philadelphia Bible College. All through those twelve years she had distinguished herself as gracious, cultured, and intelligent. She had earned a substantial part of her living and expenses during her schooling. Like so many other daughters, Jade, who became Dr. Bessie Jeong, wanted to repay Lo Mo, who had made her career possible. She volunteered to supervise the new Peninsula Baby Cottage during the summer before going to Los Angeles General Hospital as an intern.

"The Chinese never forget a kindness," Donaldina repeated a favorite phrase to Lorna, "They pay their respects and give back full measure for all they are given."

The gospel of giving had taken root in the minds and hearts of many of her daughters, she observed with deep satisfaction. In the Home she expected further fruits as a result of the earnest teachings of Mrs. Robinson, to whom responsibility for evangelizing the girls was assigned. When Grace Chan, an especially receptive new resident, made her decision "to give my life to God," she helped other girls. Asked who among her young disciples prayed most earnestly, Grace replied, "Suey Mui. She rises and goes out on the roof garden to pray alone at night for herself and for those in China who have not yet learned to know Jesus."

Mrs. Robinson confirmed her words, "I know of no one whose prayers I love better to listen to than those of little Suey Mui. She was recently pleading most earnestly with God for her own torn and distressed country and closed her prayer with 'Oh Lord help us to have the spirit of Stephen who died praying for mercy on those who stoned him to death.' "

In a story accompanying her annual report, Donaldina quoted those experiences, adding,

We hope that Christian friends who have always had the light of God in their lives and who have had a life-time of experience in testing the value and power of prayer, will remember this young rescued Chinese girl and ask that God will make of her a great blessing to the women of her own race even though it may be within a limited sphere of service in San Francisco's Chinatown or in her own country.

In the midst of pathos and problems Donaldina sometimes found a wedge of time to slip in pure fun. One evening she and Lorna and two others planned to attend a play. She challenged them to a race to see which pair could reach the theatre first. In order to win, she hailed a taxi and paid fifteen cents to ride through the Stockton Street tunnel.

With unemployment a major problem in the United States, Chinese girls found themselves pushed entirely out of the job market. Women who formerly hired household help were doing their own work. China lacked skilled dressmakers and cooks, however, and the Home was equipped to prepare its daughters in these fields. Every worker who might go to China Donaldina counted as a missionary.

By the end of 1932 five young girls and three children in the Home awaited deportation. Because Donaldina could establish no family connections in the Orient for them, she spurred her Board of National Missions to act in concert with Dr. Mary Stone, and Miss Jennie Hughes of the Bethel Mission in Shanghai. She was jubilant when joint planning finally promised a branch of Bethel Mission in Kow Loon, a village across the harbor from Hong Kong. At last a Chinese "Annex of '920' " promised to challenge the hold of Hong Kong's iniquitous slave clearing house.

Because the directors of the Bethel Mission did not speak Cantonese, they requested Miss Tien Fuh Wu's help for six months. Donaldina consented, seeing a double opportunity: to establish the long-projected receiving home for her wards and, more immediately, to get her eight deportees across the Pacific. She maneuvered ways to finance the trip, booked "special steerage" on the steamship "President Coolidge" at the reduced rate of $67.50 plus $5 head tax for each of six girls, and "special second class" for Auntie Tien and the youngest child, who would share her cabin.

Donaldina saw the travelers off on December 2, 1932. In a sentimental mood, she likened Auntie Wu to a Moses leading her small "Israelites" in Exodus from "920" to China. With the help of Tien's vivid letters she followed them. In Honolulu they were entertained by Mrs. Li and Mrs. Sieu, former daughters of the Home, and visited with Professor S. C. Lee and a former teacher at Ming Quong Home, Chi Oi. Tien wrote:

You can imagine how very pleased the girls were to have Chinese fruit [gathered in Mrs. Li's garden] and to be able to get on land. At noon we all went marketing as the steerage food is very poor, especially breakfast and lunch. We bought some canned fish, preserved ducks, coffee and condensed milk so I hope we will get along until we get to Hong Kong.

In another letter to Lo Mo, Tien described two "congenial and gentlemanly" Chinese men, whom she befriended by sharing her seasick remedy, salted olives and ginger. Veteran missionaries, Dr. and Mrs. Taylor, led worship services

for my people, especially for our own girls and the steerage folk. Dr. Taylor gave the story of the Prodigal Son. It was a new experience for him to speak in English and have me interpret it for him. We had a goodly group of men, women and children; and I hope God spoke to the hearts who were there. . . .

After visits in Japan and Shanghai the wanderers reached Kow Loon only to learn that the flat rented for them was not available. But, Tien reported,

I cast it [my anxiety] upon the Lord . . . [A friend at Peniel Mission took them in.] We have running water, a bath tub, bedrooms and a parlor. The kitchen is our sorrow for there is no sink. The Chinese stove we are trying to cook with is a trial, we have to use charcoal and wood and they smoke so that our eyes hurt. . . . It is quite safe as we are only a block away from a police station. . . .

We met a very interesting couple, Mr. and Mrs. Chung, the wife is very interested in slave girls and has a school for them. We are to visit her school and dine with them tomorrow.

Dr. Stone wrote of her pleasure in the group, informing Donaldina that she had vaccinated them for their protection, and that "Miss Wu is like a little general, having secured a flat and made all the arrangements before we arrived from Shanghai." Donaldina laughed at the apt title for saucy little Tien. She missed her salty wit and her devotion, the more so because Lorna was also away, recovering at home from a depleting case of flu. Thinking of her two staunch helpers, she asked herself if it could be possible that nearly thirty years ago she, Donaldina Cameron, had visited with her family after her first year of service at "920." She was twenty-six then, just Lorna's age. Her sixty-fourth birthday, coming in July, reminded her of her approaching retirement.

Tien came home in time for Lo Mo's birthday cake, which Annie baked as usual. She brought word that at the last minute Bethel had not been able to raise funds for the new receiving home, so she had placed all her wards in other homes or schools before leaving China. Celebrations broke the somber mood fostered by depression hardships. At Thanksgiving Donaldina arranged a lively party, inviting friends without families, and Lorna's parents from Seattle. At opposite ends of the long table Donaldina and the genial Mr. Logan prepared to carve a turkey. They raced to see who could serve half of the guests first. Whether a tie resulted because of equal skill or by the gentleman's gallantry, no one was willing to judge. A guest of honor, the Chinese Consul, "a very charming gentleman and a good sport," contributed to the fun.

A flu epidemic raced through the Home in December, but Donaldina's annual report read,

> At Christmas time over fifty children with their mothers from the poorest families of Chinatown were invited as guests. . . . The Chinese girls of the Home, under the guidance of Miss Fung and Mrs. Robinson, prepared a simple, vivid pageant with story, music and pictures giving the Christmas message. Gifts for every visiting child were provided by members of the four clubs within the Home, also a paper bag of simple Chinese food for each mother.

Her tight summary did not reflect the weeks of excitement that preceded that bright evening, or the afterglow that lasted for days. The children and older girls helped concoct simple costumes, and found no trouble imagining a Galilean hillside as backdrop for the stage. Need for hope in the quiet audience made the tinsel star gleam with promise. Donaldina wept when some of the mothers gave profound thanks for what she knew to be the only food in their homes. She and her staff directed them to city, state, or federal emergency relief programs that provided subsistence budgets to the destitute. In this time of suffering, family problems increased and doors opened to let in the wise and sympathetic counselors from "920," who did much personal work.

But, the annual report advised:

Necessary measures of economy have handicapped . . . visiting out-lying and isolated Chinese Communities for personal contact and evangelization. . . . Hospitality in the Mission Home has had to be reduced to the lowest minimum of expense.

Travel in the interests of rescue work and "follow up" . . . are cur-tailed owing to lack of funds.

And so the year ended not in triumphal climax, but in sus-pense. Her sixty-fifth birthday seemed only an hour away, and so much must be rounded off before she stepped down. Stepped down! How could she live separated from her daughters and the Chinese people she had known and served for thirty-eight years?

Unreal, impossible! "My blood is the mortar of these bricks," she cried. But the present, and the claims of the present, were the important issues.

She was heartened by a premonition that Kwai Ying, the young slave girl who came to the Home shortly before Christmas, would contribute toward her chief aspiration, ending the slave trade.

CHAPTER NINETEEN

Broken Blossoms

1933-1935

Donaldina, her staff, federal authorities, and The City's police dared to hope that the slave traffic was nearly throttled. But on December 13, 1933, Kwai Ying had rushed in off the street, her short hair awry, with a tale of oppression as grim as any Donaldina had heard during the past forty years. The girl had been bought in China, promised a good job in America as a waitress, and taken aboard the liner "President Cleveland" bound for Seattle.

En route, an agent guarded her and forced her to memorize a fake family history from a "coaching book," containing photos of her pseudo father and eight brothers and sisters. She learned details of their "home" in China, what clothes her "father" wore, what possessions he prized, the number of pigs, chickens, and rice paddies belonging to the family, and births, deaths, and marriages for twenty years. She studied sketches and descriptions of her "family's" village, which showed temple, school, cemetery, public wells, and fields. Having absorbed the whole, Kwai Ying flung the telltale book into Puget Sound before landing.

Her guard warned her of terrible reprisal if she failed to carry out directions. And the worst possible fate would overtake her if she went with Fahn Quai to the big brick house. Girls were tortured there and fed poisoned food, she was told.

On the Seattle dock, Kwai Ying recognized her "father," Mr. Lee, and a "sister," who waved. Timidly she waved back. A sailor brushed her arm, whispering, "If you ever need help go to Kum Mai Lun [Chinese for Cameron], who lives at Mission Home." Though startled, the girl stored the two names in her memory.

She answered the questions of port authorities and was turned over to her "father" and "sister," who accompanied her aboard a train to California. On the trip Kwai Ying was awed by high mountains, their trees a rising green. In valleys she watched in vain for rice fields; in towns the boxy houses and strange white faces made her long for China.

At last, in San Francisco's Chinatown, the alien scenes gave way to familiar shops and streets. She saw pagoda roofs and amber lamps; she heard the click of an abacus and the musical language of her homeland.

She and her "sister" were guided to the Jackson Street apartment of a middle-aged Chinese couple, whom Kwai Ying assumed owned the restaurant where she expected to become a waitress. She met another "sister," Wong So, who laughed bitterly at her happy plans. The wife asked Wong So to come with her on an errand, and Kwai Ying did not see her again. But soon she learned the reason for Wong So's cynical laughter. She too was escorted by the wife and discovered to her horror that she was merchandise for sale.

Several times Kwai Ying was required to take off her clothes, though she protested violently. Prospective buyers walked around her and looked her over. No, the price was too high. She was beautiful, well formed. But she was spirited. The risk of buying a girl who might run away or seek rescue was too great. Their last girl had let herself be led off by that white devil at the Mission. No! Better to await a more docile slave.

Finally two hard-faced women purchased Kwai Ying, pressing $500 into her hand. The wife snatched the money. Unwittingly, Kwai Ying had sold herself for the cost of her passage to America. $4,000 additional were promised and paid to the wife three days later.

Kwai Ying was instructed in her profession, "The Night Life," and for several weeks was conducted from one hotel to another, where she was forced to earn $25 a night and turn over $21 of it to her owners. Subtle as well as gross pressures were brought to bear to make her accept her lot. A conspirator from China wrote Kwai Ying this letter:

Hong Kong, China

Ying Sister:

Many flocks of birds have flown from the south. You, who are in another country, wishing to be coming home, must be very home-sick. It must be pitable for you, being so far away from home and relatives. Even while I am writing you, my tears streaming down mingle with yours. However, the rice is cooked, the wood has been made into a boat, and dumb boy has eaten "wong-lin" [bitter herb] for he can't tell of the bitter taste, therefore, you must be patient, and be submissive to your mistress. As for home folks don't worry. Tell Mr. Shim Chong, to thank him for me to write for you, to help those who can't write. Winter has come and snow has come like flakes. Be sure to dress warmly. Your mother and grandma are always getting after us to wear more clothing. My graduation day is coming soon, but has to see whether my luck comes my way or not. Hope you will write me often.

From big sister MEI LON

But Kwai Ying took neither solace nor advice from her Job's comforter. She had refused to become a prostitute in Hong Kong. She would resist that fate here. Sickened by her ordeal, she watched for a chance to escape. It came one late afternoon in December. She was told she must "entertain" at a big party and was left in a beauty shop to have her bobbed hair marcelled. Boldly she ordered that only the ends be curled, and, taking advantage of the few minutes before her escort returned, dashed into the street, and hid among white Christmas shoppers.

Every Chinese form on Grant Avenue loomed as a possible pursuer. Swaying lanterns pointed fingers of light at her. A salesman taking a jade pin from a display window seemed to reach for her. She asked a little boy how to get to the "Mission Home." Following his direction, she fled up Washington Street and knocked at the door of a big house, asking for Kum Mai Lun. It was the Methodist Home, Gum Moon. Hysterical, Kwai Ying refused to leave. Surely her owner would be looking for her. The sympathetic deaconess accompanied her to Donaldina.

Assured of her welcome and safety, Kwai Ying described her
ordeal to Donaldina. "Protect me," she pleaded. "I cannot go
back. Every night men kept coming, first one, then another and
another and another! I shut my eyes against them. I thought I
must be dead and suffering the horrors of the next world."

Donaldina put her arms around the young girl. Perhaps Kwai
Ying could summon the courage to witness for herself and for
her Chinese sisters, and halt this abomination at last. The men
and women she named were offenders of long standing.

Donaldina phoned Arthur J. Phelan, head of the Immigration
department's legal division. Inspector Kuckein, with Ernest
Tsang, Chinese interpreter, came at once to the Home. Kwai
Ying managed to tell them her story. Hearing the names of the
girl's deceivers, the two men excitedly hurried back to the Ap-
praiser's Building with their notes. Shortly afterward they
phoned Donaldina that A. J. Zirpoli, Assistant United States
Attorney in San Francisco, believed the girl's testimony identified a large ring. To clinch its case the department insisted on
irrefutable proof, and detectives would have to compile solid
evidence before they could bring the case to court. Donaldina
was restrained from rescuing Kwai Ying's colleagues until the
government investigation was complete. Not until March of
1935, more than a year later, did Immigration men advise Donaldina that they had sufficient information to proceed. If Kwai
Ying would testify in court, they were convinced they could con-
vict her captors, and break a powerful slave ring.

Their evidence wove a net around a respected hardware merchant on Grant Avenue, Wong She Duck. With henchmen on
both sides of the Pacific, he masterminded a bold and expensive
operation. He was rich and powerful and merciless. Only United
States law, with the aid of little Kwai Ying, stood a chance of
breaking his evil hold over many exploited lives.

The granite look stiffened Donaldina's face. "We shall do our
part," she replied. "I am not surprised that Wong She Duck has
this power. For years girls have mentioned his name. But we
must ask your protection. Retaliation is sure when it becomes
known that one of our daughters has challenged a man like that."

Chinatown learned that the hardware merchant, who had

eleven partners, and who had prospered for twenty-five years, was under arrest and had posted $3,000 bail in federal court. Though the quarter appeared serene to tourists, police and Immigration agents sensed a restiveness and anxiety. Men scudded along streets carrying messages to tong headquarters. Other sharp-eyed fellows lounged against doorways, or strolled with exaggerated casualness through streets and alleys. At night, groups of slave girls exchanged their bright robes for black and dark green sahms, and were hustled into cars and driven to valley towns.

On March 5, 1935, in the gray stone Post Office Building, Judge Graham took the bench for the United States government. Wong She Duck, his wife Kung She Wong; Fong She, an alleged moneylender, and procuress, Yee Mar, the two women who had bought Kwai Ying, were brought before him, charged with transportation of women in interstate commerce for immoral purposes and conspiracy for their transportation.

Donaldina, Auntie Wu, Lorna, and Esther Fung surrounded Kwai Ying, even in the elevator, because they feared some last-minute duplicity by Wong She Duck. At the door of the wood-panelled courtroom government attorneys Phelan and Zirpoli met them, and led Donaldina and Kwai Ying to the witness table.

The prosecution and its witness began to present evidence amassed through the long year since Kwai Ying's flight. Early days of the trial went quietly. When the girl was called, Donaldina smiled reassuringly. Kwai Ying kept her eyes on Lo Mo's face, and through interpreter Ernest Tsang, calmly recited her story, giving dates and addresses of her captor's apartments and names of the hotels where she had been required to work. She told of parties and guests she had served and of the money she earned and turned over to her owners.

Donaldina marveled. A brave girl, daring to face the most skilled criminal lawyers that Wong She Duck's wealth could buy! Kwai Ying must realize that she would be killed were she to step outside "920" without guards. Yet she chose to testify in hope of sparing other girls her awful experiences.

Tedious days of cross-examination had stirred constant rustlings in the courtroom, but on March 14 the audience sensed a change. Everyone leaned forward, intent, listening. Each word reverberated through the silence, as the defense lawyers led Kwai Ying through a maze of details about her early life in China. They tripped her over her assertion that she had been sold in Hong Kong to Wong She Duck's agent.

Suddenly counsel for the defense thundered. She had seen no transaction! She could prove nothing! And had she not sworn to Immigration authorities in Seattle that she came of her own free will to this country? She had perjured herself to get sympathy, and falsely accused innocent people!

His heavy features expressionless, Wong She Duck took the witness stand and blandly brushed aside the girl's testimony that she had stayed in his apartment. He had seen her once, yes, with an acquaintance, but he naturally thought she was his, his. . . . He left the accusation unstated. Who could believe that an ignorant female, fresh from Hong Kong, and moreover, one of her low estate, could accurately remember all those addresses and dates? Or even that she was capable of telling the truth?

"It has been written that the liar feeds well his memory."

Prosecution interjected, "It has also been written that the caged bird studies and remembers each movement and watches for every crack of escape."

Other defendants asserted, "The girl lies!"

Character witnesses glazed Wong She Duck and the other defendants with virtues and good names. Once more the defense attorney called Kwai Ying to the stand. His questions bored in, sharp, intense. He pressed her for dates, places, people. Kwai Ying hesitated, tried to answer, floundered under the cruel rain of words, and fell silent, covering her face with trembling hands.

Judge Graham intervened. Did the witness wish to say more on her own behalf? She shook her head. Prosecuting attorneys rested their case. His face grave, the judge instructed the jury. Hours passed. At last they returned. The jury could not agree on the guilt of the accused. Ten voted "aye" and two "nay."

Ernest Tsang drove Kwai Ying and her four protectors home. As they reached Chinatown, Kwai Ying shrank against Donaldina to avoid curious eyes watching to see how a discredited slave girl and her famous protector took defeat. Lo Mo comforted her, but she was thinking: "Where can we turn now?"

Kwai Ying sighed. "If only we could find Wong So, the girl I met in Wong She Duck's apartment. She was stronger than I."

For more than a year authorities had sought Wong So, the "sister." Donaldina saw it as an act of Providence that, three days after Kwai Ying's trial ended in a hung jury, Wong So was located in the Salinas Valley and brought to "920." The staff recognized immediately that she was made of sterner stuff than most slaves. She answered questions deliberately, giving no clues by gesture or expression. But she was bitter against her betrayers. She had been bandied about for more than a year by a cruel master. She was eager to expose him and the people behind him. If she could keep her balance under the vicious and confusing cross-examination that had crumpled her "sister," her evidence against Wong She Duck would be irrefutable.

Heartened by Wong So, Kwai Ying agreed to take the stand again, and another girl from the Home, who recognized the picture of Wong She Duck as the man who had sold her, volunteered to testify against him.

With help from the staff of "920" and their attorneys the girls prepared thoroughly. Wong She Duck's counsel had discovered the power of Donaldina and Tien to fortify their witnesses, and had secured court orders barring their presence from the trial room. Donaldina accepted the news grimly, but said, "There is One higher than I Who will be present." She was needed in Chicago. She would go.

On April 31, two months after the first trial, Lorna and Esther accompanied the girls to court. A new judge, Walter C. Lindley, was to hear the case. Certain of Kwai Ying's claims were inadmissible a second time. But the government, having investigated the operation of the ring in China, offered new proof that supported the girls' assertions that they had been purchased by the same man in Hong Kong. They were met by the same "father" in Seattle. Both were identified as procurers who dealt with Wong She Duck.

Wong So took her chair, brushing her short hair behind one ear. She made her statements with vigor, and she stood up under fire. Moreover, she bore herself with a dignity that was unshakable. For three uncertain days tension stretched nerves taut. The press paid little notice until, on Thursday, May 2, Carolyn Anspacher summarized a sensational aspect of the trial on the back page of the *Chronicle*. The headline read: "Huge Profit Made in Selling Girls." The article said:

Traffic in Chinese slave girls brings enormous profits, according to the testimony of one of them before a jury in Federal Judge Walter C. Lindley's court yesterday.

Wong So, imported, she said, from China, told the story of how she brought only $500 "Hongkong money"—about $250 American—in China and was resold here for $4000.

She was the star witness in the second trial of Wong She Duck, for 25 years a hardware merchant; his wife, Kung She and two so-called women "capitalists" accused in dealing in slave girls.

That night the staff and many of the girls at "920" found it hard to sleep. On Friday morning Inspector Kuckein phoned to tell them the verdict was a resounding "guilty." Lorna wired the good news to Donaldina. Household routine was ignored, bed making and dusting waited, looms quieted, sewing machines stopped. Excited voices chattered and the three girls who had testified were hugged and kissed as heroines. A particular hush fell over the lunch table following prayers of thanksgiving.

The papers gave no play to the momentous decision. Headlines concerned the Great Depression: " 'Gimme Mobs' Fill Capitol." News stories featured plans of the Works Project Administration that promised jobs to the unemployed. Lorna wrote her family in Seattle, expressing the Home's joy, as well as her compassion for the convicted Chinese, at the trial's end:

May 3, 1935

Dearest Family,

Just a few lines to share with you our news. Inspector Kuckein called up a little while ago to say that the jury had just brought in the verdict in our case, and it is that all four defendants are guilty. The man gets two years in the penitentiary, $5000 fine, the women each a year and a day, and at the end of their sentences they will all be deported. It is dreadful to think of their fate—not so much their sentences, but just their going on in sin and darkness. But we do rejoice that justice at last has been done in this case.

. . . This judge has been very fair and clear in his rulings, and this morning his instructions to the jury were fine. The three girls were fine on the stand. I'm sure their demeanor impressed the jury, and they told their stories very clearly and convincingly. I think the defendants were expecting the verdict. One of the women came up Monday evening to see Auntie. Auntie was out, so she didn't stay, but the relative who came with her is a church member. He said she had repented, and wanted to confess. It might have gone better with her if she had confessed even at that late date, but the others wanted to stick it out, finally, and she did. As a matter of fact, all of them probably would have pled guilty if their attorneys had not urged them to go on with the trial. They negotiated secretly for some time.

This decision will have a far-reaching effect. Girls may hear of it, and learn that they can run away. The slave owners will be frightened and deterred from bringing more girls. And it will make the officials much more alert in checking up on them when they apply for admittance. It was pretty much of a blow to the Seattle office as formerly conducted, to have to admit that these three girls were falsely landed after examination there.

We feel quite limp now. We've been so tense, following the case day by day in court. There hasn't been time to do much else. We've wired Lo Mo the results. She is in Chicago now, will be in Pittsburg next week. . . .

Much, much Love,

LORNA

Wong She Duck's ring had included an estimated thirty persons who procured girls in China and distributed them in the United States. No one could calculate the number of others who had merchandised flesh to remote communities.

Months later the impact of the trial stirred public interest. In 1935 and 1936 several authors roused sympathy with sensational articles about "broken" or "trampled" blossoms and the waning slave traffic. The case evoked the far-reaching effects Lorna predicted; word had spread through the underground to imprisoned girls, convincing them they could escape; most importers decided penalties had grown too great to risk; and Immigration officers had tightened their scrutiny of possible impostors.

Distasteful as she found notoriety, Donaldina believed the Broken Blossoms case had exposed pernicious undercurrents of the slave trade in Chinese society as explicitly as the 1906 earthquake had revealed the rank cellars and passageways that tunneled under the quarter. Impressment continued in The City and more so in country settlements; bigamy among the Chinese remained common. But the tap root of the system was cut. The daughters of Cathay could believe that a ray from Liberty's torch in New York's harbor gleamed across the land to them.

After the fanfare of the famous trial and its fortunate outcome, Donaldina considered the next significant development of the year to be the visit of two Christian evangelist missionaries from China, the Misses Alice Lan and Betty Hu. The care of her little ones and the support of these missionaries in Chinatown must be her thrust in the short time left to her.

CHAPTER TWENTY

The Old Order Changeth

1934-1942

While the Broken Blossoms case was hanging fire, Lo Mo's sixty-fifth birthday had come and gone. She refused to allow the big celebration her family and friends wished, plunging instead into arrangements for the sixtieth anniversary of the Occidental Board's founding of the Mission Home, the "Lok Sup Jow." She called together committees from Presbyterial, Synodical, and Advisory Board, including such stalwarts as Julia Fraser, Mrs. McMeekin, and Mrs. Marshall. With Lorna chauffeuring, Donaldina drove all over the Bay Area to attend planning meetings. In May of 1934 large crowds came to "920" for events that spread over three days. Those who attended never forgot a series of tableaux, called "Sixty Years, Sixty Minutes," portraying the Home's history. As was true of the "pictured Years" in the Jubilee of 1920, many of the figures, including Lo Mo, Sergeant Manion, and "920"'s staff, played themselves.

A few weeks later Donaldina's birthday had come as an anticlimax, acknowledged only by a family party. Though the Board of National Missions recorded their Director's official retirement, they did not declare her post vacant, or ask her to move out of the corner room on the second floor. She continued her duties, gradually relinquishing responsibilities to Lorna Logan.

After some months she rented an apartment nearby on Clay Street. New letterheads appeared listing Donaldina Cameron, Special Director Chinese Case Work; Lorna Logan, Director; and Tien Fuh Wu, Chinese Associate. But everyone knew that Donaldina continued her long reign. Lorna, who revered her, and Tien, loyal since her childhood commitment, "Don't cry, Lo Mo. I help you," carried on in amity. Lorna was regarded as an extraordinary harmonizer, an adaptable woman who accepted the ideas and ways of those around her while quietly pursuing her own direction. She thoroughly enjoyed the Chinese, with whose customs she was familiar because of her sister, Florence Logan, a missionary to China. Rarely did Lorna ruffle Donaldina, though the two directors' duties often overlapped. But forthright Tien occasionally "caught it" from Lo Mo, as did others; for under the heavy load of instant life-and-death decisions, authority had become Donaldina's prerogative. It sometimes extended beyond responsibility.

When a young mother in Chinatown appealed to "920" to rescue her baby daughter, sold by her husband in Locke, near Sacramento, Donaldina set out with Lorna, Mae, and Hung Mui to search for the child. They found her in a disreputable hovel with a woman who refused to surrender her. Learning they must wait until the next day for legal help, the rescuers stayed overnight at the Y.W.C.A., where Lo Mo read the notice of a play she wanted to see. "I'll treat you tonight," she said gaily.

Intent on pleasing Lo Mo, Mae and Hung Mui slipped downtown and got tickets. Returning breathless as Donaldina entered the dining room, they held them up, crying, "Surprise!" Lo Mo's smile disappeared. Her face reddened with an angry blush. "I told you the play was my treat. This is the kind of thing one simply does not do!"

Dinner passed wordlessly, after which Donaldina picked up the check, uncontested, and with her back stiff, marched to the cashier. The play restored the spirit of fun. Next day the party placed the baby for whom they had come in a shelter until a court order for release was issued.

On clear days Donaldina sometimes found time to walk up the hill from her apartment and look across the Bay at the blue water patched by fog shadow and laced with froth. Few San Franciscans could afford pleasure boating, but steamers carried travelers and cargo under the new bridges being built, and ferry boats, like over-sized white gulls, plied the Bay up to Sausalito and across to the East Bay.

"Don't men do wonderful things?" Donaldina marveled, as she looked at the huge pillars and cables of the Golden Gate Bridge and at the Bay Bridge's spans, some cantilevered, leaping toward the Oakland shore.

But her growing Chinese family seemed the greatest wonder of all. She foresaw that as the Broken Blossoms case had heralded the end of the terrible slave traffic, need for the Home would diminish. About twenty-five girls still lived at "920." Some would remain for months, a few for years, before they could marry or make their own living. Others still held in bondage might seek the Mission. But their number would dwindle, because orphanages and schools were beginning to admit Chinese children. "The old order changeth, giving place to the new." To better ways, she hoped. And to buoy her own spirits she thought, my father made a new beginning at sixty, and so can I!

While she lent strong support to her staff as they made the transition toward community work, the "Mother of Chinatown" devoted many of her days to visiting, counseling, and advising her grown daughters and their families. She had become "Ah Pau" (grandmother) to a second generation with half-grown children of their own. Parents took boys and girls to Grandmother's house after school to give her drawings or show her "A" papers or bring her valentines. "Ah Pau" served tea and sometimes her favorite cookies, thin sweet rounds that her own Mae Wong made best.

"Lo Mo could talk to anyone," people said, "the littlest child, the most important adult."

Each day Donaldina looked forward to her mail. Letters came from China where her girls from the Home served as Bible Women, teachers in Christian schools, nurses, secretaries, dressmakers, and store clerks. They had become wives of farmers and business and professional men, in Canada and Mexico, as well as in the United States. But what had happened to daughters from whom she did not hear, the girls who had not responded to her in the Home? And where were the lost ones who were bodily stolen or legally taken from her? Lost not only to her but to all eternity? She would pray for them. Somewhere they might still live and be saved. Some planted; others reaped.

She thought of the series of feature articles about the Home and its work recently printed in the *San Francisco News*. Three thousand girls rescued by her, the writer claimed. Who knew? She had never counted. She wished reporters would stop romanticizing her as a "living legend" and crediting her with courage and resourcefulness beyond human ken. She had told them over and over it was not her work! It was always God's work; and dedicated people had stood four square behind her through the past forty-two years.

Her associates and her daughters still carried on. Dr. Bessie had finished her internship, refused an attractive professional offer, and had come back to supervise the new Baby Cottage, although she had recovered only recently from polio. Fortunately she had escaped being crippled. Her return seemed providential. The Home, built with funds contributed by agencies, organizations, and individuals, neared completion at 740 Thirty-seventh Avenue in the Richmond district of The City. Both Dr. Bessie and the Board wished to name it in Lo Mo's honor, but on her insistence it was christened "Mei Lun Yuen," which means "Beautiful Garden of Family Relationships."

Donaldina's eyes filled with tears as she remembered a slave girl's share in the new home. She had borne a baby boy some months after coming to "920," and not long afterward had earned $1.50. One dollar she wrapped in red paper and sent as her son's gift for his care.

To further changes in the work during the late thirties Donaldina responded with mixed feelings. The fine Ming Quong Home was nearly ten miles from Oakland's Chinatown, and as the girls had grown older, the distance prevented their entering fully into life of the Chinese Presbyterian Church; they were cut off from many social contacts, which were important if they were to come into their cultural heritage and meet eligible suitors.

Mills College needed to expand its campus and in exchange for the Ming Quong building gave the Board of National Missions a choice corner lot in Oakland at Ninth and Fallon Streets, near Lake Merritt, and a large rambling house on a four-acre country plot near Los Gatos. Donaldina approved the transfers

Lo Mo, near the end of her career, with Hope Chow, about 1931.

and admired Oakland's graceful new building with curved Chinese roof, and the blue porcelain Chinese "Foo Dogs" on guard by the steps. Forty girls of all ages moved in.

In 1934 a small group of Ming Quong girls, threatened with tuberculosis, had been transferred to a rented house, Sunshine Cottage, in the warm dry climate of Los Gatos. After the Mills exchange they and a few small orphaned boys took over the larger country quarters with Mary Bankes, Lucille Reber, a new recruit, and Hung Mui Chew in charge. Mrs. Jun Bok Lee came weekly from Oakland to teach Chinese tradition and the language.

During the late thirties fewer girls were residing in "920." Donaldina was confronted with pressure from her community, as well as her denomination, to surrender the building to other uses. She petitioned for a new and smaller residence. Her Board suggested a rented house. She strongly resisted the idea. Chinatown interests at last broke the deadlock by reminding her that she had once agreed that "920" would serve admirably as a school. They presented evidence of great need for larger quarters for the Chinese language school. For the dwindling Mission operation Donaldina's Board agreed to build a new Home, then reversed themselves and insisted on renting smaller quarters. She had no choice but to capitulate. It was a bitter disappointment. Almost at the same moment her young director received an offer to spend a year in China, where she hoped to learn the language more fully and steep herself in the Chinese way of life. In that time of stress Donaldina wrote Lorna, vacationing in Seattle, a rambling letter, revealing her feelings with a freedom she allowed herself only with intimates:

February 24th, '37

Lorna dearest;

. . . I do not think we have done wrong in continuing to plead for a NEW building instead of attempting to make shift in an old rented building that would not fit our most urgent needs.

What sorrow of heart (and I fear on my own part, sin of heart) would have been saved if only those most closely concerned with our Chinese work had made a different approach to this entire situation;

but "there is a land of beginning again" from which no one is excluded! And I've set my sails for that happy shore!

About your going to China Lorna dear, I talked last night at very peaceful "Staff Meeting" and I felt that the concensus of opinion was for your trip to China this year, since your wonderful friend Mrs. Brooks is ready to finance you. . . .

Of course Lorna it is going to be difficult to spare you, and humanly speaking my courage fails me at the thought! But 'God IS ABLE' I've proved that beyond any shadow of doubt. We can have May this year, and she will be more help and comfort to both Tien and me than ANY OTHER person we could ever find to help us carry on while you . . . are away.

. . . I've talked to my precious sisters about this plan, and they, as ever, wish to put this work and my convenience before their own heart's desires, they love you, Lorna, and fully realize that you are not thinking of running away to China for a happy personal jaunt, but to better prepare for the great task of making God's love known to our Chinese people in this country. Your own dear sister's life, bears witness to the vital importance of doing what we have longed to have you do, even if only for one year. My three months in Canton were worth all the preceding ten years that I had spent in this local Chinatown! Let us continue to pray about it Lorna, I know you do.

Finally our decision rests with our Board. . . .

Dr. Van Nuys preached one of his unforgettable sermons last Sabbath on Nehemiah's struggle to rebuild the wall of Jerusalem, he made it so clear that building for God always means a battle with the forces of unbelief and unrighteousness, and that forces without and within the Church of God assail our faith and courage. . . .

So Lorna dear if only we can ALL set ourselves the great task anew, of "earnestly repairing" what sin, misunderstanding and human frailty had destroyed within the circle of our own field of service for God, and in our personal contacts with lives we touch, I am sure that "our labor will not be in vain" and that this precious work of salvaging lost lives will go forward under new, different conditions, but with the old spirit of faith and love to guide and bless.

It was cheering to read that you are "stepping out" once more! Don't you need some more garments in which to deck yourself? I suppose that selubrious Washington is already bursting with spring loveliness ! ! ! ! ! !

Ever faithfully your,

Lo Mo

Having worked through her feelings of protest, self-justification, and penitence, Donaldina, with Tien's help, supervised limited community services for a year and a half. Lorna spent a year in China, then Mae was absent for four years, studying at the Los Angeles Bible Institute and graduating in 1942.

In May of 1939, Tien, Lorna, Esther Fung, Dorothy Calecod, the housekeeper, and six remaining residents moved from "920" into two upstairs flats at 144 Wetmore Street, above a garage extending the full length of the building. The "slumgullion closet," a repository for odds and ends, was emptied, personal belongings were packed, and the ring of keys, grown heavier with each new lock installed over the years, was surrendered.

At last Donaldina's responsibilities to the Home were discharged. Other obligations waited. Her three older sisters, now more than eighty years old, needed her care, especially the artistic Helen, who was frail and kept much to herself. After forty-five years in San Francisco, Donaldina forsook her "good grey city" to live with the Misses Cameron in Oakland.

On her seventieth birthday, July 26, 1939, her Chinese family called her back for a party. For the first time in her nearly half century with them she permitted a public celebration. As always, Annie insisted on making the cake, but it was so large she had to use the pans and oven of a neighborhood baker. At the banquet with her own and her adopted families Donaldina listened to accounts of remarkable accomplishments at the four centers where the work still continued. Two branches of Ming Quong Home, at Oakland and Los Gatos, sheltered and trained young Chinese girls and boys; Mei Lun Yuen cared for babies and preschoolers in The City; and from the Mission on Wetmore Street, Chinatown felt new and benevolent influences. A new Chung Mei Home in El Cerrito, near Berkeley, built when their former property had been bought for the site of a Bay Bridge approach, had recently dedicated a mural to Donaldina in its gymnasium entrance, and she gladly claimed some of the home's residents and graduates as her stepsons.

"I am glad I did not settle for matrimony," she said to her dinner partner.

"Why not?" he asked, startled. "Does marriage seem unattractive?"

Donaldina laughed, thinking of the men she had loved, and of the men who had tried to pay her court in recent years. "Not at all. I just meant that I could not have had all this. If I had my life to live over again I'd do it the same way. Only I'd be better prepared."

Though she visited San Francisco infrequently, she kept in close touch with the Mission's work. In 1938 the last slave girl to enter "920" at first resisted the Home's religious teachings. More than a year later Donaldina learned of her decision to become a Christian, and that she had turned down a suitor who wanted her as his second wife. She rejoiced at this proof that power to change lives still flowed through the Mission.

The next annual report indicated that power was channeling into new directions. Lorna had written:

The type of work carried on by the Mission Home these more than sixty years has not been primarily aimed at leadership training. It has dealt with slave girls, delinquents, and the maladjusted of all sorts, the poorest material, it would seem, from which to develop Christian leadership. That there have been results in the development of Christian leaders is something to make us humbly wonder anew at the love and power of God, and the dynamic effect of His gospel.

Now as one phase of the Mission Home's work seems to be ended, and we are entering upon a somewhat different program, it is interesting to note that there are now in service the following who have come through the Home into places of Christian leadership: . . ." [She listed fifteen names of teachers, missionaries, a doctor, and community leaders.]

Lorna and her staff needed all possible cooperation to tackle Chinatown's new problems. Population had remained fairly stable because of traffic to and from the Orient. But when the Japanese invaded China, refugees poured into The City: few returned to their native land. A survey showed that in the tight little quarter an average of 20.4 persons used one bathroom, and 12.3 persons shared one kitchen. Men still outnumbered women, by a ratio of three to one.

While the staff of "920" pressed for changed conditions, Lorna's report stated, ". . . we must also be ready to help those involved in the sins and sorrows that are a natural outcome of the present system." A further conflict lay unresolved:

Racial relationships remain an acute problem. The violence of the days of the Kearny riots [in the late nineteenth century] has given place to a patronizing surface enthusiasm for the Chinese that just as firmly keeps them from living beyond the crowded confines of China-town, and from employment outside the Chinese community except as cooks. On the other hand, the Chinese community is so large and self-sufficient that to a large extent its members have almost no di-rect contact with Americans. . . .

A familiar hymn ran through Donaldina's mind, "In Christ There Is No East or West." Lorna was one who could live that spirit. The Mission's new labors lay in the right hands. That knowledge comforted her, for she found it necessary to relin-quish all close association with the work. Helen became acutely ill, and died, and the three remaining sisters, Donaldina, Annie, and Catharine, decided to move to the Peninsula, nearer Sister Jessie Bailey and niece, Caroline, in Los Gatos, and their nephew Allan Cameron and his family, in Palo Alto. In Palo Alto they bought a large lot on which stood a small grey cottage, at 1020 California Avenue, across from open fields. Annie and Donal-dina would occupy the existing house, and they would build a redwood cottage for Catharine, who had gathered numbers of stray cats she could not bear to abandon. Before they moved, on June 7, 1942, Donaldina attended what she expected to be her last official function, the naming of "920" in her honor. Much against her inclination, she had yielded to community pressure.

Dear old "Auntie" Wing, or T'sang T'sun, who had shared in laying the cornerstone of the building in 1873, and for the post-earthquake building in 1907, took her place beside Lo Mo. In an emotional service, Lo Mo's girlhood friend, Evelyn Browne Bancroft, read a scripture, Dr. John Creighton, minister of old First Church, offered prayer, Miss Donaldina Lew sang, and Sergeant Manion talked about Miss Cameron's contributions to Chinatown. Dr. Ezra Allen Van Nuys presided, and other repre-sentatives of the quarter and of the Presbyterian denomination paid her tribute. Donaldina expressed hope that the spirit of past commitments might prosper again in future use of the historic place. A tablet bearing the title "Donaldina Cameron House" was placed inside the entrance of "920." After the war a bronze plate with the name was mounted outside on the corner of the building by Mrs. Lloyd and several other members of the former Board. The large meeting room long called The Chapel was christened Culbertson Hall in memory of Lo Mo's valiant predecessor.

At the age of seventy-five Donaldina and her two sisters moved into what she expected to be the anonymity of retirement. But like most people whose charm and vitality have made them famous, Donaldina continued to attract both friends and strangers.

CHAPTER TWENTY-ONE

Durable Fires
1941-1959

During the anxious years of world wars Donaldina's sympathies circled the globe. She grieved for suffering friends in China, under attack since 1937; and when the Battle of Britain began, her Scottish blood fired with righteous wrath. She had been at the point of applying for United States citizenship, but decided to retain her loyalty to the British crown as a gesture of moral support to a beleaguered people. The break would have been hard on her sisters, for Annie still referred to the Fourth of July as "the day we don't celebrate." Donaldina beseeched God to restore peace to the land of her heritage, and, in 1941 when the United States joined the Allies, to uphold a right spirit in the country she had served. War, she believed, was wrong. Yet, when people she loved were endangered, she wanted them protected.

Other sad conflicts distressed her. Thousands of Japanese, some of them her daughters and their families, were trucked off to detention centers in California and Nevada. They were allowed little time to order their affairs or to store their possessions. Word filtered back that the centers amounted to concentration camps with only subsistence facilities. Donaldina deplored the attitudes of revenge and contempt expressed against the Japanese. Some Caucasians who came to Chinatown jeered at all Orientals. In defense, some Chinese wore buttons printed with the words, "I am Chinese."

Unable to play an active role, Donaldina found the war years trying. As always, when stopped by dilemma, she looked for fresh opportunity. She could help her sisters be happy. They liked living in Palo Alto and enjoyed landscaping a place of their own. Nephew Allan gave them initial help, and with a fine gardener, Giulio Gamba, they planted the front yard with an olive tree and three birches, each named for a sister. The property was called "Heatherbroom," because of the Scotch broom and heather along the front walk. Roses from the Oakland home edged the path; in bloom, they were noted among "the sights of California Avenue." The sisters chose a weeping willow tree and a pine for the back yard, bright annuals in beds near the house, and Shasta daisies along the driveway. The little grey and brown cottages looked as vital as the white-haired sisters who tended them.

Though the war drove prices up before ceilings and rations were imposed, Donaldina faced no money problems. Because friends insisted on offering gifts to supplement her meager missionary pension, she finally confided that her welfare and that of her sisters had been provided for by friends.

Some years earlier, when she was on a speaking tour in Southern California, Mr. and Mrs. Cecil Gamble, of the Proctor and Gamble company, had invited her to become a house guest in their Pasadena home at 4 Westmoreland.[1] Always a missionary-minded family, the Gambles had entertained Donaldina often, had supported her work, and admired her selfless life. Then they wished to reward her personally. One sunny morning at the breakfast table they presented a surprise, a substantial gift of stocks, which they hoped would secure her future support and that of her maiden sisters. The stocks' value grew, and the dividends provided a comfortable income.

Though she could have afforded more luxury, Donaldina lived simply, sometimes protesting she ought to sell all she owned and send the money to China. Upholstered occasional chairs and her favorite wickers circled the small living room. She considered a piano, a fireplace, and the blue Chinese rug from her room at "920" elegance enough. Over a doorway into the hall she hung a wooden plaque that read, "Yet Will I Rejoice."

No matter how bad the news or the weather might be, Donal-

---

[1] Later opened to the public as a landmark of the 1900 period.

dina reflected cheerfulness. When she went to market, sales-people on California Avenue or El Camino Real brightened. She liked to walk along El Camino Real, "the Highway of the King," because it was the route of Father Serra and the early Spanish mission fathers. At a favorite bakery, noticing that a salesgirl's hands were always cold, she said, "Let me warm them" and chafed them in both her own. The service became a regular ceremony.

The friendly Cameron sisters attracted a great deal of company. Devoted friends ran errands for Donaldina during the war, especially when gas was short and public transportation poor. After the war, people assumed that her advancing age was beginning to limit her. She curtly refuted the idea, walking the half mile to J J and F's market, and trudging home with her full shopping bag. If she accepted someone's offer to market for her, the good Samaritan might discover she had picked up cake or a plant for herself, or to deliver as a present to another of Donaldina's friends. Though Annie and Donaldina were fond of animals, they did not share what they silently considered Kathie's excessive devotion to the seventeen cats she was said to own. Donaldina, with her "love for every living thing," dropped a few grains of rice for a "dear little mouse" who escaped the cats. At sunset she often crossed the street with a handful of grass for the cow in the field, but being afraid of cows, she stood behind the pasture fence.

Caroline Bailey, a librarian in San Jose, who lived with her widowed mother, Jessie, in Los Gatos, was almost a daughter to her aunts, enjoying their wit and always ready to help. Her voice so resembled her Aunt Dolly's that telephone callers often mistook her for Donaldina. She inherited the expressive eyes and well-cut features of her Scottish forebears, and shared their close-knit loyalty and their talent for happiness.

For Donaldina the decade between 1940 and 1950 was marked with severe losses. Many of her foster sons served in the armed forces, a number with distinction. Some were killed in battle, and because Lo Mo or Auntie Tien was named as next of kin, they received the tragic telegrams that began "We regret to in-form you. . . ." A rose garden was planted at Chung Mei Home in memory of its fallen sons.

In 1945 Jessie died; in 1947 Catharine, and three years later Annie, at the age of ninety-six, leaving Donaldina, at eighty-one the youngest and last surviving of the seven children. Dear though all her family had been to her, the loss of Annie, her second mother, caused the deepest bereavement of her life. But "she lived very near her dead," her friends said of her, not in morbidity but enriched by their memory and gladdened by a firm anticipation of joining them in the future. All of her family had been buried in Evergreen Cemetery in Los Angeles, and she provided plots for herself and for Caroline on one side of her and Tien on the other. Asked if having so many dear ones "on the other side" made her anxious to hurry across, she replied, "No, I am more familiar with things here."

"When I die," she said, "sing 'Oh Love that Will Not Let Me Go,' and send only a few red roses to recall those last lines, '. . . and from the ground there blossoms red/life that will end-less be.' " She added, "In the next life I shall ask for the gift of song." Lacking that gift in this life, she had never been able to master the Chinese language with its many intonations, though she understood much that she heard.

Years later she wrote on the subject of immortality:

How greatly blessed we all are to have our deep faith and love centered in that ultimate home to which we all believe we are travel-ing while we are here. Having many dear family connections over there, it is a happy inspiring thought to know that we are journeying toward reunion with them. And in the meantime, we do love this beautiful, wonderful world in which we are now sojourning.

Brother Allan's widow Lucy had remarried and been wid-owed again. Partially paralyzed, she lived in the corner house, next door to Donaldina. One of Lucy's sons provided nursing care, and another son, Allan, and his wife and son, Allan, who lived only a few blocks away were always on call. But Donaldina felt a "sacred trust" to do for her what she could. Tien com-plained that she wore herself out and refused to accept invitations away from home because of Lucy, who lived until Donaldina was nearly ninety.

At Christmas the two Allans trimmed the evergreen on Donaldina's back lawn with lights whose glow was visible from the homes of their mother and aunt.

Through her niece, Caroline, her nephews Allan, Kenneth, and Donald Cameron and their children, and her friends in her "beautiful, wonderful world" Donaldina responded to vigorous younger lives. She retained her ability to charm people of any age. When calling at a crowded mental hospital, she persuaded case workers to let her use their office so that she might have a private visit with a dear friend who was a patient.

A witty family of fellow Scots, Dr. Alexander Miller, a young Stanford professor of theology, his wife, Jean, and their son, David, became part of Donaldina's Peninsula family. Dr. Miller died, but "dear Jean" and "dear David" remained devoted to her for the remainder of her life.

She regularly saw or heard from Lorna, Tien, or Mae, and through them followed the Mission's work. After V-J Day in 1945, Chinatown had received an influx of war brides from the Orient, sometimes happy and hopeful, often bewildered or frightened. The Mission's staff opened its arms to them as Donaldina had embraced her forsaken slave girls. Within a short time the counseling service at 144 Wetmore Street found itself being called upon for more than could be provided. In 1947 the Board decided to resume use of Donaldina Cameron House for Presbyterian programs, and add staff. Hip Wo Language School found space in the Methodist Church. In 1947 a group-work program began; in 1949, after remodeling of the building, Lorna, Mae and Tien moved back. Christian education and case work were undertaken. Donaldina was enormously gratified. A proper restoration.

For the first time in "920" 's 76-year history a man, vigorous F. S. Dick Wichman, joined the staff. He and his wife, Lois, and two little children, John and Anne, occupied one of several apartments remodeled from bedrooms on the third floor.

Dick, an enthusiastic young minister, who for five years had been program director of the Chinese Y.M.C.A., opened a new

*Richard Hee, a foster grandson; Dick Wichman, director of
"920" 's social service center, named Donaldina Cameron House;
and Lo Mo, 1953.*

*Lorna Logan of the happy
laugh, Lo Mo's successor
and head of the Christian
Service Department of
the reorganized "920."*

division in the House under the Department of City and Industrial Work of the Board of National Missions. Concurrently, as collegiate pastor of the Chinese Presbyterian Church around the corner on Stockton Street, he brought back the intimate relationship of local church and Mission. Lorna retained direction of an autonomous social service division renamed the Christian Service Department.

Donaldina attended an official open house of the reinstated "920" with a feeling of welcoming her prodigals home. She liked and trusted Dick and was pleased that the Board of National Missions had expanded the work. As Dick developed his ideas, she neither demanded nor criticized. She advised when asked, and Dick often read her endorsement or disapproval by implication. When she addressed him as "My dear Dick," she liked what he was doing. When she began "My dear Dr. Wichman," he knew she withheld her blessing.

Through strong leadership the work prospered. Dick, Lorna, Mae, and Tien lived and worked in amity under one roof, making the wider services of the House known and influential in Chinatown. But all were firm individuals, and there were times of disagreement and hurt feelings when Donaldina was asked for counsel.

Children in Chinatown knew Miss Cameron's name, a household word, and they enjoyed what had become an adventurous legend, painted in murals on the hallway of the House. But Dick regretted that they did not know Lo Mo as a person. So he asked her to tape a message that he could play for a junior high group.

"She'll know how to talk to these kids," he said.

Donaldina did not like gadgetry and replied that she would prefer to come in person and talk. She would speak for five minutes. At the appointed time children packed Culbertson Hall, but Miss Cameron did not appear. Dick, always resourceful on stage, led the crowd in songs and told stories while they waited. Knowing she was subject to headaches, he feared she might have canceled her plan at the last minute. But a late train had caused the delay, and when Lo Mo stepped onto the platform where, at meetings, she had so many times shared in making life-and-death decisions for this House, she looked into a hundred and fifty friendly Chinese faces.

She realized that once again she might influence children on the threshold of life. What a wonderful moment. In her melodious voice she began to tell stories of young Chinese she had known, some their parents and grandparents, who made choices and grew up to live with the results. With rising excitement her listeners followed the words of this Pied Piper on their own hillside.

"What are you going to do with your life?" she asked them.

She led them back two thousand years and more to see children from the Scriptures: Joseph, Samuel, Miriam, and Jesus— alert, active, choosing the highest loyalties.

"What are you going to do with *your* life?"

She told them true stories about Auntie Wu and Miss Mae. They laughed at "my saucy little Tien who learned so quickly," and "my dear bright Mae." Donaldina spoke of brave children and happy children and of the wonder of loving one another in the Christian family.

As her promised five minutes stretched into sixty minutes, she talked as an affectionate Ah Pau (grandmother), a bold adventuress, a comrade who charmed and challenged her own into their future. Not a rustle disturbed the hall. No child wriggled or sighed during the hour.

"What will you do with *your* life?"

CHAPTER TWENTY-TWO

Yet Will I Rejoice
1959-1968

Donaldina often thought about her daughters' choices. Mae Wong had served her people wonderfully over the years. After she finished her schooling at Wheaton Academy in Illinois, she had wanted to become a nurse, so she could take her religion and healing skills to China. "But Lo Mo needed me," she said, and postponed her training until a future time, a time that never came. Instead she had expanded the work of the Industrial Department, and later joined the Christian Service staff. She was not wholly content. Donaldina recalled how, soon after World War II, Mae observed bewildered war brides and refugees pouring into The City. After giving an immigrant woman who had failed in her suicide attempt the courage to live, Mae had said, "I don't need to go to China. God has brought all these girls here. Now I am satisfied, Lo Mo. I know that I am spending my life where God wants me."

Always Mae tested her decisions by Lo Mo's guidelines: Is this what you really want to do? Can you choose anything better? Have you prayed about it?

In 1954 Mae decided on an heroic stand. After changed laws permitted Chinese to become American citizens, she confessed that she had entered the United States illegally a quarter of a century earlier, and asked the court's mercy. Her plea was honored; she was naturalized, and led a community "Confessional" movement of Chinese immigrants without papers. She discovered shocking numbers had cowered in lifelong fear of being discovered and deported. Encouraged by her example and sympathetic coaching, hundreds came under the protection of the American flag.

Donaldina would have liked to help Mae, and she could have filled several days a week with meetings, speaking dates, luncheons, and teas. But she avoided most, for high blood pressure made her miserable when she came under stress or grew overtired. Occasionally she braved the consequences. She attended the dedication of a stained glass window depicting her and Dr. William Speer, pioneer of the work in Chinatown, in the Stewart Chapel of San Francisco Theological Seminary in San Anselmo. And she enjoyed special events in Los Gatos Ming Quong Home. When the need for an orphanage had ended, that home became a center for emotionally disturbed children.

When Tien Wu retired in 1952, Donaldina gave her Catharine's cottage across the drive. Because cordial Tien loved to talk about Lo Mo and "920," guests or reporters were deflected to her. Occasionally Donaldina granted interviews. At ninety-four she said:

I had such dear, dear friends among the Chinese. We had so much private, secret cooperation from the right living, right thinking Chinese. I take no credit to myself. I did have one gift which I poured into my life—LOVE. I'd been loved since childhood, and I offered love to those who needed it. The Chinatown I knew is no longer. In many ways, despite its evil, it was admirable and appealing and very romantic. I have something of a dowager's love of old San Francisco.

At ninety-eight, queried about her cloak-and-dagger ventures, she minimized them. "Oh yes, there was that side of it. Things got into the newspaper. But it was the work that was important. I don't like epitaphs!" she added sternly. *"The work* is what I want people to know."

Members of Lo Mo's adopted family she had always with her. In order to see loved faces and to enjoy cherished scenes, she covered every inch of her living room walls with pictures: a painting of Scottish moors, a prized photograph of her mother, one of Annie, others of relatives, and scores of her Chinese family and their children, grandchildren, and great grandchildren. As new snapshots and photos arrived, she filled the mantel,

Lo Mo's grown "daughters," left to right, Ah Lon, Tien Wu,
Ah Ching, Ah Tye.

Donaldina's "dear, bright Mae Wong," who found her place. "Now I know I am spending my life where God wants me."

"Auntie" Tien Wu pouring tea at a church social function.

the tables, every surface. Cherubic Chinese babies smiled at dignified Old World Scots and American friends.

Memories were renewed by a continual flow of visitors. Virginia Borland, daughter of Attorney Robert Borland, who had served the Home for so many years, often called to see her. Donaldina asked for a picture of Virginia in Chinese costume at the age of four, when she first came to play with Lo Mo's Chinese daughters. They recalled later times together. For more than thirty years after Borland's death Donaldina praised his effectiveness and loyalty to her work.

Borland had viewed her with an almost worshipful admiration. He was always willing to put other matters aside to go to her aid, postponing appointments with paying clients, canceling parties at the last minute. Mrs. Borland confessed to Donaldina, "For many years I've been devoted to you, but I hated you when I was young. I was jealous of you!" she said. "You came first with my husband."

Donaldina tucked her hands in her sleeves in the Chinese manner. "Oh, just a little missionary?"

The Borlands had realized that Lo Mo gave so much of herself that she needed friends to renew her enthusiasm. They always attended parties at the Home in formal dress, she in long skirts and he in white tie and tails. One evening a band played Scottish airs to please Miss Cameron and her sisters, leading off with "The Campbells Are Coming." Annie was indignant, and Borland stopped the playing, explaining that to a Cameron the song was tantamount to playing "Marching Through Georgia" at a Confederate ball. He later told a friend. "I don't know the Cameron men, but if they are anything like the Cameron women, I wouldn't want to march into battle against them."

When Borland died in 1933, Donaldina's grief was such that she could scarcely walk by his office, and she held the mystical belief that he helped her "from the other side" to solve a difficult case. When she was eighty-eight she made the 120-mile trip by bus from Palo Alto to San Rafael to visit his widow during her illness, bringing comfort and some nourishing bird's nest soup.

Inspector Manion's daughter, Agnes, who became Sister Mary

Clement of the Sisters of Mercy, also held a warm place in Donaldina's circle. She recalled many hours of play in the Home while her father conferred with Miss Cameron. In her teens Agnes had talked with her about dedicating her life to the Church, and at her graduation Donaldina stepped for the first time across the threshold of a Catholic church. She went again when Sister Mary Clement took her vows. On his death bed Donaldina's father had exacted a promise that she would never enter a "Popish" church, for he remembered tales of persecution trials in Scotland. But Donaldina felt that if he had known the Inspector and other fine Catholics, he could have been freed of his bitterness, as she was. Word of Manion's death so crushed her that she went to bed for the day.

She was pleased with news of the second marriage of two Chinese friends, Mrs. Wok Jun Lee, the teacher who for years had taught Chinese culture at the Tooker and Ming Quong Homes, and Mr. Linn, "a delightful man," widower of Ida Lee, also a teacher and musician in the Homes. The bride hesitated, because Chinese widows rarely remarry. But Mr. Linn persuaded her that she "should be proud to be loved." He had first known her at the Tooker Home, when, at Ida's request, she entertained him while he waited for his date. When she had run out of conversation, she served him a plate of grapes.

As she grew older, Donaldina declined to see all but her relatives and closest friends. She turned down an offer of a dear friend to bring a bagpiper to play for her. "I yearn to hear the pipes," she said, "but I have not the emotional strength to stand it." She sent her love "to enfold you," adding, "how much your constancy and love do help me you cannot fathom."

Tien Wu hovered near, dusting the house, tending her as faithfully as Lo Mo would allow. Donaldina permitted only what she could not manage herself. She wanted to do the helping. "Allow me the comfort and privilege of sharing your life's difficulties," she cried to a friend, "And, oh, my dear, I hope the day will hold for you some of the peace and happiness our Father wills for us all!"

The habit of looking for alternatives when desires were

blocked served her well. At the age of ninety-one she wrote to Lorna Logan, who regularly corresponded, phoned, or visited her:

Earlier today I was thinking how very much I would like to have a really quiet good long visit with you, when we might speak freely, and at length about the dear Chinese people whom we both love . . . now comes your dear note, which you need not have felt called upon to write! But I am glad to have [it]. . . .

Your message gives me a clearer insight into your life of so MANY problems, and great opportunities dear Lorna; but it must sometimes be somewhat bewildering and oft-times wearying!

Recently the conviction has been very definitely laid upon my heart that PRAYER is my greatest, and still available, opportunity to help with the mission so dear to my heart, for our Chinese people here and in China.

It seems hard to be unable to take any active part but Prayer CAN be active, and is so vital!

Later she said, "The spiritual life is a tremendous reality to me. I've lived it. I've seen it." She did not complain about her growing frailty; she alluded to limitations deprecatingly or with humor.

Today I am supposed to be "hors de combat" (and I really was, during the early part of this day) but one or two urgent matters, which could not well be sidetracked pressed me to arise! Now stimulated by black coffee and toast, I am getting two or three letters off my mind; my (not too serious) but limiting infirmities (!!) make visitors difficult!

Or she wrote, "Today I have fully 'arisen from my ashes'—the mental and physical 'slump' of the past few days." More and more often in her letters or telephone conversations she said, "Dear Caroline was here yesterday," or "Caroline will be here soon." To a friend insistent about sewing for her, she said gently, "I hope you won't. Caroline takes such pleasure in selecting my clothes." Unobtrusively, in the family's loyal tradition, her niece and nephew stood by.

Occasionally the old independence flared. A new friend told Donaldina of an attachment for her telephone which amplified

*Donaldina Cameron, at age 91 in 1960, loving and teaching
a little one, to the end.*

sound. She was pleased and consented to have it installed. The friend ordered the service and made the mistake of paying the charge of $12 for a year as a birthday present. Donaldina refused to let the telephone representative into the house. Wearing the old granite expression, she said, "I don't need it!"

Often when she knew of a friend in trouble she "longed greatly to send someone who could bring comfort and reassurance of God's care . . . ," and asked her former colleagues to take messages and gifts for her.

"Dolly frankly loved material things," Caroline said, explaining her. She gave princely gifts, gorgeous Chinese robes, exquisite jewelry, pottery, carvings. Because Donaldina had never earned more than $100 a month, the recipients realized she was bestowing her own presents. When a friend tried to return a fine jade ring, Donaldina cried, wounded, "Dear friend, do you think that I would give you anything that I didn't value for myself?"

Yet she never hesitated to recruit for her Homes' needs. When friends were disposing of furniture, she remarked, "I lay covetous eyes on that kitchen table."

Donaldina was proud of "920" 's continued witness. In May of 1965, Lorna Logan testified on an immigration bill before a House of Representatives committee, in Washington, D.C. She urged revision of the law, which long had discriminated against Chinese. In December a bill was passed which eliminated the national quota system under which, since 1943, only 105 Chinese per year had been admitted. The new law allowed 20,000 per year from any country, without regard to race or national origin.

That same year Lorna, her sister, Florence, and Mae Wong moved from busy "920" into apartments. Lo Mo wrote a motherly letter:

It is difficult to bring myself to think of you, Lorna dear, and Mae, living elsewhere instead of at the old "Mission Home", but in so many ways, I am quite sure, it will be less strenuous life and better for your health. Already Mae has written how quiet her little apartment is, so soothing to her.

Of you, Florence, dear, I am very often thinking, . . . (specially when I am getting my own simple little meals here at home) and am wondering how you are faring as "chief cook" for yourself and Lorna in your apartment home.

But it will take you all three some time to become fully adjusted. . . . However, our lives here on this dear old planet are ever prone to change, and so I trust you will already be feeling at home in your recently acquired residence.

I am truly thankful Mae is in the same building because I would not feel quite happy if she were living by herself in an unfamiliar apartment house.

Until she was ninety-five years old Donaldina claimed her memory was good. But by the age of ninety-seven she admitted she had taken to making lists. Her hearing dimmed, she grew frail, but she looked often at the motto above the hall doorway, "Yet Will I Rejoice," and her eyes, now faded to light blue, shone.

"I did not want to live so long," she said. "Ninety-seven is a ghastly age! But my Creator blessed me. I enjoy people." She retained her keen interest in the Mission. In her ninety-eighth year she wrote to Lorna:

I am very happy to have your very interesting account of the opportunities that are constantly opening up for Christian service among the poorer Chinese of our community. . . .

It is a very real comfort to me to have had this letter, Lorna, dear . . . and I am going to hold you closer than ever to my heart and ask our unfailing help from above to strengthen you in spirit, mind and body for the many, often difficult problems, you are trying to meet.

May I just say a word from my heart that I think you have the personality, and I am quite sure you have the mentality, and I believe you have the spirituality, all of which combined make you a great blessing to our Chinese community.

So much of my heart is still there between Sacramento and Clay Streets and between Powell and Kearney, in particular.

. . . So often every day my mind travels to that bit of San Francisco where I spent so many vitally interesting and often very anxious years of my life.

Nearly every letter included a "love gift" of money for the work, to "do with as thou wilt. . . ."

Though Donaldina suffered painful arthritis in her knees, she rarely complained except to say that "age limitations are such a grievous hindrance—I cannot do for those I love the personal things that my heart prompts." She talked with Tien about going into a retirement home. Tien discouraged her, telling her she had for too long lived alone and independently to be happy in an institution.

Donaldina protested, "After all, I lived in an institution many years."

"Yes," Tien replied, "But *you* were the boss!"

On Donaldina's ninety-eighth birthday her little house could scarcely hold the flowers that arrived. Her excitement grew with every bouquet, every florist's delivery. Opening a box from Hawaii, she held up a pikaki lei. "Oh do smell this wonderful fragrance," she said, passing it around to friends who had dropped in with good wishes. "Sit down. Let's have some refreshments."

Tien set out small glasses of chilled grape juice and passed a plate of Mae's cookies. Donaldina took her hand. "She was born honest," she said. "I remember the first time I saw her. She was about ten, but so little. The older girls had put her up to taking some fruit from the kitchen, promising to own up if it was missed. But they didn't. When Miss Culbertson asked for the guilty party, this little thing stood up and said, 'I did it.' And those miserable older girls never said a word!"

The friends laughed. But Tien was reproachful. "I never tell things about you, Lo Mo!" She moved to gather up the glasses, but Lo Mo put an arm around her. "This is what Mission can do."

In October of 1967 Donaldina fell and broke a hip. After a few weeks it became evident that it would not heal. Caroline remained with her aunt in the hospital most of the time, spelled off by Tien and close friends. Daughters and "920"'s staff often visited.

"How dear of you to come," Donaldina would begin. Tell me about. . . ." She listened, eager to remain active through those she loved. She once wept with happiness when Mae brought word that a daughter she had feared far from the fold had returned to church loyalties.

In a letter Dick Wichman told of his and his wife, Lois's call on her in the hospital:

> She was a joy to talk with, effervescent with appreciation for loved ones and the care of hospital personnel. She reminisced about the "lovely" episodes in her life. . . . Every topic . . . included God's Grace, as might be expected; for no one walked life more aware of His constant companionship. Her dedication to people was still the drive of life as she inquired into the well-being of dozens of friends and staff. She ministered to us more than we to her.

Her friends later wished she could have known that both she and Lorna would be selected by the *San Francisco Examiner* as "Woman of the Year" and given awards in memory of Phoebe Apperson Hearst, one of the original benefactresses of Donaldina's Occidental Board; and know that Lorna would be elected the first woman Moderator of the Presbytery of San Francisco.

The old habit of taking care of people never wavered. "Let me warm your hands," she told a visitor who had come in out of the crisp November air.

Shortly before Christmas, Ah Ching and Ah Tye, who had been members of Lo Mo's quartet sixty years earlier, visited her. Noticing that she was in need of a manicure, they sat on either side of her bed, each doing a hand, and began to sing her favorite hymns and Christmas carols. Tien and Caroline joined. Nurses gathered in the doorway.

"You make me so happy!" Lo Mo said.

On the morning of January 4 she asked Tien to get her clothes, saying that she wanted to go home. Tien suggested they first have their devotions. From "Daily Light" she read, "In my father's house are many mansions. If it were not so, I would have told you. I go to prepare a place for you and if I go and prepare a place for you, I will come again and will receive you unto myself that where I am there you may be also. . . ."

She talked with joyous anticipation of going to that other home and of reunion with family and friends.

And Lo Mo took her leave.

CHAPTER TWENTY-THREE

The Legacy
1968-

For all who loved Lo Mo a stillness fell across the earth when she left them. Disbelief was followed by solace. She was freed from the fetters of earth and age.

They asked one another, "Do you remember. . . ?" She always looked so nice. How quick she was. The funny things she said. Her granite expression. She never gave up. How she held your cold hand in both her warm ones and smiled at you. Her wonderful eyes. She was so certain of The Way. She loved us every one and brought out our best.

Not surprisingly, though they were surprised, Lo Mo's spiritual heirs recognized in one another—at "920," in Peking, in New York—her stamp, her hallmark, her sign, resemblances as manifest as the Camerons' chiseled features: a light in the eye, a warm voice, the touch of kindness, an air of confidence, laughter, expectancy, joy.

Perhaps their reflection of her was in no way extraordinary—for Lo Mo had faithfully reflected an Image, too.

Selected Bibliography

Books

Altrocchi, Julia. *The Spectacular San Franciscans.* New York: E. P. Dutton & Co., 1949.

Asbury, Herbert. *The Barbary Coast.* New York: Alfred A. Knopf, 1933; Pocket Books, 1947.

Bronson, William. *The Earth Shook, The Sky Burned.* Garden City, N.Y.: Doubleday, 1959.

Buck, Pearl B. *My Several Worlds.* New York: John Day, 1954.

Caen, Herbert E. *Baghdad-by-the-Bay.* Garden City, N.Y.: Doubleday, 1949.

_____. *The San Francisco Book.* Boston: Houghton Mifflin, 1948.

Carruth, Gordon, and Associates. *The Encyclopedia of American Facts and Data.* Sixth Edition. New York: Crowell, 1972.

Chen, Kwong Min. *The Chinese in the Americas.* New York: Overseas Chinese Culture Publishing Co., 1950.

Chen-Tsu Wu (Ed.) *"Chink."* New York: Times Mirror, 1972.

Dickson, Samuel. *Tales of San Francisco.* Stanford, Calif.: Stanford University Press, 1957.

Dillon, Richard. *The Hatchetmen.* New York: Coward-McCann, 1962.

Dobie, Charles C. *San Francisco's Chinatown.* New York: Appleton-Century, 1936.

Drury, Clifford M. *Presbyterian Panorama: One Hundred and Fifty Years of National Missions History.* Philadelphia: Board of Christian Education, 1952.

Genthe, Arnold. *As I Remember.* New York: Reynal and Hitchcock, 1936.

Glick, Carl, and Hong, Shen-hwa. *Swords of Silence.* New York: Whittlesey House, 1947.

Hansen, Gladys C., and Heintz, William F. *The Chinese in Cali-

fornia: A Brief Bibliographic History. Portland, Ore.: Richard Abel, 1970.

Hom, Gloria Sun. *Chinese Argonauts: An Anthology of the Chinese Contributions to the Historical Development of Santa Clara County.* Los Altos, Calif.: Foothill Community College, 1971.

Hoy, William. *The Six Companies: The Chinese Consolidated Benevolent Association.* San Francisco: Privately printed, 1942.

Irwin, Will, and Genthe, Arnold. *Pictures of Old Chinatown.* New York: Moffat, Yar and Company, 1908.

Jackson, Joseph Henry (Ed.) *The Western Gate: A San Francisco Reader.* New York: Farrar, Straus and Young, 1952.

Kahn, Edgar M. *Cable Car Days in San Francisco.* Stanford, Calif.: Stanford University Press, 1940. (Oversize ed., 1944)

Lewis, Oscar. *San Francisco, Mission to Metropolis.* Berkeley, Calif.: Howell-North Books, 1966.

McLeod, Alexander. *Pigtails and Gold Dust.* Caldwell, Ida.: Caxton Printers, 1947.

Nee, Victor G., and Nee, Brett de Bary. *Longtime Californ'.* New York: Pantheon Books, 1973.

Shepherd, Charles R. *The Ways of Ah Sin.* Old Tappan, N.J.: Fleming H. Revell, 1923.

————. *The Story of Chung Mei.* Valley Forge, Pa.: Judson Press, 1938.

Soule, Frank. *The Annals of San Francisco.* New York: D. Appleton and Co., 1966.

Sung, Betty Lee. *Mountain of Gold.* New York: Macmillan, 1967.

Thomas, Gordon, and Witts, Max Morgan. *The San Francisco Earthquake.* New York: Stein and Day, 1971.

Wicher, Edward A. *The Presbyterian Church in California* (1849-1927). Frederick H. Hitchcock, The Grafton Press, 1937.

Wilson, Carol Green. *Chinatown Quest.* Stanford, Calif.: Stanford University Press, 1931, 1950.

Wong, Jade Snow. *Fifth Chinese Daughter.* New York: Harper, 1950.

Magazines

"A San Francisco Landmark: She Rescued Girls from Tongs' Vice Lords," *The Progress,* April 26, 1975.

"Cameron House—Lo Mo's Legacy: Love, Service," *East-West,* January 17, 1968.

Chu, George. "Chinatown," *San Francisco Magazine,* June 1969.

Cooper, Katherine, "Incidents and People of Early San Francisco," *Grizzly Bear,* August 1914.

De Witt, Jack. "Smashing the Slave Girl Traffic," *Real Detective,* June 1936.

Dosch, Arno. "The 'Uplift' in San Francisco," *Pacific Monthly,* September 1907.

Fong-Torres, Ben. "Chinatown Youth," *San Francisco Magazine,* June 1969.

Hammack, Valentine C., as told to Dean S. Jennings. "Broken Blossoms," *Famous Detective Cases,* October 1935.

Jennings, Dean S. "Smashing California's Yellow Slave Traffic," *True Magazine,* January 1936.

Martin, Mildred Crowl. "Cameron House," *San Francisco Magazine,* June 1969.

Robinson, Henry. "The City at the Golden Gate," *Overland Monthly,* January 1873.

"San Francisco Economic Conditions, as seen by a stranger," *Pacific Monthly,* January 1864.

Slater, Paul. "Chinatown's Newspapers," *San Francisco Magazine,* June 1969.

Strother, E. French. "Setting Chinese Slave Girls Free," *The California Weekly,* February 26, 1909.

Presbyterian Publications

"Annual Meeting of Occidental Board," *Woman's Work,* July 1908.

Brown, Mrs. P. D. "Dr. John Gillespie," *The Occident,* April 26, 1899.

_____. "Our Annual Meeting," *The Occident,* March 7, 1900.

Buchanan, Alice L. "Conference on 'Cause and Cure of War,' " *Women and Missions,* March 1936.

Burnham, Mrs. T. H. "The February Meeting," *The Occident,* March 8, 1899.

Cameron, Donaldina. "For the Guild of Intercessors," *Outreach,* May 1952.

_____. "Rescue Work of Occidental Board," *Woman's Work,* January 1911.

"Christmas at the Chinese Church," *The Occident,* January 24, 1900.

Cochran, Jean Carter. "Those Narrow Missionary Interests," *Women and Missions,* March 1936.

Current, quarterly news sheet of Cameron House, 1972-75, *passim.*

"Donaldina Cameron Dies in Her Ninety-Ninth Year," *Presbyterian Life,* March 1, 1968.

"Editorial About an English Visitor to the Home," *The Occident,* December 1899.

"Extra Penny a Day" (Tract issued by Home Missions of Presbyterian Church about 1900)

Field, Mrs. Mary H. "A Bit of Romance at '920,' " *The Occident,* February 7, 1900.

"From San Francisco, Notes from Headquarters," *Women and Missions*, June 1920.

Hamilton, Frances S. "The Quiet Heart," *Woman's Work*, June 1916.

Harrington, Janette F. "Family of Six-Hundred," *Presbyterian Life*, November 15, 1954.

Kelley, Mrs. L. A. "Story of Sickness and Death in the Home," *The Occident*, January 10, 1900.

Latham, Edith D. "At the Door of the House on the Hill," *Woman's Work*, June 1918.

_____. "Our Oriental Christians in California," *Women and Missions*, July 1920.

Laughlin, Annie B. (Mrs. J. H.) "Three Chinese Women in San Francisco," *Woman's Work*, August 1909.

Logan, Lorna. "I Have a Problem," *Outreach*, May 1957.

Manion, Inspector John J. " 'Lo Mo,' Mother of Chinatown," *Women and Missions*, January 1932.

Martin, Mildred Crowl. "At the Heart of Life," *Concern Magazine*, May-June, 1969.

Martin, Mrs. C. S. "Chinese New Year in the Home," *The Occident*, April 26, 1899.

"Notes on the Twenty-Seventh Annual Meeting of the Occidental Board," *The Occident*, April 11, 1900.

Page, Bessie R. (Mrs. E. S.) "The Occidental Board," *Woman's Work*, June 1915.

Pinney, Laura Y. (Mrs. H. B.) "Occidental Board Campaign," *Woman's Work*, September 1911.

Robbins, Pauline. (Mrs. E. V.) "Help for Chinese Women and Children in San Francisco," *Woman's Work*, June 1912.

Roberts, Mrs. J. B. "Reception to Missionaries," *The Occident*, March 8, 1899.

Shepherd, Charles R., Th.D., "The Passing of the House on the Hill," *Revelation*, March 1940.

Smith, Bertha M. "They Call Her Fahn Quai, 'The White Spirit' " (Pamphlet reprinted from an article by the Board of Foreign Missions in the *American Magazine*)

Tooker, Mrs. Mary Fitch. "The New Woman in China," *Woman's Work*, February 1910.

_____. "Methods of Approach," *Woman's Work*, June 1912.

Watkins, Eleanor Preston. "Home for Chinese Girls Dedicated," *Women and Missions*, February 1926.

Wilson, Carol Green. "Home Coming Day at Ming Quong," *Women and Missions*, August 1930.

Wright, Emma G. (Mrs. C. S.) "The Occidental Board After Earthquake and Fire," *Woman's Work*, June 1906.

Miscellaneous Papers and Statements

Abbot, Kenneth Albert, thesis: "Cultural Change, Psychological Functioning and the Family: A Case Study on the Chinese-American Community of San Francisco," University of California, 1966.

_____. "The Presbyterians and Social Welfare" (unpublished paper)

Cattell, Stuart H. "Health, Welfare and Social Organization in Chinatown New York." Dept. of Public Affairs, Community Service Society of New York, August 1962.

Cameron, Donaldina. Personal papers and correspondence.

Fong, March, Assemblywoman, House Resolution No. 62, January 30, 1968, Assembly of California State Legislature.

Logan, Lorna, "Into the Second Century," A Brief History of Donaldina Cameron House in Commemoration of its 100th Anniversary, 1973.

Speer, William, "An Humble Plea Addressed to the Legislature of California in Behalf of the Immigrants from the Empire of China to This State." (Date uncertain, probably in 1860's or 1870's.)

Wolfe, Burton H., "50,000 in a Ghetto; Plus the New Tongs," *The California Liberal*, February 1960.

A History of the San Francisco Police Department, 1973.

Newspapers

Oakland Tribune
Palo Alto Times
San Francisco Call and *Call Bulletin*
San Francisco Chronicle
San Francisco Examiner
San Francisco News
San Jose News

Reports and Records

Annual Reports of the Mission Home to the Woman's Occidental Board of Foreign Missions, 1874-1920, written by Directors: Sarah M. N. Cummings, Margaret Culbertson, Mary H. Field, and Donaldina M. Cameron, and their assistants, matrons, and housekeepers.

Annual Reports of the Mission Home to the Board of National Missions, 1931-1939.

Annual Reports of other mission efforts from the Presbyterian Synods of Arizona, California, and Utah, as reported to the Woman's Occidental Board of Foreign Missions, 1874-1920, *passim*.

Two handwritten ledgers, records of girls entering the Home and some case histories, 1874-1910.

Robbins, Mrs. E. V. A handwritten journal of the years 1873-1913.

_____. A report: "The Occidental Board—A Retrospect and Prospect," January 1916.

Donaldina Cameron's diary for the year 1909.

Letter files of Donaldina Cameron and Lorna Logan, 1921-1939.

A file of articles and stories written by Donaldina Cameron, her staff, and wards.

Transcripts of interviews and testimony of court cases, United States National Archives, San Bruno, California.

Index